# THE FERTILIZER INDUSTRY: STUDY OF AN IMPERFECT MARKET

# THE FERTILIZER INDUSTRY

## STUDY OF AN IMPERFECT MARKET

*By*

### JESSE W. MARKHAM

*Professor of Economics*
*Princeton University*

Nashville
THE VANDERBILT UNIVERSITY PRESS
1958

To Betsy

# FOREWORD

A generation of economists has recognized that the theory of pure competition, while gaining in precision of formulation and validity of logic, has diminished in relevance to the study of price behavior in industries that lack the structural characteristics assumed in the model of pure competition or its counterpart, the model of pure monopoly. John Maurice Clark's landmark article, "Toward a Concept of Workable Competition," in 1940 advanced the idea that since pure competition is rarely attainable, some elements of market imperfection that are subject to control may in fact compensate for other elements of imperfection that cannot be eliminated. Clark suggested that many industrial markets may without being perfectly competitive still be workably competitive. The hypothesis has won the approval of many economists, and some have endeavored to find standards by which the workability of competition in a given market may be determined. Jesse W. Markham has made important contributions to this endeavor. In an article appearing in 1950 his formulation of a proposed standard of workable competition was: "An industry may be judged to be workably competitive when, after the structural characteristics of its market and the dynamic forces that shaped them have been thoroughly examined, there is no clearly indicated change that can be effected through public policy measures that would result in greater social gains than social losses."

The widespread interest of economists in giving more precise meaning to the concept of workable competition and in establishing standards by which to test competitive workability has greatly increased the need for industrial studies which will both illuminate the concept and furnish guides for public policy. Markham's *Competition in the Rayon Industry* (1952) is a pioneer study in this field of applied economics. Economists familiar with his work, and all students of industrial organization and public policy, will welcome his second contribution. *The Fertilizer Industry: Study of an Imperfect Market* reflects the professional competence and analytical ability that economists have come to associate with Markham's work. Particularly significant is Markham's finding that a vigorous antitrust policy cannot alone insure workable competition in the fertilizer industry. A positive program is called for, designed primarily to permit and promote intelligent buying of farm fertilizers. This requires a coordinated effort on the part of the various federal, state, and county agencies whose policies at present are diverse and frequently contradictory.

Vanderbilt University                                 GEORGE W. STOCKING
July 6, 1958

# PREFACE

The preparation of a detailed industry study is a tedious, painful, and often dull process. At best it affords an opportunity to apply broad principles, never to develop them. At worst it can be an outlet for the urge to describe. Few aspire to either of these attainments. Nevertheless, the incentives for this study were strong. First, while the potash and nitrogen industries have been carefully examined by others, the phosphate industry, which furnishes the one remaining principal fertilizer material, has been neglected. This was a gap that needed filling, especially since the potash and nitrogen studies could be drawn upon to round out an analysis of the entire fertilizer industry. Second, a study of the phosphate industry had from time to time been considered by both the Institute of Research and Training in the Social Sciences at Vanderbilt University and the Tennessee Valley Authority. The two institutions together offered to support such a study by furnishing research aid, travel funds, and access to data they had accumulated over the years. Finally, a long-standing controversy has surrounded the problem of filler in fertilizers; the study afforded an opportunity to explore its basis.

While I accept full responsibility for the contents of this book, it is in fact a product of many people: officials of fertilizer co-operatives and private companies, a board member and several division directors and branch chiefs of TVA, an assistant to the Secretary of Agriculture and numerous other Department of Agriculture personnel, officials of three trade associations, several economists with the Federal Trade Commission, one administrative assistant to the House Committee on Agriculture, various persons in the Departments of Commerce and Interior, and the clerical personnel attached to these companies and agencies. All have had a hand. The assistance given me by several of such persons deserves special recognition, although the point at which the names of individuals give way to the names of groups is an arbitrary one.

My debt to Dr. Harry A. Curtis of the TVA Board is especially large. During much of the time this study was in progress a vacancy existed on the TVA Board; and Mr. Gordon Clapp, one of the remaining two directors, was either abroad on official duty or on sick leave. It often fell to Dr. Curtis to perform the duties ordinarily performed by three men. During these exceedingly busy months he not only gave me unstintingly of his time when I needed information that he alone could supply but also read two versions of the manuscript carefully for technical accuracy. He is, of course, relieved of all responsibility for any technical errors the book may still contain.

I am especially indebted also to Mr. C. T. Prindeville of Swift & Company, Vice President in charge of plant food; and Mr. K. D. Jacob of the U. S. Department of Agriculture's Bureau of Plant Industry, Soils, and Agricultural Engineering. Both gave me several days of their time, much information that could not possibly have been obtained elsewhere, and they read and commented upon all or significant portions of the book.

Others who supplied me with important information include Claude A. Scroggs and Frank T. Conyers of the Farm Credit Administration; Dr. Robert Salter, Chief of the Soil Conservation Service; Louis Porter of the Production and Marketing Administration; W. A. Minor, Assistant to the Secretary of Agriculture under Secretary Brannon; A. L. Mehring of the Bureau of Plant Industry, Soils, and Agricultural Engineering; W. A. Turrentine, President of the American Potash Institute; Leland Allbaugh, Director of TVA's Agricultural Relations Division, and John Blackmore, John Mahan, Warren West, James A. Wells, and others of his staff; Vernon Ruttan, formerly an economist with TVA and now on the staff of Purdue University; Paul E. Johnson of TVA's Soils and Fertilizer Research Branch; and R. M. Crabtree, K. L. Elmore, and E. L. Newman of TVA's Chemical Engineering Division.

I also wish to express a debt of gratitude to Professors Corwin Edwards of the University of Chicago and George W. Stocking of Vanderbilt University and to Dr. Stefan Robock, former Chief of the Industrial Economics Branch of TVA, for having read and commented upon the finished book. Professor Stocking's suggestions on both substance and style were especially helpful.

Finally, I wish to express my thanks for the financial aid and the services provided by the Tennessee Valley Authority, the Institute for Research in the Social Sciences at Vanderbilt University, and the Faculty Research Fund of Princeton University. The Institute provided me with typing and secretarial services and the help of two research assistants, James A. Pikl and Homer B. Fletcher, which made the writing of this book a much less onerous task than it otherwise would have been. TVA supplied certain research and travel funds that made the study possible. The Faculty Research Fund of Princeton financed the typing of the final draft. None of these organizations has in any way tried to shape the conclusions reached in the study. They are entirely my own.

J. W. M.

Princeton, New Jersey,
July 6, 1958

# TABLE OF CONTENTS

11

# LIST OF TABLES

# LIST OF ILLUSTRATIONS

# Part I

## INTRODUCTION

# CHAPTER 1

# THE PROBLEM AND THE ISSUES

MOST economists identify agriculture with the purely competitive price model. For agricultural product markets this is understandable. Farmers are so numerous that none can perceptibly influence price by altering his rate of output. From the point of view of *structure,* agriculture is perfectly competitive.

Public policy has long recognized, however, that atomistic structure alone is not enough to assure economical resource allocation in agriculture. As early as 1839 the federal government assumed responsibility for disseminating to farmers certain plants and seeds and for providing to farmers certain statistical services they could not perform for themselves. In 1862 Congress created in quick succession the Department of Agriculture and the land-grant college system; and in 1887, with the enactment of the Hatch Act, launched a program whereby state agricultural experimental stations would be established and supported by federal funds. The Smith-Lever Agricultural Extension Act of 1914 provided for the diffusion of technical know-how developed at experiment stations. The Capper-Volstead Act of 1922 legalized certain concerted action among agricultural producers. The Agricultural Marketing Act of 1929 ushered in the period of agricultural price stabilization through direct government action. The New Deal brought in much new farm legislation, the most important statutes being the various Agricultural Adjustment Acts, the Bankhead-Jones Research Extension Act (1935), the Bankhead-Jones Farm Tenant Act (1937), the Hope-Flanagan Act (1946), and the agricultural provisions of the act creating the Tennessee Valley Authority (1933).

While some of these laws, notably those providing price supports, sought to circumvent or lessen the rigors of competition, most of them aimed at implementing it. With the passage of the Homestead Act of 1862 the United States committed itself to the family-unit farm. But the family-farm operator ordinarily was not equipped to conduct research or experimentation. He was unacquainted with the techniques of business entrepreneurship and handicapped by habit and lack of information. He usually did not innovate and frequently was slow to adopt the innovations of others.[1] Agriculture was structurally akin to perfectly

---

[1] This is *not* to say that *no* family-farm operators innovate. Many do. It does say that most family-farm operators do not; or if they do, they have not yet convinced those entrusted with formulating agricultural policy that they do; otherwise, many agricultural programs would be discontinued as merely duplicating what the average farmer already does for himself.

competitive models, but it was singularly imperfect on other counts. To overcome these imperfections, attributable in part to the industry's atomistic structure, government agencies have attempted to perform the innovating and knowledge-disseminating functions of a competitive market. Entrepreneurship in agriculture has for many decades been divided between farm operators on the one hand and public agencies on the other, with the latter probably playing the more dynamic role.

## A. The Central Policy Problem

This is an economic analysis of the fertilizer industry; and, for reasons set forth below, it assigns a pivotal position to the phosphate- and mixed-fertilizer components of the industry. Fertilizers are an important factor of production for farmers. In 1951 they spent 6.8 cents out of every dollar of their previous year's income on fertilizers. In the South Atlantic states, where agriculture is more dependent on fertilizer, the proportion is fourteen per cent. For farm income derived from crops dependent on fertilizers, such as grains, cotton, and tobacco, the proportion is also higher than for farm income generally. In recent years fertilizer has accounted for about eleven per cent of the total expenditures made by grain farmers and has ranked as the third most important cash outlay; machinery costs and taxes of all kinds have ranked first and second respectively.[2] The financial success of many farmers is affected in no small way by the kinds and quantities of fertilizers they buy and how efficiently they use them.

Like most manufacturing industries the fertilizer industry is subject to public policy as expressed in the anti-trust laws; unlike most industries it is also subject to a positive policy consisting of various government programs. The purpose of anti-trust is to attain the social benefits of competition; the purpose of positive fertilizer policy is to reduce the social costs of market imperfections outside the scope of anti-trust, especially the high degree of imperfect knowledge on the demand side of the fertilizer market, and to further technological innovation in the production and use of fertilizers.

Such positive government action antedates any clear formulation of its objectives; it even antedates the anti-trust laws. Since the 1880's, state governments have exercised regulatory powers over fertilizers sold within their borders, their purpose being to protect farmers from the high costs of unwise purchasing. The federal government has actively engaged in fertilizer research since about 1900 and has produced and distributed fertilizers since 1933. As the pace of governmental activity quickened

---

[2] U. S. Department of Agriculture. *Farm Costs and Returns, 1955.* Agriculture Information Bulletin No. 158 (June, 1956), p. 42.

in the 1930's, objectives with respect to fertilizers—which collectively may be loosely described as a national fertilizer policy—gradually evolved. However, an express statement on national fertilizer policy did not appear until November, 1941, when the U. S. Department of Agriculture's Interbureau Co-ordinating Committee on Fertilizer issued its first report.[3] A second national policy statement appeared in 1945,[4] and a third in 1952.[5] National policy, as broadly defined in these statements, was to encourage increases in fertilizer production to meet future needs as estimated by the Department of Agriculture; to develop research and action programs leading to more efficient production, distribution, and use of fertilizers; and to place certain responsibilities for attaining these objectives on federal agencies and the land-grant colleges.

The public's stake in the success of this policy should not be obscured by postwar agricultural surpluses. Efficient agriculture is itself a desirable public-policy objective. It is also a necessary objective. The President's Materials Policy Commission estimates that the American people will require forty per cent more agricultural production in 1975 than they did in 1950, and that much of the increase must come from greater and more efficient use of fertilizers.[6]

Meanwhile, anti-trust has been administered with considerable vigor. In 1906 the Virginia-Carolina Chemical Company and sixty other phosphate and mixed-fertilizer producers were charged with cartelizing the domestic fertilizer industry through a Canadian corporation. In 1926, and again in 1941, the Department of Justice found certain phosphate and mixed-fertilizer producers to have violated the anti-trust laws. In the 1926 case thirty-seven defendants paid fines of $95,000, and in the 1941 case sixty-nine defendants paid fines of $259,852. In 1916 the Federal Trade Commission published its first study of the fertilizer industry, including all its various components. One of its principal findings was that profit margins on certain grades of fertilizer were excessive. The Commission published another comprehensive study in 1950, in which it stated that previous anti-trust action against various components of the fertilizer industry had freed competition of some but not necessarily all undue restraints. In 1945 and 1946 the Commission found two phosphate-rock export associations to have engaged in activities in violation of either the anti-trust laws or the Webb-Pomerene Act, or both, and issued recommendations to both associations; one of the associations complied by

    [3] U. S. Department of Agriculture. *Report of the Interbureau Co-ordinating Committee on Fertilizer* (November 1, 1941). See especially summary and recommendations, pp. 90 ff.
    [4] U. S. Department of Agriculture, Committee on National Fertilizer Policy. *A National Policy for Fertilizers and Liming Materials* (February 12, 1945).
    [5] U. S. Department of Agriculture, Office of the Secretary. *A National Program for More Efficient Use of Fertilizer and Lime* (September 11, 1952).
    [6] U. S. President's Materials Policy Commission. *Resources for Freedom*. Vol. I. A Report to the President (Truman. Washington, 1952), pp. 45-46.

adjusting its activities, and the other complied by dissolving itself. Nearly all the large nitrogen and potash producers have been parties to consent decrees with the Department of Justice. A sulphur export association has received and acted upon recommendations from the Federal Trade Commission that it put an end to certain restrictive practices tending to injure competition.

These two policies of public control—anti-trust and what we shall call positive fertilizer policy—are the subject of this study. Both policies have the common purpose of reducing the social costs of market imperfections, but each is addressed to imperfections arising from a different source. Anti-trust policy seeks to reduce social costs by attacking monopoly and restraints of trade, imperfections which interfere with producing the "ideal" output.[7] Positive policy seeks, for the most part, to reduce social costs by fostering more rational purchasing and use of fertilizers by farmers. And both policies, although by different means, seek to foster technological innovations which reduce the costs of plant nutrients to the farmer: anti-trust by fostering the competitive environment conducive to more efficient fertilizer production; positive policy by government research on fertilizer production and use.

The central thesis of this study is that market imperfections giving rise to these two policies cannot be appraised independently. The value of a fertilizer depends almost entirely upon the quantities of plant nutrients it contains. It would seem elementary that producers would seek to produce plant nutrients at the lowest possible unit cost, and that farmers would buy them at the lowest price offered. Actually, however, a large proportion of fertilizer sales is made on the basis of the price per ton of total material instead of the price per unit of plant nutrient. This means that farmers do not buy plant nutrients at the lowest prices at which they are available in the market, and that producers do not produce them at the lowest possible cost.

For nearly a century this problem has been expressed as a simple question: Why is there so much sand in the farmer's fertilizer? The public debates this problem has precipitated have been like the age-old question of which came first, the hen or the egg. Producers have contended that they would produce more economical fertilizers if farmers would buy them. Spokesmen for farm organizations have argued that farmers would buy more economical fertilizers if producers would put them on the market. No doubt both contentions have some basis in fact, but there is persuasive evidence that farmers do not purchase fertilizers rationally even within the range of alternatives producers supply. Hence, as a

---

[7] Cf. William J. Baumol, *Welfare Economics and the Theory of the State* (Cambridge: Harvard University Press, 1952), pp. 24-59; and A. C. Pigou, *The Economics of Welfare* (4th ed., London: Macmillan & Co., 1929) esp. Part II.

practical matter, producers have little or no incentive to increase the plant-nutrient content of fertilizers so long as demand reflects irrational consumer choice; on the other hand, they have every incentive to do so when demand reflects rational judgment, unless they make industry-wide agreements to keep quality low. In short, effective competition among producers cannot reduce the profit incentives for selling adulterated fertilizers so long as farmers buy as they do, and no producer of adulterated fertilizers could survive if farmers bought as they should. Under these circumstances effective anti-trust administration is not enough. Indeed, it is not altogether clear how enforcement of the anti-trust laws affects resource allocation in the fertilizer industry in the face of irrational demand for the industry's output, but it is certain that competition alone cannot assure the "ideal" output. Hence comes the necessity for the simultaneous appraisal of both anti-trust and positive policy.

That farmers buy fertilizers unwisely requires at the outset a brief tentative explanation. The following factors, which extend beyond ordinary economic motivations, help to explain it: most fertilizer output has been used in the South on row crops, and in the past half-century row-crop farming has not been sufficiently profitable to attract efficient entrepreneurs. The typical farm operator, and particularly the row-crop farmer of the South, has viewed farming as "a way of life." But a way of life involves customs, mores, preconceptions, and perhaps even superstitions. When purchasing fertilizers, farmers have frequently employed such criteria as smell, types of packaging, their relationship with the seller, and what their predecessors have used, rather than the cost per unit of plant nutrient. Since the agronomic sciences were developed only a few decades ago, these criteria were not so irrational in the latter half of the nineteenth century as they now appear. But the buying habits of that period, irrational though they were, persist.

Irrational demand patterns seem to have laid a dead hand on the fertilizer manufacturing industry itself, where entrepreneurs have bowed to custom rather than striven for the rewards of innovation. Given such patterns, however, capitulation to them may well have been the most profitable course to follow. While, as this study will develop, other forces have contributed to the persistent production and use of uneconomical fertilizers, they all stem in whole or in part from the foregoing environment factors.

### B. The Problem of Measuring and Allocating Social Costs of Market Imperfections

If for no reason other than that of co-ordinating and assigning priorities to the two public policies toward the fertilizer industry, it would be useful to measure quantitatively the social costs of various market imperfections. Alternative policies ultimately mean alternative government action and budgets. The minimum acceptable sound policy calls for allocating a given amount of public funds so that the net product of government is maximized, an ideal policy for equating the marginal costs of each government operation with its marginal social product.

This study proposes a less ambitious set of quantitative measures than the ideal—or even the acceptable minimum—public policy envisages. Even if all the required data were available—which is not the case—the problem of assigning the social costs of all market imperfections to the purview of anti-trust on the one hand or to positive policy on the other would still remain. For example, it can be shown that fertilizer producers could produce the annual outputs of plant nutrients at considerably lower costs than they actually produce them. Should the unnecessary costs be attributed to imperfect knowledge on the demand side of the market, or to imperfect knowledge or trade restraints on the supply side? When we can assume that buyers buy their fertilizers in terms of price per unit of plant nutrient, we can also assume that sellers, whether monopolists or competitors, attempt to minimize the production costs of plant nutrients at all possible rates of output. To behave otherwise would be inconsistent with the assumption that sellers attempt to maximize their profits. However, when buyers buy fertilizers in terms of the price per ton of total material, presumably producers attempt to minimize the production costs of tons of total material, but then the production costs of plant nutrients are not minimized. Here, while the social costs of using inefficient fertilizers may be quantitatively measured, the particular market imperfection to which such costs should be assigned is a matter of judgment. They may be attributed to imperfect buyer knowledge, imperfect seller knowledge, insufficient or misleading seller advertising, or a combination of them all.

However, it is possible to make judgments about social costs which produce useful approximations. The fertilizer industry comprises commercial firms and farmer-owned co-operatives. It can be assumed that the latter, in the absence of restraints on the sale of fertilizer materials which can only be obtained outside the co-operative, sell their owner-members fertilizers in the most efficient forms they demand them. The federal government produces efficient high-analysis nitrogen and phosphate fertilizer materials in Tennessee Valley Authority plants and makes them available to co-operatives; co-operatives can buy potash on the open market. Special conditions may distort the measure somewhat—the government may *require* co-operatives to distribute efficient fertilizers, and members of farmer co-operatives may differ from farmers generally—but otherwise the amount by which unnecessary social costs would be reduced if all commercial firms sold the kinds of fertilizers that farmer co-operatives sell is principally attributable to market imperfections on the supply side of the fertilizer market. The amount by which unnecessary social costs would be even further reduced if all firms, co-operative and commercial, sold the most efficient fertilizers they could produce may then be attributed to imperfect knowledge on the demand side of the fertilizer market.

Some of these unnecessary social costs can be measured with reasonable accuracy and their cause identified. Fertilizer producers offer for sale the three principal plant nutrients—nitrogen, phosphate, and potash—in various concentrations and combinations. The price per unit of each plant nutrient, or particular combination of plant nutrients, varies considerably with the degree of concentration. When farmers buy their plant nutrients in a more costly form than they could buy them in alternative forms that sellers offer, we may reasonably attribute the unnecessary costs to imperfect buyer knowledge. Here buyers have a choice but exercise it irrationally. Such costs come under the purview of positive fertilizer policy.

It is possible to measure within reasonable limits the fertilizer industry's monopoly profits. It need scarcely be pointed out that this is never a simple problem, but it is somewhat less complex in the case of most of the components of the fertilizer industry than in the case of many other industries. The nitrogen, phosphate, sulphur, potash, and mixed fertilizer industries are old industries. Most of the significant product and process innovations, especially in the production of nitrogen and phosphate fertilizer materials, have originated in government research. A very small portion of the profits the industry earns can be considered rewards for the innovation of private entrepreneurs. Moreover, production techniques are well known and not especially complex, and the cost of entry into most segments of the industry relatively low. For these reasons most of the profits various segments of the fertilizer industry may have earned above the competitive rate of return can be considered monopoly profits. The industry practices which create them come under the purview of anti-trust policy.

This study attempts to measure the unnecessary social costs the production and sale of fertilizers involve and to identify the market imperfections which account for them. While the results may not approach slide-rule accuracy, they indicate the tasks of anti-trust and positive policies more clearly than could be indicated without them. A tolerably accurate conclusion that the annual social cost of imperfect knowledge amounts to $x$ million dollars and of trade restraints to $y$ million dollars provides a basis for sounder public policy than the less precise conclusion that market imperfections cost society much or little.

## C. Organization of the Fertilizer Industry

The fertilizer industry, broadly defined, comprises all producers, processors, and mixers of fertilizer nitrogen, phosphate and potash—the three principal plant nutrients. Producers and processors of a fourth material, sulphur, might also be included on the grounds that the most important phosphatic fertilizer material, superphosphate, is produced from approximately equal quantities of sulphuric acid and phosphate rock. While this study encompasses all four materials, it focuses on the phosphate industry. For the purpose of appraising market imperfections, this approach has a distinct advantage. Over three-fourths of the phosphate rock produced in the United States is consumed as fertilizer. The American farmer buys most of his fertilizers as mixtures of nitrogen, phosphate, and potash. A large portion of the mixed-fertilizer industry is integrated with the production and processing of phosphate rock. Producers of nitrogen and potash do not sell significant quantities of their output to farmers.[8] Instead, they sell to integrated phosphate producers and fertilizer mixers who in turn sell to farmers. Even the nitrogen and potash which farmers buy as straight materials usually reach them through these channels. A large part of this study is concerned with fertilizer markets in which farmers are buyers, and in these markets integrated phosphate producers and mixers are the sellers. For this part of the analysis nitrogen and potash can conveniently be considered as factors of production for the suppliers.

The phosphate industry, including its vertically integrated parts, comprises three industrial processes: rock mining and beneficiation (preparing for smelting), the manufacture of phosphatic materials, and the manufacture of mixed fertilizers. The first of these consists of extracting phosphate rock from the ground and processing it for further manufacture. The second consists principally of the manufacture of ordinary and concentrated superphosphate. Ordinary superphosphate is produced from approximately equal parts by weight of phosphate rock and a standard grade of sulphuric acid. Nearly half of the ordinary superphosphate plants in the United States produce their own sulphuric acid. These plants are buyers of sulphur. The remaining plants are buyers of sulphuric acid. Concentrated superphosphate is produced by mixing phosphate rock with phosphoric acid—which itself is produced from phosphate rock—or by the electric furnace method. The phosphorus in superphosphates is much more readily available to growing plants than that in phosphate rock. The available phosphorus in rock is estimated at from three per cent to

---

[8] For example, the Spencer Chemical Company sums up its sales policy as follows: "Spencer Chemical Company, as a primary producer of nitrogeneous fertilizer materials, has followed the well-established practice of selling its nitrogen fertilizer materials through fertilizer manufacturers." *The Fertilizer Industry and Spencer Chemical Company*, Spencer Chemical Co., Kansas City (September, 1949).

ten per cent by weight, while that in ordinary and concentrated super-phosphate is respectively about twenty per cent and over forty per cent. The third process consists of the manufacture of mixed fertilizers from superphosphate, nitrogen, and potash. About seventy-six per cent of the phosphorus, forty-five per cent of the nitrogen, and ninety per cent of the potash used as fertilizer in the United States are sold to farmers as mixed fertilizers. But whether farmers purchase these fertilizer materials separately or as mixed fertilizers, they generally purchase them from mixed fertilizer producers, the largest of which also produce phosphate rock and superphosphate.

The degree of concentration varies among the three processes, and the large phosphate rock companies account for most of the vertical integration. In 1949 there were thirty active phosphate-rock mining companies in the United States. The seven largest accounted for slightly over eighty per cent of total output, the six largest for about seventy-five per cent, and the five largest for seventy per cent. In 1950 the ordinary super-phosphate industry comprised eighty-one independent firms, of which the four largest accounted for 35.6 per cent of total output. At the same time seven commercial firms and the Tennessee Valley Authority produced concentrated superphosphate. The four largest concentrated superphos-phate producers account for sixty-nine per cent of total output; the Tennessee Valley Authority, the second largest producer, accounted for nineteen per cent. In 1954 the four largest superphosphate producers, ordinary and concentrated combined, accounted for fifty per cent of total shipments, and the eight largest for seventy per cent. In 1954 the ferti-lizer mixing industry comprised approximately 750 independent firms; the largest four accounted for twenty-seven per cent of total output and the largest eight for forty-four per cent. In 1950 six large integrated companies accounted for approximately seventy per cent of the total phosphate rock output, fifty per cent of the output of ordinary and concentrated superphosphate, and thirty per cent of the output of mixed fertilizer. An additional thirty-two per cent of the plants producing super-phosphate were integrated with mixed-fertilizer plants, but few of the firms involved produced phosphate rock. The trade identifies these verti-cally integrated firms and the nonintegrated firms which compete with them at each stage of manufacture as the phosphate-fertilizer industry; it identifies the components of the industry as the phosphate rock, the superphosphate, and the mixed-fertilizer industries.

Phosphate-fertilizer producers consume about one-fifth of the total United States output of sulphur in the production of superphosphates. Those that operate their own acid plants buy sulphur in the crude; those without acid plants buy sulphuric acid, often from their integrated rivals.

Phosphate-fertilizer producers and independent mixers consume about ninety-four per cent of the total output of potash and, in peacetime, about fifty per cent of the total output of nitrogen.[9] Most of the potash and nitrogen they buy goes into the manufacture of mixed fertilizers; the rest is sold as separate materials. The nitrogen, potash, and sulphur industries are not integrated with the phosphate and mixed-fertilizer industry.[10] In fact, fertilizer manufacturers initially obtained these materials from foreign sources. Fertilizer manufacturers and distributors buy their nitrogen requirements from producers of natural and synthetic nitrogen. Their chief source of natural nitrogen is Chilean sodium nitrate; their chief sources of synthetic nitrogen are products of the chemical industry, such as ammonia and solutions, ammonium nitrate, and ammonium sulfate. They obtain their sulphur and most of their potash requirements from domestic mining companies.

The markets in which integrated phosphate and independent mixed-fertilizer producers buy these fertilizer materials are characterized by high concentration of control. Domestic natural sulphur production has been concentrated in the hands of from two to four sulphur-mining companies. In 1951 four companies accounted for nearly ninety-eight per cent of total output. Until World War I a German cartel supplied nearly all the potash consumed in the United States. In the interwar period a French-German importing agency and from one to three domestic producers supplied the market; and as late as 1952 three large and six small domestic mining companies supplied about ninety per cent of the market, and foreign sources supplied the remaining ten per cent. Before World War I a Chilean nitrate cartel was the fertilizer industry's principal supplier of nitrogen. At the outbreak of World War II Chilean sodium nitrate and the output of two domestic synthetic-nitrogen producers accounted for over ninety per cent of the nitrogen consumed by fertilizer manufacturers. Concentration of control over nitrogen declined after World War II, principally because of the federal government's policy in disposing of the nitrogen plants it had built during the war.

Concentration of control on both the supply and demand sides of these markets raises certain problems for anti-trust policy; but, unlike the markets in which integrated and independent mixers sell to farmers, these markets do not raise for positive policy the important problems of imperfect knowledge and irrational demand. Mixers generally produce particular grades of mixed fertilizer from the cheapest available sources of plant nutrients. While these are not the most economical fertilizers,

[9] In wartime, when explosives production increases, the percentage is much lower.
[10] The International Minerals and Chemical Corporation and the Tennessee Valley Authority are two exceptions. International is a large integrated producer, producing phosphate rock, superphosphates, and mixed fertilizers. It also operates a small potash mine. TVA produces phosphate rock, concentrated superphosphate, nitrogen, and a variety of fertilizers, principally for experimental and educational purposes.

they nevertheless are produced from materials in which plant nutrients cost the least per unit. In comparison with farmers', mixers' demand reflects more perfect knowledge and less irrational choice.

The public policy problems on which this study focuses can now be summed up in precise terms. The primary raw materials used in the manufacture of fertilizers are phosphate rock, sulphur, potash, and nitrogen-bearing products. The final products farmers purchase consist of mixed fertilizers (graded according to units of nitrogen, phosphoric acid, and potash) and straight fertilizer materials. Phosphate-rock mining companies are the only producers of primary materials which are vertically integrated with the manufacture and sale of final fertilizer products. These companies and independent mixers buy other primary materials and sell manufactured fertilizers to farmers. The markets in which they buy are characterized by high concentration of control, and their suppliers have pursued policies which have precipitated numerous anti-trust suits. The markets in which phosphate-rock mining companies and independent mixers sell are characterized by considerably less concentration on the selling side, but by a high degree of imperfect knowledge and irrational choice on the demand side. These facts would seem to support the hypothesis that the principal instruments of public policy toward the materials markets should be the anti-trust laws, and toward the final-products markets should be the anti-trust laws and something more—positive programs for reducing the social costs of irrational choice. This study appraises public policy toward the fertilizer industry, seeking to ascertain its consistency with this hypothesis, the effectiveness with which it has dealt with both problems, and how it should be reformed.

# Part II

## ORGANIZATION AND STRUCTURE OF THE INTEGRATED FERTILIZER INDUSTRIES

## CHAPTER 2

# THE PHOSPHATE-ROCK INDUSTRY

APPROXIMATELY seventy-six per cent of all phosphate rock sold in the United States finds its way into the fertilizer industry, either for direct application or as a principal ingredient of mixed fertilizers.[1] Its value as a fertilizer derives from its phosphoric acid (hereafter called $P_2O_5$) content. For economic and other reasons foreign-produced phosphate rock has not entered the United States in substantial quantities since about 1909; the domestic phosphate-rock industry, therefore, is virtually the only source of $P_2O_5$ for the manufacture of phosphatic fertilizer materials and mixed fertilizers.[2]

### TABLE 1

#### ESTIMATED PHOSPHATE RESERVES OF THE UNITED STATES BY STATES, 1946 [a]

##### (Thousands of Long Tons)

| | | |
|---|---:|---:|
| Florida, total reserves | | 5,081,839 |
| Land Pebble | 3,491,580 | |
| Hard Rock | 1,540,259 | |
| River Pebble | 50,000 | |
| Western States, total reserves | | 7,984,892 |
| Idaho | 5,736,335 | |
| Utah | 1,741,480 | |
| Montana | 391,323 | |
| Wyoming | 115,754 | |
| Other States, total reserves | | 224,129 |
| Tennessee | 194,468 | |
| Arkansas | 20,000 | |
| South Carolina | 8,798 | |
| Kentucky | 863 | |
| Total United States reserves | | 13,290,860 |

[a] From Federal Trade Commission, Phosphate Export Association: *Report and Recommendations,* Appendices C and D. 42 FTC 555. 853-54 (1946).

## A. GEOGRAPHICAL DISTRIBUTION OF PHOSPHATE ROCK

Important phosphorus-bearing rock deposits are found in several states in the United States, nine of which have an estimated reserve of about thirteen billion long tons (Table 1). While estimated reserves in the West must be considered as scarcely more than guesses, surveys show that more than ninety per cent of the nation's reserves are located in Florida and in the four western states of Idaho, Montana, Utah, and Wyoming, and about two per cent are located in Tennessee. But under recovery methods and geographical demand patterns that have prevailed for over

[1] U. S. Department of the Interior, Bureau of Mines, *Minerals Yearbook,* 1952.
[2] Small quantities of phosphorus enter the fertilizer industry in the form of basic slag, a by-product of the steel industry, and in the form of such organic matter as bone meal and tankage.

half a century, the location of commercial sources of phosphate rock differs considerably from that of potential sources. For example, although only thirty-eight per cent of the estimated reserves were located in Florida in 1949, the state supplied over seventy-five per cent of all phosphate rock consumed in the United States. Similarly, Middle Tennessee accounted for only about two per cent of the nation's total phosphate reserves but supplied over fifteen per cent of total domestic consumption. On the other hand, Idaho, Wyoming, Utah, and Montana accounted for sixty per cent of the nation's total reserves but supplied only nine per cent of the domestic market. Except for the period 1868-1900 when South Carolina (where phosphate deposits were first discovered in the United States) was an important source (Table 2), Florida and Tennessee have been the chief sources of phosphate rock. In recent years the rock output of the western states has increased; but until the outbreak of World War II the combined annual output of Idaho, Montana, and Wyoming seldom equalled two per cent of total domestic production.

Florida phosphate deposits are of two general types—land pebble and hard rock. Competition between Florida pebble rock and other phosphate-rock fields has been severely limited by costs of transport and differences in recovery costs. Hard rock does not compete with pebble rock in the domestic market because of its higher recovery costs; its costs merely set a high upper limit to pebble-rock prices.[3] Tennessee rock competes with Florida pebble rock only in a limited area because of its high recovery costs and low grade. Under 1946 cost conditions and freight rates, competition between western and pebble rock was limited to an area adjacent to a line running southeast through the United States from a point located slightly east of the upper Mississippi River.[4] Historically this market-boundary area has consumed a very small percentage of the total output of phosphatic fertilizers. The area east of this line accounts for eighty per cent of total domestic $P_2O_5$ consumption, and depends on pebble-rock producers for nearly all of its supply of phosphate.

## B. Control of Phosphate Resources Before World War I

*The Florida Fields.* The Florida pebble deposits are located principally in an area extending almost sixty-five miles north and south and about thirty miles east and west, which includes large portions of Polk, Hillsborough, Hardee, and Manatee counties, and small portions of Sarasota, DeSota, and Highlands counties; their geographical center is in the approximate vicinity of Nichols, Florida. The hard rock deposits are located in an area roughly parallel to the Gulf coastline of Florida, extend-

---

[3] Hard rock has competed with pebble rock in foreign markets because of its higher bone phosphate-of-lime (BPL) content, and since 1950 limited quantities have been sold in the domestic fertilizer market.
[4] See Figures 3 and 4, pp. 136-37.

ing about 115 miles from Suwannee and Columbia counties in northern Florida southward to Pasco county. The maximum width of the field is about thirty miles. The average annual production of hard rock in the United States in recent years, nearly all of which has been exported, has equalled only about 1.2 per cent of land pebble production.

Ownership of the Florida land pebble deposits is fairly widely dispersed among sixty or more private companies and individuals and the federal government. Of the estimated total reserves, the seven largest operating companies control only 13.7 per cent (Table 3). However, these de-

TABLE 2

PHOSPHATE ROCK MINED IN THE UNITED STATES
1868-1954, SELECTED YEARS, BY STATES [a]

(long tons and per cent)

| Year | United States Total[c] | South Carolina | | Florida | | Tennessee[d] | | Western States[e] | |
|---|---|---|---|---|---|---|---|---|---|
| | | Long Tons | Per Cent | Long Tons | Per Cent | Long Tons | Per Cent | Long Tons | Per Cent |
| 1868 | 12,262 | 12,262 | 100.00 | | | | | | |
| 1870 | 65,241 | 65,241 | 100.00 | | | | | | |
| 1880 | 211,377 | 211,377 | 100.00 | | | | | | |
| 1888 | 451,567 | 450,754 | 99.82 | 813 | .18 | | | | |
| 1890 | 510,499 | 458,118 | 89.74 | 52,381 | 10.26 | | | | |
| 1893 | 941,368 | 495,564 | 52.64 | 438,804 | 46.61 | | | | |
| 1894 | 996,949 | 450,108 | 45.15 | 527,653 | 52.93 | 19,188 | 1.92 | | |
| 1895 | 1,038,551 | 431,975 | 41.59 | 568,061 | 54.70 | 38,515 | 3.71 | | |
| 1900b | 1,491,216 | 329,173 | 22.07 | 706,243 | 47.36 | 454,491 | 30.48 | | |
| 1905 | 1,947,190 | 270,225 | 13.88 | 1,194,106 | 61.32 | 482,859 | 24.80 | | |
| 1910b | 2,654,988 | 179,659 | 6.77 | 2,067,507 | 77.87 | 392,588 | 14.79 | | |
| 1915b | 1,835,667 | 83,460 | 4.55 | 1,358,611 | 74.01 | 389,748 | 21.23 | | |
| 1920b | 4,103,982 | 44,141 | 1.08 | 3,369,384 | 82.10 | 621,396 | 15.14 | | |
| 1925b | 3,481,819 | 2,147 | .06 | 2,929,964 | 84.15 | 464,240 | 13.33 | 72,631 | 2.09 |
| 1928 | 3,523,356 | | | 2,909,264 | 82.57 | 573,265 | 16.27 | 40,827 | 1.16 |
| 1929 | 3,787,255 | | | 3,100,505 | 81.87 | 647,711 | 17.10 | 39,039 | 1.03 |
| 1930 | 4,036,197 | | | 3,361,786 | 83.29 | 607,814 | 15.06 | 66,597 | 1.65 |
| 1931 | 2,666,509 | | | 2,155,903 | 80.85 | 393,925 | 14.77 | 116,681 | 4.38 |
| 1932 | 1,698,148 | | | 1,500,891 | 88.38 | 152,533 | 8.98 | 44,724 | 2.63 |
| 1933 | 2,359,635 | | | 2,039,531 | 86.43 | 296,411 | 12.56 | 23,663 | 1.00 |
| 1934 | 2,898,238 | | | 2,464,969 | 85.05 | 394,311 | 13.61 | 38,958 | 1.34 |
| 1935 | 3,159,328 | | | 2,598,337 | 82.24 | 493,501 | 15.62 | 67,490 | 2.14 |
| 1936 | 3,462,837 | | | 2,645,819 | 76.41 | 737,866 | 21.31 | 79,152 | 2.85 |
| 1937 | 4,261,416 | | | 3,179,588 | 74.61 | 942,158 | 22.11 | 139,670 | 3.28 |
| 1938 | 3,860,476 | | | 2,722,927 | 70.53e | 999,551 | 25.89 | 137,998 | 3.57 |
| 1939 | 3,987,920 | | | 2,791,360 | 70.00 | 1,057,570 | 26.52 | 139,040 | 3.49 |
| 1940 | 4,068,077 | | | 2,782,956 | 68.41 | 1,120,551 | 27.54 | 164,570 | 4.05 |
| 1941 | 4,922,183 | | | 3,417,900 | 69.44 | 1,301,067 | 26.43 | 203,216 | 4.13 |
| 1942 | 4,818,938 | | | 2,984,503 | 61.93 | 1,568,162 | 32.54 | 266,273 | 5.53 |
| 1943 | 5,369,967 | | | 3,274,266 | 60.97 | 1,868,407 | 34.79 | 227,294 | 4.23 |
| 1944 | 5,200,002 | | | 3,486,482 | 67.05 | 1,413,246 | 27.18 | 300,274 | 5.77 |
| 1945 | 5,399,739 | | | 3,814,935 | 70.65 | 1,260,849 | 23.35 | 323,955 | 6.00 |
| 1946 | 7,168,839 | | | 5,280,402 | 73.65 | 1,316,107 | 18.36 | 572,330 | 7.98 |
| 1947 | 9,110,989 | | | 6,381,282 | 70.04 | 1,489,980 | 16.35 | 1,239,727 | 13.61 |
| 1948 | 9,388,160 | | | 7,184,297 | 76.53 | 1,499,547 | 15.97 | 704,316 | 7.50 |
| 1949 | 8,877,474 | | | 6,695,407 | 75.42 | 1,403,469 | 15.81 | 778,598 | 8.77 |
| 1950 | 11,114,159 | | | 8,597,227 | 77.35 | 1,472,017 | 13.24 | 1,044,915 | 9.40 |
| 1951 | 10,775,032 | | | 8,211,820 | 76.21 | 1,424,516 | 13.22 | 1,138,696 | 10.57 |
| 1952 | 12,064,892 | | | 9,205,138 | 76.4 | 1,444,737 | 11.9 | 1,415,017 | 11.7 |
| 1953 | 12,503,830 | | | 9,331,002 | 74.6 | 1,518,912 | 12.2 | 1,653,916 | 13.2 |
| 1954 | 13,821,100 | | | 10,437,197 | 75.5 | 1,633,226 | 11.8 | 1,750,677 | 12.7 |

[a] 1868-1927: PEA: "Report and Recommendations," Appendix A 42 FTC 555, 851-52 (1946); 1928-54: U. S. Department of Interior, Bureau of Mines, *Minerals Yearbook*, 1928-54 issues.
[b] United States totals include, for certain years prior to 1928, production in Utah, Alabama, Arkansas, Kentucky, North Carolina, Pennsylvania, and Virginia in addition to production in the states included in the table. Therefore, individual percentages will not total to 100 per cent for all years.
[c] Production in western states from 1906 through 1924 is included in United States totals but cannot be shown separately without disclosing confidential data.
[d] Includes small quantities of apatite from Virginia in 1941-47 and 1949, and some matrix of washer grade in 1941-43.
[e] Includes small quantities of apatite from Virginia and phosphate rock from South Carolina.

## TABLE 3
### DISTRIBUTION OF OWNERSHIP OF ESTIMATED FLORIDA LAND-PEBBLE PHOSPHATE DEPOSITS, 1946 [a]

| | Acres | Reserves (millions of tons) | % Total |
|---|---|---|---|
| Seven active companies[b]............. | 163,881 | 477.3 | 13.7 |
| Eleven inactive companies[c]........... | 52,628 | 250.0 | 7.2 |
| Forty-two local corporations and individuals........................... | ........ | 300.0 | 8.6 |
| Inactive field[d]....................... | ........ | 2,464.3 | 70.5 |
| TOTAL....................... | ........ | 3,491.6 | 100.0 |

[a] Compiled from Moody's *Manual of Industrial Investments,* and various publications of the Bureau of Mines.
[b] American Agricultural Chemical Co., American Cyanamid Co., Coronet Phosphate Co., International Minerals and Chemical Corp., The Phosphate Mining Co. (Virginia-Carolina Chemical Co.), Southern Phosphate Corp. (Davison Chemical Corp.), and Swift & Co.
[c] Includes Davison Chemical Corp. and Virginia-Carolina Chemical Co., both of which have active subsidiaries (see note [b]).
[d] Includes a very small portion of foreign holdings and large portions in the public domain subject to federal leasing laws. Prior to June, 1946, no individual or company could lease more than 2,560 acres; in June, 1946, the maximum number of leasable acres was doubled.

posits involve the lowest recovery costs of any in the field, and for years have been the center of rock-mining operations. The remaining reserves are largely inactive and widely scattered. About 55,000 acres are in the federal domain and may be leased and operated by private firms and individuals. A small part is in the custody of the Tennessee Valley Authority.

In spite of wide dispersion in ownership, control of Florida land-pebble-rock production has been highly concentrated in the hands of about seven or eight producers for more than fifty years. For a decade after phosphate rock was discovered in Florida in the 1880's, competitors were numerous. As early as 1892 they numbered more than a hundred.[5] By 1913 the number of independent pebble-rock producers serving the domestic market had dropped to eleven; and, through vertical integration, pebble-rock production had become concentrated in the hands of a few large commercial fertilizer producers.[6] Of the 2.06 million tons of Florida pebble rock mined in 1913, the largest producer, the International Agricultural Corporation, accounted for 32.8 per cent; the two largest producers for 48.4 per cent, the three largest for 56.5 per cent; and five large commercial fertilizer producers accounted for 62.8 per cent (Table 4).

*The Tennessee Fields.* By 1913 the same firms that had rapidly increased their holdings in Florida had also begun to dominate the phosphate-mining industry in Tennessee. Four of the fourteen companies operating in Tennessee in that year were large fertilizer manufacturers; and three of these

[5] Carroll D. Wright, *The Phosphate Industry of the United States,* Sixth Special Report of the Commissioner of Labor, March 20, 1893, pp. 91, 110-31.
[6] FTC. *Report on the Fetrilizer Industry* (Washington, 1916). 100 ff.

TABLE 4

FLORIDA PEBBLE ROCK MINED BY FIVE LARGE
COMMERCIAL FERTILIZER PRODUCERS, 1913 [a]

| Company | Tons Mined | Per Cent of Total Pebble Rock Mined | Per Cent of Total Rock Consumed in United States |
|---|---|---|---|
| American Agricultural Chemical Co...... | 320,675 | 15.6 | 18.1 |
| Virginia-Carolina Chemical Co........... | 167,165 | 8.1 | 9.5 |
| International Agricultural Corp.[b]........ | 673,277 | 32.8 | 38.1 |
| Swift & Co............................. | 70,000 | 3.4 | 4.0 |
| Armour Fertilizer Works................ | 60,000 | 2.9 | 3.4 |
| Total—5 large fertilizer companies....... | 1,291,117 | 62.8 | 73.1 |
| Total—United States................... | 2,055,482 | 100.0 | 116.3 |

[a] Federal Trade Commission. *Report on the Fertilizer Industry*, 1916, pp. 96 and 101.
[b] Corporate name changed later to International Minerals & Chemical Corp.

were simultaneously the largest producers of commercial fertilizer, the largest producers of Tennessee rock, and the largest producers of Florida pebble rock. The American Agricultural Chemical Company, the Virginia-Carolina Chemical Company, and the International Agricultural Corporation, through their own operations and those of their subsidiaries, controlled 56.5 per cent of the Florida pebble output, fifty-five per cent of the Tennessee rock output, and nearly fifty per cent of the total domestic output of phosphate rock of all kinds. Swift & Company and Armour Fertilizer Works—two other large fertilizer and Florida pebble-rock producers—owned significant phosphate deposits in Tennessee but at least until 1916 had not begun regular mining operations.

*Causes of High Concentration.* Early concentration of control in phosphate rock was due in part to the normal attrition of high-cost producers. Many small-scale operators who entered the fields during the rush soon discovered that the deposits could not be mined profitably—the actual yields were far smaller than expected. Their exit was hastened by the rapid decline in the price of phosphate rock. Between 1881 and 1915 the price fell from $7.00 to less than $3.00 per ton, and from $6.30 to $2.50 in the first seven years of operations in the Florida fields. But both concentration and vertical integration were also increased by mergers. Complete data on the number of phosphate-rock company mergers in this period are not available, but there is evidence that enough occurred to alter measurably the structure of the industry. The American Agricultural Chemical Company acquired sixteen companies on the date of its incorporation in 1893, most of them fertilizer companies. By 1913 it had acquired control of the Pierce Phosphate Company and the Palmetto Phosphate Company, both pebble-rock producers, the Peter B. and Robert

S. Bradley Company, a hard-rock producer, and the American Phosphate Mining Company, principally a Tennessee rock producer.[7] The International Agricultural Corporation acquired controlling interest in thirteen large companies soon after its incorporation in 1909. By 1913 it had also acquired the Florida Mining Company and the Prairie Pebble Phosphate Company, both pebble-rock producers, and the Independent Phosphate Company and the Volunteer State Phosphate Company, both Tennessee rock producers. The Virginia-Carolina Chemical Company, formed in 1895 by a merger of over thirty mixed-fertilizer and fertilizer-materials producers, by 1913 had acquired interests in the Ammo-Phos Corporation (which in 1915 acquired the Amalgamated Phosphate Company with mines around Chicora, Florida) and in the Charleston (S.C.) Mining and Manufacturing Company, which operated mines around Charleston, South Carolina, and Fort Meade, Florida. Also by 1913 Swift & Company had acquired the State Phosphate Company of Bartow, Florida, and the Royster Guano Company and American Cyanamid Company had acquired other fertilizer firms.

## C. THE INTERWAR PERIOD

The degree of concentration in the phosphate-rock mining industry did not change significantly between the two world wars, but the relationship among the producers, primarily in response to developments in the international market, underwent changes that further tended to lessen competition.

For several years after the large integrated fertilizer producers had gained control over a substantial portion of the phosphate-rock industry they operated at arm's length; at least there is no evidence that they colluded to restrain trade in the domestic market. However, developments during and following World War I provided them with impelling reasons for doing so. The discovery of extensive high-grade phosphate deposits in North Africa in 1917 threatened to drive United States producers out of the European market, the most lucrative market they had until World War I interrupted international trade. Suspension of normal trade during the war years had reduced annual United States rock exports from over one million long tons (1910-14) to slightly over one-tenth of one million long tons by 1918. At the war's end they faced a common rival, North African phosphate, and they saw the necessity of making peace among themselves. The Webb-Pomerene Act of 1917 and the patent rights to an important recovery process granted one of the large producers in 1925 enabled them to do so.

*Formation of Export Associations.* Confronted with rebuilding a foreign

[7] *Ibid.*

market in the face of strong potential competition from a rival source having a tremendous freight advantage, United States producers, now reduced to a manageable number, banded together under the legal sanction of the Webb-Pomerene Act to protect their mutual interests abroad. In 1919 they formed three export associations: the Phosphate Export Association (PEA), to export high-grade Florida pebble phosphates; the Florida Pebble Phosphate Export Association, to export standard-grade Florida pebble phosphates; and the Florida Hard Rock Phosphate Export Association (Hardphos), to export Florida hard-rock phosphate. Both of the pebble-rock export associations used the same office building and were under the same management; and since some companies produced both high-grade rock (seventy-two per cent bone phosphate of lime content or over) and standard-grade rock (seventy per cent BPL or less), the two associations had duplications in membership (Table 5). By 1933 the mem-

TABLE 5

MEMBERSHIP OF PHOSPHATE EXPORT ASSOCIATION
AND FLORIDA PEBBLE PHOSPHATE
EXPORT ASSOCIATION, 1919-45 [a]

| Company | Membership in Phosphate Export Association[b] | Membership in Florida Pebble Phosphate Export Association[c] |
|---|---|---|
| American Agricultural Chemical Co. | Sept. 3, 1929—Oct., 1945 | Mar. 6, 1919—July 1, 1933 |
| American Cyanamid Co. | Mar. 21, 1929—Oct., 1945 | Mar. 6, 1919—July 1, 1933 |
| Coronet Phosphate Co. | Feb. 13, 1919—1927 Jan. 1, 1941—Oct. 1945 | Dec. 22, 1922— April 12, 1926 |
| International Mineral and Chemical Corp. | Feb. 13, 1919—Oct. 1945 | Mar. 6, 1919—July 1, 1933 |
| The Phosphate Mining Co. | Feb. 1919—Feb. 1926 Aug. 1933—Oct. 1945 | Mar. 6, 1919—Feb. 1926. |
| Southern Phosphate Corp. | Feb. 1920—Oct. 1945[d] | May 2—Oct. 31, 1925 Mar. 11, 1930—June 30, 1933 |
| Swift & Co. | Dec. 1, 1933—Oct. 1945 | Not a member |
| Armour Fertilizer Works | Jan. 3, 1922—Nov.30, 1924[e] | Not a member |
| Ore and Chemical Corp. | May 1, 1929—Feb. 9, 1933 Aug. 8, 1933—Dec. 31, 1940 | Not a member |

[a] PEA, "Report and Recommendations," 42 FTC, 555, 569-74 (1946). FTC, *Report on International Phospate Cartels*, 1946.
[b] Voluntarily dissolved in October, 1945.
[c] Absorbed by Phosphate Export Association July, 1933.
[d] Resigned its membership for a brief period in 1926.
[e] Ceased operating in 1924.

bership of both pebble-rock associations had become identical, at which time PEA absorbed the standard-rock association. From April, 1921, to July, 1923, and from December, 1933, until the voluntary dissolution of PEA in October, 1945, the hard-rock (Table 6) and pebble-rock associations worked in close harmony with each other.

TABLE 6

MEMBERSHIP OF HARD ROCK PHOSPHATE
EXPORT ASSOCIATION, 1919-45 [a]

| | Date of Membership |
|---|---|
| Dunnellon Phosphate Mining Co. | 1932—June, 1945 |
| Societie Anonyme La Floridienne[b] | 1919-22 |
| (J. Buttgenbach & Co.) | 1933—June, 1945 |
| C. & J. Camp, Inc. | 1919-25 |
| | 1933—June, 1945 |
| Cummer Lime and Manufacturing Co.[c] | 1919-25 |
| Mutual Mining Co.[c] | 1919-33 |
| Dunnellon Phosphate Co.[c] | 1919-26 |

[a] Florida Hard Rock Phosphate Export Association, "Report and Recommendations," 40 FTC, 843, 847-49 (1945); Federal Trade Commission, *Report on International Phosphate Cartels*, 1946.
[b] Formally in and out of the Association, but a member for all practical purposes from 1919 to 1945.
[c] Inactive after date of resignation from association.

PEA, as previously indicated, was organized to protect the mutual interests of its members in foreign markets. According to the findings of the Federal Trade Commission,[8] minimum export prices were fixed by the council of the association, comprised of one representative from each member company. No member was permitted either to quote prices or independently to negotiate inquiries received on phosphate-rock exports. Each member had a fixed quota for each grade of rock and the quota of each new member was determined by agreement. The association was empowered to examine the books and records of its members at any time, and it required each member to submit monthly reports on exports and cancellations. The council administered a special fund, set up from pro rata deposits by member companies, to liquidate fines imposed upon members for breaching the association's rules and regulations. In short, PEA was organized like a cartel, empowered to control the marketing of virtually all the domestic pebble rock sold outside the United States. In only four years between 1919 and 1945 did pebble-rock exports not under the direct control of PEA amount to as much as twenty per cent of total United States rock exports; in only nine years did they exceed eleven per cent.

With but few exceptions, the principal United States producers of phosphate rock, knit together through common membership in an export association, entered into and honored exchange agreements among themselves, both in their domestic and foreign phosphate-rock business. Hardphos, whose members sold almost their entire output outside the United States, had an organization similar to PEA's.

*Pre-Cartel Activity.* By 1920 it was evident that French North African miners were in a position to offer Florida mine operators serious competition in the European phosphate market. Their location gave them a decided freight advantage in most of Europe and their production and loading

[8] PEA, "Report and Recommendations," 42 FTC, 577 (1946).

costs per ton are reported to have been at least one dollar lower.[9] As early as January, 1920, PEA attempted to open negotiations with French North African operators to insure "some kind of an equitable arrangement between the African and American miners that might be advantageous to all concerned, looking to the stabilization of prices, the elimination of long-term contracts, c.i.f. sales and competitive offerings intended to break down prices." [10] To present a united front in negotiating with French North African producers, American hard-rock and pebble interests—Hardphos and PEA members—formed a joint association in 1921. Their initial suggestions to the North African interests, although favorably received by both the French government and French miners, resulted in no formal action. The French miners had more business than they could handle and they could not determine from their early development operations what their long-run competitive position in Europe would be. PEA recognized the necessity for lowering prices on rock to Europe as an interim measure. Hardphos refused to follow PEA's price reductions and the joint association was dissolved in June, 1923.

For a year or so following 1923, the position of each major rock-producing group selling in the European market remained relatively stable. But by 1925, PEA members felt the impact of increased competition from North African producers. Whereas the actual tonnage of Florida pebble sold in Europe remained relatively constant between 1920 and 1925, North African shipments over the same period increased from 1.82 million long tons to 4.0 million long tons (Table 7). PEA authorized its European sales director to reopen negotiations with the French and in April, 1925, authorized its president to make an agreement with them. The governors of Algeria, Tunisia, and Morocco, and the producers of low-grade phosphate rock in Algeria and Tunisia approved the proposals, but the producers of high-grade rock in Morocco would not join in the agreement. To prod the Morocco group into action PEA voted in October, 1926, to sell 200,000 tons of phosphate rock per year in Europe at reduced prices.

Soon another development threatened to further disturb the European market. Early in 1927, Coronet Phosphate Company, a member of PEA, entered into a contract with Metallgesellschaft (a large German industrial firm, hereafter referred to as Metall) to handle its European sales.[11] Coronet then resigned from PEA. Metall immediately began an intensive sales campaign in Europe. Confronted with a common rival, PEA and the North African group resolved their differences and, after several unsuccessful attempts, prevailed upon Metall to co-operate with them. Metall dropped its independent sales policy in Europe; and in 1929 the

---

[9] FTC, *Report on International Phosphate Cartels*, 1946, p. 29.
[10] *Ibid.*
[11] PEA. "Report and Recommendations." 42 FTC 555, 600 (1946).

TABLE 7

FLORIDA PEBBLE, FLORIDA HARD ROCK, AND NORTH AFRICAN PHOSPHATE EXPORTS, 1919-40

(in 1,000 long tons) [a]

| Year | PEA Shipments | Shipments Outside PEA | Total | Per Cent of Total Exports | Hardphos Shipments | Hard Rock Shipments Outside Hardphos | Total | Per Cent of Total Exports | North African Shipments | Per Cent of Total Exports |
|---|---|---|---|---|---|---|---|---|---|---|
| 1919 | 57,158 | 73,816 | 130,974 | .... | 138,768 | 102,383 | 241,151 | .... | .... | .... |
| 1920 | 416,602 | 269,164 | 685,766 | 24.03 | 261,545 | 84,693 | 346,238 | 12.13 | 1,822.4 | 63.84 |
| 1921 | 297,548 | 270,867 | 568,415 | 23.05 | 117,764 | 13,484 | 131,248 | 5.32 | 1,766.0 | 71.62 |
| 1922 | 334,222 | 193,711 | 527,933 | 16.11 | 113,500 | 34,698 | 148,198 | 4.52 | 2,600.3 | 79.36 |
| 1923 | 506,205 | 138,934 | 645,139 | 17.06 | 117,969 | 41,063 | 159,132 | 4.21 | 2,976.9 | 78.73 |
| 1924 | 560,534 | 101,974 | 662,508 | 15.13 | 63,285 | 81,808 | 145,093 | 3.31 | 3,570.6 | 81.55 |
| 1925 | 664,363 | 29,887 | 694,250 | 14.32 | 74,295 | 75,575 | 149,870 | 3.07 | 4,002.6 | 82.58 |
| 1926 | 613,273 | 26,599 | 639,872 | 13.15 | 45,265 | 62,475 | 107,740 | 2.21 | 4,119.5 | 84.64 |
| 1927 | 693,234 | 90,546 | 783,780 | 13.56 | 51,596 | 74,129 | 125,725 | 2.18 | 4,869.1 | 84.26 |
| 1928 | 643,274 | 169,941 | 813,215 | 15.01 | 24,075 | 60,430 | 84,305 | 1.56 | 4,520.2 | 83.43 |
| 1929 | 822,905 | 238,510 | 1,061,415 | 16.92 | 16,970 | 47,405 | 64,375 | 1.03 | 5,146.2 | 82.05 |
| 1930 | 954,030 | 189,746 | 1,143,776 | 18.25 | 14,108 | 51,655 | 65,763 | 1.05 | 5,059.2 | 80.71 |
| 1931 | 725,316 | 103,715 | 829,031 | 21.05 | 13,700 | 27,075 | 40,775 | 1.04 | 3,069.3 | 77.92 |
| 1932 | 477,886 | 64,605 | 542,491 | 14.72 | 27,840 | 16,215 | 44,055 | 1.20 | 3,098.5 | 84.08 |
| 1933 | 686,449 | 100,131 | 786,580 | 18.94 | 37,015 | 4,275 | 41,290 | 0.99 | 3,325.3 | 80.07 |
| 1934 | 873,790 | 26,216 | 900,006 | 19.88 | 93,399 | none | 93,399 | 2.06 | 3,534.0 | 78.06 |
| 1935 | 936,911 | 36,816 | 973,730 | 22.63 | 102,411 | none | 102,411 | 2.38 | 3,225.8 | 74.98 |
| 1936 | 990,697 | 22,066 | 1,012,763 | 22.42 | 119,725 | none | 119,725 | 2.65 | 3,384.8 | 74.93 |
| 1937 | 944,361 | 3,299 | 947,660 | 19.65 | 68,560 | none | 68,560 | 1.42 | 3,800.7 | 78.93 |
| 1938 | 953,683 | 7,992 | 961,675 | 21.83 | 121,065 | none | 121,065 | 2.74 | 3,323.4 | 75.43 |
| 1939 | 774,399 | 32,985 | 807,384 | 18.00 | 86,621 | none | 86,621 | 1.93 | 3,592.7 | 80.07 |
| 1940 | 664,597 | .... | .... | .... | 19,355 | none | 19,355 | .... | .... | .... |

[a] PEA, "Report and Recommendations," Appendix L, 42 FTC 555, 862 (1946); and FTC, *Report on International Phosphate Cartels*, 1946, pp. 15-16.

company, through its American subsidiary, Ore and Chemical Corporation, joined PEA. The three producing groups, their principal differences resolved, had laid the foundations for an international cartel agreement as early as 1929; but when European consumption rose and prices remained stable throughout 1929 and 1930, they did not work out its details at that time.

*The International Cartel Agreement.* Developments within each major phosphate producing group and in the international phosphate market after 1930 apparently convinced both PEA and the North African producers that a cartel arrangement would be to their mutual advantage. The world-wide depression reduced North African rock exports from about five million to three million long tons between 1930 and 1932 (Table 7). PEA exports declined by one-half. The decline in demand and competition from outside PEA and the North African group caused a substantial reduction in prices. The devaluation of the United States dollar in 1933 nearly wiped out the competitive advantage that the North African producers' location had given them; but since the gap between their delivered costs and those of PEA members had not closed, PEA was still anxious to reach an agreement with the French North African group. Before a cartel agreement could be effective, representatives of the several groups had to assure each other that they represented their respective producing areas. They therefore set about putting their own houses in order.

In 1933, four United States producers outside PEA sold pebble rock abroad. The Phosphate Mining Company had withdrawn from the association in 1926. Since that time its sales had been confined principally to shipments of standard-grade rock to Japan. Coronet Phosphate Company had resigned from the association in 1927, when it contracted with Metall to handle its sales in Europe. Metall, through its subsidiary the Ore and Chemical Corporation, had slipped in and out of the association to suit its own convenience between 1929 and 1933. At the time PEA and the French producers began preliminary negotiations in July, 1933, Metall was offering stiff competition to both groups in the European market. Swift & Company had never been a member of PEA, although the association had acted as Swift's sales agent in the Japanese market. Hardphos was independent of PEA. PEA's preliminary tasks seemed to be clearly defined. It had to induce the independent pebble producers to join the association, and it had to work out a co-operative arrangement with Hardphos. Taking first things first, PEA turned its attention to pebble-rock producers outside the association.

In applying for readmission to PEA, the Phosphate Mining Company imposed certain conditions as a prerequisite to its acceptance of membership.[12] The principal condition was that it be allowed a sufficiently large quota to meet its outstanding Japanese contracts. PEA's acceptance of these conditions, with slight modification, brought the Phosphate Mining Company back into the association in August, 1933.

Negotiations to secure the application of Metall for readmission to PEA were also successful. Metall, however, reserved the right to withdraw from the association upon the expiration of its contract with Coronet, an action which would leave Coronet's exports outside the association's control. PEA met this contingency by obtaining Coronet's promise to apply for membership when its contractual arrangement with Metall terminated.[13]

When PEA began negotiating with Swift & Company, counsel for Swift objected on legal grounds to the activities of PEA, particularly to its participation in foreign agreements. After several lengthy conferences at which lawyers representing Swift raised many questions concerning PEA's past and proposed activities, Swift applied for membership on December 1, 1933, reserving the right, however, to withdraw at the end of any year on sixty days' notice.[14] Although its regulations required six months' notice prior to the withdrawal of a member, PEA made an exception of Swift and immediately approved its application.

In the meantime, the French North African producers had also reached an agreement among themselves. Around the middle of 1933, Algerian and Tunisian mine operators, prompted by the devaluation of the United States dollar, formed the Comptoir des Phosphates d'Algerie et de Tunisie. The Office Cherifien des Phosphates (OCP), the government-financed Morocco company, could not become a full-fledged member of the Comptoir because of its semi-official status; however, it entered into an agreement with the Comptoir which provided that the commercial director of OCP in Paris would serve as general director of sales for both OCP and the Comptoir. Having disposed of these preliminary steps to an effective cartel arrangement, PEA and the French turned their attention to the details of the cartel itself.

The International Phosphate Cartel, initiated by the Florida pebble and North African phosphate producers in December, 1933, functioned according to the provisions set forth in six specific agreements.[15] Three of these served as a basis of cartel control of the European market: (1) the French Agreement executed by the French and PEA on December 12, 1933; (2) the Hard Rock or Paris Agreement between Hardphos and the African-American group reached on December 1, 1933, which was

[12] PEA. Transcript of Testimony, pp. 680-83. 42 FTC 555 (1946).
[13] PEA. "Report and Recommendations." 42 FTC 555, 604 (1946).
[14] *Ibid.*, p. 690.
[15] *Ibid.*, pp. 605-19.

incorporated into the French Agreement and made conterminous with it; and (3) the Curaçao Agreement between the three parties to the French and Paris agreements and Mÿnmaatschappÿ Curaçao, entered into on June 19, 1934.

Three other agreements, collectively referred to as the Japanese Agreements, served to control the prices and quantities of phosphate rock entering the Far Eastern market: (1) the Japanese or Pacific Low Grade Agreement ratified by PEA, Kosseir (Societa Egiziani per L'Estrazione ed il Commercio dei Fosfati) of Alexandria, Egypt, Safaga (Egyptian Phosphate Company) of London, England, and the North African Group, on February 13, 1934; (2) the Kosseir Agreement between Kosseir and the North African Group, reached on January 1, 1937; and (3) the Pacific High Grade Agreement between all the parties to the Pacific Low Grade Agreement on the one hand and the Pacific High Grade Group, consisting of the British Phosphate Commission, La Cie Francaise des Phosphates de L'Oceanie, and Christmas Island Phosphate Company, Ltd., on the other, signed on April 15, 1937.

The French Agreement served as the basic instrument of cartel control, the other five agreements being essentially amendments to it. Executed on December 12, 1933, it was to remain in force until December 31, 1943, but was automatically renewable for five-year periods if neither party gave notice of termination at least two years prior to the date of expiration. Although the war interrupted its operation in 1939, the agreement was not formally dissolved until December 31, 1944, six months after PEA had officially notified other parties of its rescission of the agreement in June, 1944.

From its birth in December, 1933, to its unofficial termination in 1939 the cartel was plagued with competition from nonmembers, first from producers located in Curaçao, and then in succession from those located in Egypt, on the Ocean, Nauru, Makatea, and Christmas islands in the Pacific, and in Russia.[16] Its efforts to support prices invited competition, and each new competitor had to be placated and absorbed. In the end, all except the Russian interests became parties to the cartel agreement; but as competition was throttled in one area, it appeared elsewhere. Successive compromises and Russian competition called for frequent revisions of price and quota schedules. While the cartel undoubtedly managed to maintain international prices above a competitive level, it never circumvented all the strong competitive forces that confronted it. As an international cartel it was only moderately successful.

*The International Cartel and the Domestic Market.* Harmonious rela-

16 For a detailed account of the cartels activities see Federal Trade Commission, *Report on International Phosphate Cartels,* 1946.

tions among United States phosphate producers in the export market affected their relations in the domestic market. PEA and Hardphos representatives were also the officers of domestic phosphate-mining companies. As representatives of the associations they had access to export price, sales, and other records, and frequently met to discuss them and related matters. Since the rock destined for export came from the same mines as that destined for the domestic market, producing firms could hardly consider export prices and shipments unrelated to prices and shipments in the domestic market.

More important, since *all* exports by domestic producers were applied against the quotas allowed PEA and Hardphos, the export associations had a strong incentive to limit, by whatever means possible, the number of phosphate producers engaged in foreign trade. This entailed limiting the number of phosphate producers selling in the domestic market. The export associations used two methods to restrict entry: indirect restriction by charging foreign consumers discriminatory prices as against domestic consumers and direct restriction by denying potential competitors the use of certain processes and terminal facilities.

The pricing of phosphate rock in domestic and foreign markets during the early twenties and after the formation of the cartel was consistent with the pricing policy of a discriminating monopolist. In some parts of Europe intensive cultivation creates a relatively inelastic demand for phosphate and other fertilizer materials. In the United States, on the other hand, the possibility of substituting new land, or more land and labor, for fertilizer creates a more elastic demand for fertilizer. Under such conditions, a monopolist behaves rationally only when he equates his marginal cost to marginal revenue in each of his separate markets, charging higher prices in the market having the less elastic demand. The Florida phosphate group pursued a pricing policy after it formed PEA consistent with that of a discriminating monopolist.

Between 1919 and 1922, after the formation of PEA but before serious competition developed between United States and North African producers, phosphate rock destined for European markets sold for an average price of $7.33 per long ton f.o.b. mines, or eighty-one per cent higher than the average domestic f.o.b. mine price of $4.05.[17] Competition in the European market, particularly after 1925, gradually eliminated the price differential; the average price of rock shipped to Europe for the period 1929-33 was $3.12, while the average domestic price for the same period was $3.03. After 1933, a significant differential between export and domestic prices again appeared, which increased as additional sources of supply were brought under the cartel's control. In 1933

[17] PEA. "Report and Recommendations." 42 FTC 555, 765 (1946).

the export price of Florida pebble rock was \$2.81 per ton, or only 1.4 per cent higher than the domestic price of \$2.77. By 1937 the export price had increased to \$4.45 per ton, or to over twice the domestic price of \$2.14.

In none of its several investigations[18] of the export associations did the Federal Trade Commission find that the discriminatory pricing policy in itself restrained domestic trade. In fact, the Commission concluded the opposite to be true: since the volume of each domestic producer's exports was limited by the by-laws of PEA to a percentage of the total quota allowed all PEA members, an expansion of output by any member would have been channelled into the domestic market, thereby reducing prices. The Commission concluded: "It is apparent that the cartel agreements, by restricting exports, indirectly depressed prices in the domestic market." [19] Moreover, since the exporting Florida producers had to compete with Tennessee rock producers, who had a freight advantage over Florida rock producers in certain interior areas in the domestic market, but who were barred from foreign markets because of prohibitive transportation costs to Atlantic ports, "domestic prices tended to remain on a low competitive level." [20]

In view of the Commission's findings that both PEA and Hardphos measurably *increased* their export business through the cartel agreements, one could of course just as logically argue the other way; i.e., had the associations not joined the cartel, domestic producers would have sold less rock in Europe and Asia and more rock in the United States, thereby depressing domestic prices to an even lower level. Furthermore, there is no logical basis for concluding that even the low discriminating monopolists' price is lower than a competitive price. However, the important economic consideration is not whether the cartel agreement resulted in higher or lower domestic prices that would have otherwise prevailed, but whether PEA and Hardphos and the agreements they entered into made domestic prices less competitive. The evidence suggests that they did.

Before 1927, and after OPA controls were removed in 1946, domestic phosphate-rock prices were relatively flexible, averaging about three or four changes per year. Between 1927 and 1942, when nearly all the Florida producers were bound together through interlacing export associations, prices were stable, experiencing only one important change (in December, 1935) throughout the entire sixteen-year period.[21] PEA and Hardphos evidently stabilized domestic prices. But even if the Commission's conclusion that they also depressed domestic prices be accepted,

[18] Hardphos, "Condensed Report of Investigation," 40 FTC 943 (1944); PEA, 42 FTC 555 (1946).
[19] FTC, *Report on International Phosphate Cartels*, 1946, p. 58.
[20] *Ibid.*
[21] See Figure 1, p. 118.

it does not follow that price competition was not affected. If they did so, they made the phosphate-rock industry less attractive to potential producers and kept down the number of independent firms. The policy of suppressing prices in the short run in order to maintain higher prices in the long run is not altogether unfamiliar.

Obviously, however, PEA and Hardphos members needed stronger weapons than discriminatory prices to preserve their collective interests both here and abroad. They needed the power to prevent entry into any of their markets a new firm wished to enter. The findings of the Federal Trade Commission indicate that the associations had such power and used it effectively.[22] The most important sources of such power were (1) control by one of PEA's charter members of the flotation-process patent; (2) control by Hardphos members of the Fernandina, Florida, Terminal facilities; and (3) long-term contractual arrangements between PEA and its members which provided that, while the French Agreement was in effect, no member, except Swift & Company and Ore and Chemical Corporation, could resign from the association or dispose of its mineral deposits without first arranging for the continuation of PEA's control over the export of rock from the deposits affected.

The flotation process for phosphate-rock recovery was patented in 1928 by the Phosphate Recovery Corporation,[23] a joint subsidiary of International Agricultural Corporation and the Minerals Separation North American Corporation. The process reduced considerably the cost of recovering pebble-phosphate rock, and its use became a prerequisite to entering or remaining in the industry on a competitive basis.

In its investigation in 1944 the Federal Trade Commission found considerable evidence that the Phosphate Recovery Corporation, by issuing exclusive licenses to PEA members and refusing to license nonmembers, restricted entry to the phosphate industry after the 1934 cartel agreement had been reached. Prior to 1933 the Phosphate Recovery Corporation had licensed several Florida and Tennessee phosphate-rock producers to use the flotation process on a royalty basis. These contracts contained no exclusive clause. But when the French Agreement was drawn up in December, 1933, both PEA and the North African Group apparently recognized the threat of potential competition to the cartel from non-PEA members in the Florida fields. The agreement provided

[22] PEA, "Report and Recommendations," 42 FTC 555 (1946).
[23] In the course of the Pope Committee's *Hearings Before the Joint Committee to Investigate the Adequacy and Use of Phosphate Resources of the United States,* pursuant to the Pub. Res. 112, 75th Cong., 3rd Sess. (1938), considerable controversy arose over who actually first adapted the flotation principle to phosphate-rock recovery. Oliver C. Ralston, a Bureau of Mines Engineer, testified that the Bureau had laid much of the groundwork for phosphate-rock recovery by the flotation process, but had stopped its experimentations when convinced that private concerns had become sufficiently interested to carry the work on to completion (pp. 991-96). On the other hand, Charles E. Heinricks, one-time assistant to the president of the Phosphate Recovery Corporation and at the same time an employee of the International Agricultural Corporation, testified that the Phosphate Recovery Corp. and other operators were justified in claiming all credit for the development of the process (pp. 960-61).

that PEA's quota would be charged with all pebble-rock shipments from the United States to Europe, whether or not such shipments originated with PEA members. When the agreement was submitted to PEA members for ratification, the Phosphate Mining Company refused to approve it unless the Phosphate Recovery Corporation limited the use of its flotation process to the then existing membership of PEA.[24]

In the meantime, however, Pembroke Chemical Company, controlled jointly by Metall and the English firm of Allbright and Wilson, had applied to the Phosphate Recovery Corporation for a license to use the flotation process at its recently acquired Florida mine. Caught in the period of transition from nonexclusive to exclusive licensing, Phosphate Recovery turned to International Agricultural Corporation, its parent company, for advice. International solved this threat to both the domestic and foreign market by directing Phosphate Recovery to construct and operate a flotation plant for Pembroke, by agreeing to take eighty per cent of Pembroke's output, and by persuading all the members of PEA except the Phosphate Mining Company to apply the remaining twenty per cent against their export quotas on a pro rata basis. International then agreed to absorb in its quota the tonnage the Phosphate Mining Company would lose as a result of Pembroke's exporting twenty per cent of its output.[25]

With the threat of Pembroke's entry into the industry as an independent firm removed, the Phosphate Recovery Corporation began issuing exclusive licenses to PEA members. By mid-1934 it had negotiated exclusive license agreements with all PEA members except the Phosphate Mining Company and International. Phosphate Mining used its own process until 1940, when it obtained an exclusive license to use the flotation process. International, the parent company of the licensing firm, simply had the Phosphate Recovery Corporation construct flotation plants on its properties. However, all the exclusive license agreements provided that International could obtain at any time an exclusive license on the same terms as other PEA members.

What effect the exclusive-license agreements had on the structure of the phosphate-rock industry cannot be precisely determined, since it is quite likely that a number of inactive firms, aware of the exclusive nature of the licensing agreements, never applied for licenses to use the flotation process. However, the proceedings before the Federal Trade Commission produced evidence that at least two potential producers, in addition to Pembroke, were barred from working their Florida deposits because they

---

[24] The Phosphate Mining Company at that time owned the patent rights to its own electromagnetic recovery process. The company stated that it would abide by the same practice it required of the Phosphate Recovery Corporation, i.e., limit the use of its process to PEA members. See PEA, "Report and Recommendations," 42 FTC 555, 632 (1946).
[25] *Ibid.*, pp. 644-59.

were refused licenses. In the latter part of 1934, International refused Armour Fertilizer Works, a large producer of fertilizer, a license to use the process to mine its then-inactive Florida pebble fields because "an option had already been given to the present producers in the Florida pebble field for the exclusive rights to this process." [26] Armour was refused a license, even though it had already been licensed to use the process in its Tennessee fields and had formerly been a PEA member. In September, 1934, the Virginia-Carolina Chemical Company, another large producer of fertilizers, while negotiating a renewal of its phosphate-rock contract with the American Agricultural Chemical Company, threatened to reopen its mines. Virginia-Carolina had mined its Florida rock fields until 1920, but since that year had purchased all its Florida rock, principally from the American Agricultural Chemical Company. During negotiations over the new contract, AAC increased price from $1.95 to $2.25 per ton, or by slightly more than the reported per-ton royalty of $0.25 paid for the use of the flotation process. Virginia-Carolina then threatened to reopen its mines and use the flotation process, since, according to the company's cost studies, this would hold its rock costs to $2.15 per ton. An AAC interoffice memorandum of December 8, 1934, stated that V-C had underestimated its costs, which in fact would run around $2.35 per ton; but more important, "he [Virginia-Carolina] could not obtain a license to use the flotation process under the existing exclusive license agreements." [27] The two companies finally agreed upon a contract price of $2.175 per ton, and V-C continued to purchase rather than to produce its phosphate rock.[28] A similar compromise on prices was reached when V-C again threatened to reopen its Charleston Mining Company mines in 1937 and 1938.

In February, 1935, American Agricultural Chemical learned that the Swann Corporation of Anniston, Alabama, planned to open a phosphate mine on its properties outside Carbor, Florida, and to sell rock in both the foreign and the domestic markets. In anticipation of using the flotation process, President Klug of the Swann Corporation later requested a tour of AAC's Pierce plant where the process was used. AAC officials granted the request but promptly wrote a memorandum to their Florida manager carefully instructing him to dissuade Klug from following his proposed plans. They cautioned the manager particularly to volunteer no

[26] *Ibid.*, p. 637.
[27] *Ibid.*, 638.
[28] The willingness of American Agriculture Chemical to come to terms with Virginia-Carolina on prices was probably prompted by the maneuverings of Mitsui & Co., a Japanese sales agency, at the time. Mitsui alternately approached V-C and Armour with offers to sell 100,000 tons of their rock in Japan if either would reopen its inactive Florida pebble fields. Later Mitsui's American representative suggested that the company might buy either V-C's or Armour's inactive mines if they could not purchase the rock. This, wrote Mitsui's representative, would mean that "they would have a surplus to sell in the American market or wherever they wanted to sell it." Facing these alternatives, AAC lowered its price to V-C; and the International Agric. Corp. lowered its price to Armour, thereby removing the threat of two new entrants. *Ibid.*, pp. 669 ff.

information on costs or prices of rock and to use evasive tactics if Klug should broach these topics. AAC's motive was apparent from the following statement contained in the memorandum:

> It would be the natural consequence of events, if another miner should enter the field and attempt to sell rock in competition with existing miners, at figures lower than existing prices, for the present miners to be inclined to hold their business by reducing prices, even if they had to go as low as their out-of-pocket costs.[29]

The prevention of Swann's entry was not entirely dependent upon the dissuasive powers of AAC's Florida manager. Phosphate Recovery, AAC's licensing subsidiary (jointly owned with International), tested Swann's deposits and found that they did not justify extensive mining, and AAC was not put in the position of again invoking the exclusive licensing clause.

*Harphos Control of Fernandina Terminal Facilities.* Since the flotation process was not adaptable to the recovery of hard rock, cartel members had to rely on other means for restricting entry to this sector of the industry. The Fernandina Terminal Corporation of Fernandina, Florida, afforded the means.

A prerequiste to entering the phosphate hard-rock industry is access to adequate crushing, drying, and storage facilities. Until 1925, four such terminals had served the hard-rock fields: Loncala Phosphate Company, Port Inglis Terminal, Cummer Lumber Company, and Fernandina Terminal Corporation. At the time the cartel agreements were negotiated, however, the Fernandina Terminal Corporation was the only crushing, drying, and storage facility serving the hard-rock fields, the others having discontinued operations between 1920 and 1925 when a number of hard-rock mining companies closed their mines.

Fernandina was a private terminal owned jointly by C. and J. Camp and Mutual Mining Company, two hard-rock producers. In 1933, C. and J. Camp, the Dunnellon Phosphate Mining Company, and J. Buttgenbach & Company were the only active hard-rock producers in the Florida fields and constituted the complete membership of Hardphos. In negotiations preceding the Paris Hard Rock Agreement, the Fernandina terminal was frequently discussed. Both PEA and the French were concerned over potential competition from inactive hard-rock producers. Accordingly, Morgan H. Grace, then president of PEA, conferred in New York with Hardphos representatives on October 6, 1933, and the next day informed proposed cartel members: "They [Hardphos] state that through their control of the terminal which they cannot maintain unless they bring 100,000 tons a year through the terminal they can prevent any other

Hard shipper from shipping." [30] Actually, hard-rock producers had effectively controlled competition in the hard-rock fields since 1927 through restricting the use of terminal facilities, but it was tactically to their advantage to make a guarantee of control contingent upon a 100,000 ton quota in Europe. On October 11, 1933, David B. Kibler, Jr., a member of the Hardphos executive committee, wrote to Buttgenbach's Brussels office:

Mr. Fitch and Mr. Groves were in a position to state that they would not permit any other shipments through the Fernandina Terminal Corporation, and that the plant would be retained for the exclusive use of Dunnellon Phosphate Mining Company, C. and J. Camp, and Buttgenbach. We, therefore, feel that the Fernandina Terminal Corporation is in a position to keep down any further hardrock competition. You know that it is absolutely impractical for a person to build and equip a terminal plant for exporting hardrock phosphate, particularly in view of the small amount of hardrock that can be sold.[31]

With the signing of the Paris Agreement, Hardphos was given the 100,000 ton quota in Europe it requested and continued to control competition in the hard-rock industry through restricting the use of the Fernandina terminal to its members.

On November 27, 1933, C. N. Smith of Tampa, Florida, requested information of PEA regarding annual shipments of 30,000 tons of hard rock his clients wished to make from their deposits, which were estimated at 300,000 tons. PEA referred Smith's request to Hardphos members, none of whom bothered to answer the inquiry. However, Camp's reply to PEA stated that his firm was not at all surprised at developments such as this but that "we believe that with our control of certain facilities . . . it will be difficult for any one to produce phosphate on a paying basis." [32]

In 1935 the Tampa Phosphate Company requested a rate quotation on phosphate rock from its mines to Tampa from the Seaboard Airline Railway, and requested the use of the Fernandina terminal facilities in handling shipments of rock ordered by I. G. Farbinindustrie. Seaboard quoted them a satisfactory rate, but Fernandina replied that it could not serve them because contracts with other producers took up their entire storage capacity. The Tampa Phosphate Company then tried to obtain sidetrack facilities from Seaboard. Seaboard, after conferring with representatives of Hardphos and Fernandina, decided that the persons associated with the Tampa Phosphate Company were "unreliable, unworthy, and unqualified and not financially able to do anything." [33] Thereafter close co-operation developed between the railroads, Hardphos, and Fernandina Terminal, which successfully limited the hard-rock phos-

[30] *Ibid.*, p. 709.
[31] *Ibid.*, p. 709.
[32] *Ibid.*, p. 748.
[33] *Ibid.*, p. 749.

phate industry to members of Hardphos throughout the effective life of the cartel agreement.

*Other Market Restrictions.* Restrictions on the use of the flotation process and Fernandina terminal facilities were perhaps the greatest barriers to entry in the phosphate industry during the cartel period. But to maintain control over prices and output, PEA also had to control both changes in ownership of rock deposits and arbitrage between domestic and foreign markets.

To insure continuing control over the deposits owned by its members at the time the French Agreement was signed, PEA adopted a resolution whereby each member bound itself to retain membership in PEA for the duration of the agreement. The resolution took cognizance of the special concessions that had been made to Swift and Coronet to secure their membership and provided two escape clauses for other members: (1) If any member of PEA wished to resign from the association, it could do so provided it continued to export rock exclusively through PEA with the same quota it had before resignation. (2) If any member wished to dispose of any or all of its mineral deposits, it could do so only after it had arranged that the new owner would continue to live up to the retiring member's agreement regarding resignations.[34] The latter escape clause was rescinded in 1936, possibly because producers knew that it made them vulnerable to anti-trust prosecution, or possibly because none of the members of PEA at that time contemplated selling any of their deposits.

To prevent arbitrage between the domestic and foreign markets, PEA members restricted the resale of phosphate rock sold in the United States and obtained guarantees from the principal foreign producers that they would not invade the United States market. The Federal Trade Commission's investigation of 1944 revealed that each PEA member had a restrictive clause in its domestic sales contract which prohibited domestic purchasers from exporting and reselling phosphate rock.[35] The reason for such clauses is obvious. During the cartel period the average foreign price f.o.b. mines was about forty per cent higher than the domestic price f.o.b. mines. Unless PEA members prevented the resale of rock, "domestic" buyers could buy at the low price and simply offer it for sale to foreign buyers, thereby eliminating the gains to be derived from a discriminatory pricing policy. Moreover, such restrictive clauses prevented buyers of rock from competing in the domestic market with rock producers, a practice that would have complicated the task of equating production destined for the domestic market with domestic sales.

[34] *Ibid.*, pp. 620-21, 689.
[35] *Ibid.*, pp. 818-23.

As a further safeguard against disruptive forces in the domestic market, PEA obtained agreements from the French North African and Curaçao producers not to export rock to the United States.[36] The French Agreement provided that American producers had full liberty of action in the United States, and that one party to the agreement could not negotiate for sales that would harm the other group in another region (outside Europe) without the approval of both groups. The Federal Trade Commission interpreted this provision as meaning that North African producers could sell phosphate rock in the United States only if PEA approved such sales.[37] Finally, evidence uncovered by the Federal Trade Commission's investigation suggests that PEA and Hardphos, to further tighten their control over both domestic and foreign phosphate markets, had inter- and intra-association working agreements covering domestic-market quotas. In 1924 and 1925 the three members of Hardphos—Camp, Mutual Mining Corporation (which ceased mining operations in 1931), and Dunnellon—had a pooling arrangement whereby their rock output was stored together in the Fernandina terminal. The association set prices and quotas; and the withdrawals by each producer, whether sold in the United States or abroad, were applied against that company's quota.[38] This arrangement came to an end in 1926, when J. Buttgenbach, then a nonmember, insisted that its stock be segregated. Subsequently Camp became an inactive member of the association and Dunnellon resigned, leaving Mutual the sole member for the years 1926-31.

Although the Paris Agreement of 1933 did not revive an overt pooling arrangement among the members of Hardphos, the tacit understanding among hard-rock producers that stemmed from the agreement was tantamount to its having done so. The Paris Agreement provided that the Florida hard-rock producers be given a quota of 2.75 per cent of the cartel's total sales in Europe. The three members of Hardphos agreed to share the quota equally and, for all practical purposes, to extend the quota agreement to include domestic sales as well.[39] When the Paris Agreement was signed, Camp, Buttgenbach, and Dunnellon, the three members of Hardphos in 1933, agreed among themselves to apply domestic sales against their European quotas. During the cartel period, however, Camp was virtually the only producer selling substantial quantities of hard rock in the domestic market. The understanding among hard-rock producers appears to have been so thorough that Buttgenbach, a firm operating jointly with Camp, and Dunnellon customarily referred all

[36] *Ibid.*, pp. 836-37.
[37] *Ibid.*
[38] Hardphos. "Report and Recommendations." 40 FTC 863-64 (1945).
[39] *Ibid.*, p. 864.

domestic inquiries about hard rock to Camp.[40] This practice gave Camp a monopoly over the domestic hard-rock market at no sacrifice to Buttgenbach and Dunnellon, since their quotas abroad were increased by tonnages corresponding to Camp's domestic sales.

Because rock producers were aware that agreements to share the domestic market ran counter to the anti-trust laws, domestic quota arrangements were never incorporated in either of the two associations' records, and written communications concerning them were held to a minimum. Hence, evidence of domestic market-sharing agreements and information concerning their precise nature and duration are very limited. Letters from the associations' files produced during the Federal Trade Commission's proceedings suggest that the pebble producers also may have had a working agreement as to how the domestic pebble market was to be shared. For example, in April, 1935, the Pelham Phosphate Company asked Dunnellon and Camp for domestic prices on hard rock. In a letter to Dunnellon concerning the price quotation, an official of Camp, who was also a member of the executive committee of Hardphos, stated:

This whole question of domestic sales is one that will have to be handled with exceeding care because, as you know, the pebble people are working under some sort of allotment arrangement and they protect each other as to customers, and this is the reason that we have thus far hesitated to quote any price to this outfit [Pelham Phosphate Company] until we had the opportunity to discuss the matter with some of our pebble friends, as we do not want anything to happen to distract the very satisfactory relations that now exist. It is our belief that when we are in position to offer rock for domestic purposes and can compete on the pebble scale, we will co-operate with pebble and work under some plan as outlined above although, of course, this is by no means assured, but something we hope for.[41]

The same official later conferred with pebble producers on the matter of domestic sales and in September, 1935, wrote to another member of Hardphos as follows:

As you are aware, we have been making some effort to enter the domestic market because of the Camp/Buttgenbach production of concentrates and had been promised some co-operation from Mr. Burrows [of PEA]. It now seems that pebble are quite anxious to keep us out of the domestic market and, as a consequence, are suggesting our participation in this Japanese cartel, if effected, up to 25,000 tons of high grade rock, which will not affect the European quota, but will about represent the tonnage that we might sell for domestic purposes.[42]

Nothing ever came of Mr. Burrows' suggestion that Hardphos participate in the Far Eastern market, primarily because of objections raised by the North African Group.

The two letters suggest that both Hardphos and PEA encouraged their

[40] Hardphos, Exhibits 406-12. 40 FTC 843 (1945).
[41] *Ibid.*, Exhibit 155.
[42] *Ibid.*, Exhibit 156a.

members to abide by certain quotas in the domestic market, and that PEA, in procuring for Hardphos a larger European quota than the North African Group was at first willing to allow, had obtained from Hardphos a gentleman's agreement not to sell large quantities of rock in the domestic market. To make it convenient and advisable for Hardphos to keep its agreement, the cartel arrangement provided that domestic hard-rock shipments should be deducted from Hardphos' European quota. The effectiveness with which this arrangement limited sales of hard rock in the United States is evidenced by the noticeable decline in domestic hard-rock sales after 1933. For the period 1928-33, which includes all the years of the Great Depression, hard-rock sales in the United States average 13,000 tons per year; for the years 1934-39, average annual sales of hard rock in the United States were less than 1,000 tons, or substantially below the 25,000 tons per year the Camp official had estimated the domestic market would take.[43]

The Federal Trade Commission, after conducting hearings on PEA and Hardphos throughout the late months of 1944, concluded that the activities of the two associations were in violation of either the antitrust laws or the Webb-Pomerene Act, or both, and issued recommendations for the readjustment of the business of both associations.[44] Hardphos agreed in writing to readjust its business to comply with the Commission's recommendations; PEA complied by voluntarily dissolving itself on October 11, 1945.

### D. The Phosphate Rock Industry Since World War II

Several mergers and some changes in mine operations[45] have occurred since the Federal Trade Commission brought its hearings to a close. In 1945 the Virginia-Carolina Chemical Company acquired the Phosphate Mining Company through a 99.83 per cent stock purchase. In 1946 the Davison Chemical Corporation formally acquired the mining properties of the Southern Phosphate Corporation; the two companies had previously been affiliated with each other through interlocking stock ownership and one interlocking director. W. R. Grace & Company acquired Davison in 1954. In 1951 International Minerals acquired Hoover & Mason, a small producer of Tennessee rock. In 1952 the Smith-Douglass Company, a medium-sized fertilizer manufacturer, acquired Coronet. In 1948 David B. Kibler, Jr., formerly the American manager for J. Buttgenbach & Company, bought out the Buttgenbach holdings in Florida

[43] 42 FTC 860.
[44] 42 FTC 555; 40 FTC 943.
[45] The Bureau of Mines, U. S. Department of the Interior, reports significant developments in the phosphate industry annually in its *Minerals Yearbook*. I am also indebted to K. D. Jacob, Bureau of Plant Industry, Soils, and Agricultural Engineering, U. S. Department of Agriculture, for making available to me files containing details on postwar developments.

and later consolidated them with C. and J. Camp to form the Kibler-Camp Phosphate Enterprise. The new company was the only hard-rock phosphate producer in Florida in 1950, the Dunnellon Phosphate Mining Company having been inactive for several years. In 1949 Armour Fertilizer Works began preparations for reopening its Florida phosphate mine, but had produced no rock by 1953.

Since Camp and Buttgenbach had operated their mine holdings jointly from 1935 to 1948, the formal consolidation of the two companies in 1948 had no appreciable effect on the structure of the phosphate industry. International Minerals' acquisition of Hoover & Mason increased concentration. Davison's acquisition of Southern Phosphate and Smith Douglass' acquisition of Coronet left the number of rock producers unchanged, but both acquisitions increased vertical integration. Virginia-Carolina's acquisition of the Phosphate Mining Company increased both vertical integration and concentration. The reappearance of Armour among the Florida pebble-rock producers just about offset the cessation of mining operations by Pembroke. In the meantime several new entrants had begun mining the western deposits.

In 1952 the phosphate-rock industry nominally included about forty producers of phosphate rock of all kinds (Table 8), of which thirty were actively engaged in mining. Seven large Florida pebble-rock pro-

TABLE 8
STRUCTURE OF THE PHOSPHATE-ROCK INDUSTRY, 1952 [a]

| Type of Rock | Number of Active Producers | Per Cent of Total Phosphate Rock Sold or Used by Producers |
|---|---|---|
| Florida Pebble.............................. | 7[b] | 74.2% |
| Florida Soft Rock........................... | 5[c] | 0.9% |
| Florida Hard Rock.......................... | 1 | 0.3% |
| Tennessee Rock............................. | 7[b] | 15.8% |
| Western Rock............................... | 10 | 8.8% |
| Total.................................. | 30[b] | 100.0% |

FLORIDA PEBBLE ROCK PRODUCERS

American Agricultural Chemical Co.
American Cyanamid Co.
Smith-Douglass Fertilizer Co.
Davison Chemical Corp.
International Minerals and Chemical Corp.

Swift & Co.
Virginia-Carolina Chemical Corp.
Pembroke Chemical Corp.[d]
Armour Fertilizer Works[d]

FLORIDA HARD ROCK PRODUCERS

Kibler-Camp Phosphate Enterprise

Dunnellon Phosphate Mining Company[d]

FLORIDA SOFT ROCK PRODUCERS

Sea Board Phosphate Co.
Soil Builders, Inc.
Superior Phosphate Co.

Loncala Phosphate Co.
Colloidal Phosphate Co.
Kellogg Co.

## TABLE 8—*Continued*

### TENNESSEE ROCK PRODUCERS

Tennessee Valley Authority
Virginia-Carolina Chemical Corp.
Armour Fertilizer Works
Federal Chemical Co.

International Minerals & Chemical Corp.
Monsanto Chemical Co.
Owens Agricultural Phosphate Corp.

### WESTERN PRODUCERS

Idaho:

Simplot Fertilizer Co.
Anaconda Copper Mining Co.
San Francisco Chemical Co.[d]
Teton Phosphate Co., Inc.[d]
Gem State Phosphate Co.[d]
　(Idaho Farm Bureau—Gates Bros.,
　Inc.)

Western Fertilizer Association Pacific
　Supply Corp.[e]
Central Farmers Fertilizer Association
　of Chicago[f]

Montana:

Montana Phosphate Products Co.
George Relyea
Anderson Brothers Mining Co. (owned by
　Canadian Consolidation)

Soluble Phosphates, Ltd.[d]
International Minerals & Chemical Corp.[d]
Victor Chemical Works

Utah:

Pearl & Toland Phosphate Co.
Garfield Chemical & Manufacturing
　Corp.[d]

Utah Phosphate Co.[d]
Monsanto Chemical Co.[f]

Wyoming:

San Francisco Chemical Co.
Phosphate Mines, Inc.

Continental Sulphur & Phosphate Corp.

[a] U. S. Bureau of Mines, U. S. Department of the Interior, *Minerals Yearbook,* 1950; *Commercial Fertilizer Yearbook,* 1950; and unpublished records of the Bureau of Plant Industry, Soils, and Agricultural Engineering, U. S. Department of Agriculture.
[b] Includes two producers, Virginia-Carolina Chemical Corp. and International Minerals & Chemical Corp. which operate in both the Florida and the Tennessee fields.
[c] From directory of fertilizer manufacturers appearing in *Commercial Fertilizer Yearbook* (1950), pp. 83-86.
[d] Inactive in 1950.
[e] Planning large phosphate fertilizer plant in 1951.
[f] Developing deposits in 1950.

ducers mined about seventy-four per cent of all the phosphate rock mined in the United States; essentially the same producers have had approximately the same degree of market occupancy since 1913. Six of the seven also manufactured large quantities of superphosphate and mixed fertilizers. The seventh, American Cyanamid, began producing concentrated superphosphate in 1957, but has manufactured no mixed fertilizers. Two of the seven also operated in other fields. Virginia-Carolina and International both operated large phosphate mines in Tennessee, and until 1954 International operated a mine at Drummond, Montana. Completely accurate individual company data are not available, but it can be fairly accurately estimated that in 1952 the seven largest phosphate-rock mining companies produced from seventy-five to eighty-five per cent of total rock output.

While concentration of control over phosphate-rock production has not changed greatly since about 1913, the fertilizer industry, which consumes most of it, has changed its geographical center. Until recently the Southeast consumed most of the Nation's output of fertilizers. Florida and Tennessee were the only practical sources of phosphate rock. The dominant firms in both states were the same. In the last ten years the western phosphate deposits have taken on significance as the geographical center of fertilizer consumption has shifted toward the Midwest. Nineteen of the country's forty-two phosphate-rock producers are located in the western fields. None of the nineteen operates in either the Florida or Tennessee fields except International, which operates in both. While most of the western firms are of fairly recent origin—many are scarcely beyond the prospecting or developmental stage—they constitute a source of potential competition to the oligopoly that has controlled the industry in the past. This development has important implications for public policy which are explored in Chapter 7.

# CHAPTER 3

# THE SUPERPHOSPHATE AND
# MIXED-FERTILIZER INDUSTRIES

ABOUT 6.4 million of the 7.2 million long tons of phosphate rock consumed annually as fertilizer in the United States goes into manufactured fertilizers, and 0.8 million is ground at the mine and sold for direct application to the soil or as a filler in mixed fertilizers (Table 9). Nearly all the rock that goes into manufactured fertilizers is made into ordinary or concentrated superphosphate.

TABLE 9

MAJOR USES OF DOMESTIC PHOSPHATE ROCK, 1954 [a]

|  | Long Tons | Per Cent of Total | Per Cent of Total Domestic Consumption |
|---|---|---|---|
| Fertilizers............................ | 7,213,468 | 55 | 67 |
| Ordinary superphosphate............. | 5,069,176 | 39 | 47 |
| Concentrated superphosphate......... | 1,297,719 | 10 | 12 |
| Nitrophosphate...................... | 12,851 | ....[b] | ....[b] |
| Direct application to the soil......... | 774,016 | 6 | 7 |
| Fertilizer filler...................... | 13,764 | ....[b] | 1 |
| Other fertilizers..................... | 45,942 | ....[b] | .... |
| Other Agricultural Stock and poultry feed.............. | 144,257 | 1 | 1 |
| Industrial........................... | 3,407,527 | 26 | 32 |
| Elemental phosphorus, ferro-phosphorus, and phosphoric acid............ | 3,403,210 | 26 | 32 |
| Undistributed....................... | 4,317 | ....[b] | ....[b] |
| Total domestic consumption............ | 10,765,252 | .... | 100 |
| Exports............................. | 2,278,572 | 18 | |
| Grand total........................ | 13,043,824 | 100 | |

[a] Bureau of Mines *Minerals Yearbook* 1954.
[b] Less than 0.5 per cent.

Phosphate rock is manufactured into superphosphates to make more of the $P_2O_5$ in the rock readily available to growing plants. The total $P_2O_5$ content of ground phosphate rock ranges from twenty-nine to thirty-five per cent by weight, but only about five per cent to ten per cent of the $P_2O_5$ in untreated phosphate rock is soluble in a neutral ammonium citrate solution, a standard test for determining the quantity of $P_2O_5$ in a

60

given phosphate material available to plants.[1] Accordingly, a short ton of ground phosphate rock contains about sixty pounds, or three per cent by weight, of available $P_2O_5$. But combining a ton of ground high-grade phosphate rock with approximately one ton of sulfuric acid ($55°$ Baume') yields about four hundred pounds of available $P_2O_5$, an increase to twenty per cent by weight. Treating ground rock with phosphoric acid instead of sulfuric acid raises the quantity of available $P_2O_5$ per ton of product to about nine hundred pounds, or forty-five per cent. Superphosphate containing less than twenty-nine per cent citrate-soluble $P_2O_5$ is usually called ordinary or normal superphosphate; that containing from twenty-nine to fifty per cent citrate soluble $P_2O_5$ is usually called concentrated, double, or triple superphosphate.[2] In 1954 the superphosphate industry consumed 6.4 million long tons of phosphate rock and produced 2.2 million short tons of citrate-soluble $P_2O_5$; the same tonnage of rock in the raw state contained only 0.2 million short tons of citrate-soluble $P_2O_5$.

About one-third of the superphosphates produced annually in the United States is sold to farmers as straight phosphate fertilizer; the rest is used in the manufacture of mixed fertilizers containing nitrogen (N), $P_2O_5$, and potash ($K_2O$). Mixed-fertilizer manufacturers are required by the laws of the states in which they sell to label their product according to the per cent of N, available $P_2O_5$, and soluble $K_2O$ by weight it contains. For example, a ton of mixed fertilizer designated as grade 5-10-5 must contain at least 100 pounds of N, 200 pounds of available $P_2O_5$, and 100 pounds of $K_2O$, or a total of 400 pounds of plant nutrients. The remainder consists of the associated compounds of the original raw materials and inert material added to bring the product to the desired consistency and grade. The particular fertilizer materials mixers use depend on their cost per unit (20 pounds) of plant nutrient and on the desired grade.[3] Mixed fertilizers containing thirty or more units of plant nutrients generally contain some concentrated superphosphate; those containing less than twenty-five may be made from either superphosphate or concentrated superphosphate, but if they are made from the latter, large quantities of inert filler must be added to produce the desired grade.[4]

The phosphate-fertilizer industry, including rock miners and bene-

---

[1] Calculations of the availability of $P_2O_5$ in phosphate fertilizers are at best rough approximations. The use of uranium and modern tracer techniques has begun to yield more reliable calculations.

[2] Hereafter ordinary superphosphate will be referred to simply as "superphosphate"; "double" "triple," or "concentrated" superphosphate as "concentrated superphosphate"; and the two together as "superphosphates." For a brief technical description of the manufacture of various phosphatic materials, including superphosphate and concentrated superphosphate, see K. D. Jacob, "Phosphate Resources and Processing Facilities," *Fertilizer Technology and Resources in the United States*, K. D. Jacob, ed. (New York: Academic Press, 1953).

[3] See Chap. 10.

[4] For example, one ton of grade 6-12-6 fertilizer can be produced from 400 pounds of ammonium nitrate (30%), 1,333 pounds of superphosphate (18%), 200 pounds of muriate of potash (60%), and 67 pounds of lime. The substitution of 533 pounds of concentrated superphosphate (45%) for the superphosphate would give the same quantities of plant nutrients, but the total weight of the mixture would then be only 1200 pounds, leaving room for the addition of 800 pounds of inert filler.

ficiators, manufacturers of superphosphates, and fertilizer mixers, comprises over 900 independent firms. Only a few of them are vertically integrated through all three processes. Not more than ten per cent of the 750 to 800 mixers produce superphosphate, and scarcely one per cent of them mine phosphate rock. On the other hand, nearly all the phosphate-rock producers are large producers of superphosphates and mixed fertilizers. In terms of total output, in contrast with the total number of firms, a large proportion of the phosphate-fertilizer industry is vertically integrated.

For over forty years five large integrated firms, American Agricultural Chemical Company, International Minerals and Chemical Company, Virginia-Carolina Chemical Company, Swift & Company, and Armour Fertilizer Works, have been important producers of phosphate rock, superphosphates, and mixed fertilizers. The Davison Chemical Corporation (acquired by W. R. Grace in 1954), the Smith-Douglass Fertilizer Company, and the American Cyanamid Company have recently joined the list of integrated producers—Davison when it acquired Southern Phosphate in 1946, Smith-Douglass when it acquired Coronet in 1952, and American Cyanamid when it constructed a concentrated superphosphate plant in Florida in 1957. American Cyanamid does not manufacture mixed fertilizers. These eight firms have produced nearly all the output of Florida pebble and Tennessee rock. Through their various export and trade associations and patent holdings they have at times controlled substantially all domestic phosphate-rock output. The same integrated producers, along with F. S. Royster Guano Company, have produced from about forty-five to sixty-five per cent of the country's superphosphates and from about thirty-five to fifty-five per cent of its mixed fertilizers. Because of the strategic market position the large integrated firms occupy in the phosphate fertilizer industry, they are singled out for special attention in much of the subsequent discussion and analysis.

## A. The Superphosphate Industry

Fertilizer manufacturers have known the technology of superphosphate production by the sulfuric acid process for many years; they produced it in the United States as early as 1850. The early product was not well received by American farmers, partly because they were not acquainted with the appropriate methods of application, and partly because of the faulty manufacturing formulae employed. By 1900, however, annual superphosphate production capacity in the United States had reached 1.5 million tons, or the equivalent of about 270,000 tons of $P_2O_5$; and between 1900 and the first World War, capacity quadrupled. While no such spectacular increases have occurred since, capacity increased seventy-nine per cent between 1940 and 1950 (Table 10).

TABLE 10

ESTIMATED ANNUAL CAPACITY FOR PRODUCTION OF
SUPERPHOSPHATES IN THE UNITED STATES, 1900-54
(in tons of $P_2O_5$)[a]

|      | Number of Plants | Ordinary Superphosphate | Number of Plants | Concentrated Superphosphate |
|------|------------------|-------------------------|------------------|------------------------------|
| 1900 | ......           | 335,000                 | ..               | 1,000                        |
| 1910 | 256[b]           | 950,000                 | 1                | 3,000                        |
| 1920 | ......           | 1,440,000               | ..               | 7,000                        |
| 1930 | ......           | 1,600,000               | 5                | 44,000                       |
| 1940 | 145              | 1,511,888               | 8                | 180,000                      |
| 1945 | 159              | 2,067,503               | 9                | 223,400                      |
| 1947 | 176              | 2,384,433               | 7                | 220,000                      |
| 1950 | 201              | 2,594,147               | 9                | 315,616                      |
| 1952 | 213              | 2,700,000[c]            | 12               | 500,000[c]                   |
| 1954 | ......           | 1,644,515[d]            | ..               | 561,870[d]                   |

[a] 1900-40 data from *Fertilizers and Lime in the United States*, U. S. Dept. of Agriculture Misc. Pub. No. 586, p. 60; 1940-50 data from Jacob, *loc. cit.*, pp. 150, 154; *Commercial Fertilizer*, February 1951. 1952 data from U. S. Dept. of Commerce, *Facts for Industry*, December, 1952. 1954 data from Bureau of Mines, *Minerals Yearbook*, 1954.
[b] 1913.
[c] Estimated.
[d] Actual production.

Superphosphate manufacture requires a relatively simple technology and fairly modest capital outlays. A mixture of approximately 1,100 pounds each of phosphate rock and sulphuric acid yields a short ton of superphospate. The heat generated by the chemical reaction causes the loss of 200 pounds of water through evaporation. Mixing facilities and storage space are the principal physical plant requirements of superphosphate manufacturers who purchase sulphuric acid; and those who manufacture their own sulphuric acid must have co-existing acid facilities. But in either case total capital costs are low. In the Midwest sulphuric acid and phosphate rock account for about ninety per cent and plant overhead for less than ten per cent of total production costs (Table 38, p. 151). Along the Atlantic seaboard sulphuric acid and phosphate rock account for ninety-five per cent and capital and labor only five per cent of the total production costs for the average plant having a capacity of 1,000 tons per day.[5] It is estimated that such a plant, exclusive of sulphuric acid facilities, cost about $1,000,000 in 1952.[6] Since the average superphosphate plant along the Atlantic Seaboard is only one-third, and in the rest of the country less than one-sixth, this size,[7] and was constructed at lower

[5] W. H. Waggaman, *Phosphoric Acid Phosphates and Phosphatic Fertilizer* (2nd ed.; New York: Reinhold Pub. Corp., 1952), 288.
[6] *Ibid.*
[7] J. R. Adams, T. H. Tremearne, K. D. Jacob, and L. G. Porter, *Survey of the Superphosphate and Wet-Process Phosphoric Acid Industries in the United States in 1950 and 1951*, U. S. Dept. of Agriculture, in collaboration with the National Production Authority, the Bureau of the Census, and the Bureau of the Budget (mim. and n.d.), p. 8.

costs than those prevailing in 1952, the cost of entry to the industry has probably been less than one-quarter of a million dollars.

In 1950, eighty-one firms, including thirteen farmers' co-operatives, operated two hundred superphosphate plants in the United States. Ninety of the two hundred superphosphate plants produced their own sulfuric acid. In general, superphosphate plants are market oriented, their location corresponding roughly to the regional pattern of $P_2O_5$ consumption (Table 11). A considerable portion of superphosphate capacity is in the

TABLE 11

CONSUMPTION OF $P_2O_5$, ORDINARY SUPERPHOSPHATE PLANTS,
AND MIXING PLANTS, BY GEOGRAPHICAL REGION,
SELECTED YEARS [a]

| | Per Cent of Total $P_2O_5$ Consumption, 1948-49 | Superphosphate Plants | | Fertilizer Mixing Plants 1950 |
|---|---|---|---|---|
| | | Active 1940 | Active 1950 | |
| New England............ | 3.0 | 3 | 4 | 33 |
| Middle Atlantic........... | 12.2 | 15 | 14 | 91 |
| South Atlantic........... | 25.4 | 59 | 72 | 449 |
| East North Central........ | 21.0 | 28 | 45 | 107 |
| West North Central....... | 9.7 | 0 | 11 | 43 |
| East South Central....... | 15.8 | 30 | 36 | 104 |
| West South Central....... | 7.3 | 8 | 13 | 64 |
| Mountain................ | 1.7 | 0 | 2 | 31 |
| Pacific.................. | 3.9 | 2 | 3 | 121 |
| | 100.0 | 145 | 200 | 1043 |

[a] $P_2O_5$ consumption from *Fertilizer Consumption in the United States, 1948-49,* Bureau of Plant Industry, Soils, and Agricultural Engineering, U. S. Dept. of Agriculture. Plant data from K. D. Jacob, "Phosphate Fertilizer Progress," *Fertilizer Review,* January-February 1948, pp. 6, 9, and *Commercial Fertilizer Yearbook,* 1950.

hands of the large integrated commercial-fertilizer manufacturers, where it has been since 1913 (Tables 12 and 13). The six largest producers of

TABLE 12

CONCENTRATION OF CONTROL IN THE SUPERPHOSPHATE
INDUSTRY, 1913-50 [a]

| | 1913 | 1937 | 1947 | 1950 |
|---|---|---|---|---|
| 3 largest companies | 32.4% (plants) 32 % (output) | ............... | ............... | ............... |
| 4 largest companies | .............. | 33% (plants) 42% (output) | 39.5% (plants) 35.6% (output) | 39.0% (plants) 35.1%(output)[b] |
| 7 largest companies | 44% (plants) 46% (output) | ............... | ............... | ............... |
| 8 largest companies | ............... | ............... | 55.9% (output) | ............... |

[a] FTC, *Report on the Fertilizer Industry,* 1916 and 1950; 1950 data from *Commercial Fertilizer Yearbook,* 1950.
[b] Estimated from number of plants.

## TABLE 13
### NUMBER OF SUPERPHOSPHATE PLANTS OPERATED BY LARGE FERTILIZER PRODUCERS, 1913 AND 1950 [a]

| | 1913 | | 1950 | |
| | Number of Plants | Per Cent of Total | Number of Active Plants | Per Cent of Total |
|---|---|---|---|---|
| Virginia-Carolina............ | 41 | 16.0 | 27 | 13.5 |
| American Agricultural....... | 24 | 9.8 | 17 | 8.5 |
| International.............. | 19 | 7.4 | 19 | 9.5 |
| Armour.................... | 14 | 5.5 | 15 | 7.5 |
| Swift & Co................. | 8 | 3.1 | 10 | 5.0 |
| F. S. Royster.............. | 5 | 2.0 | 11 | 5.5 |
| Baugh & Sons............. | 2 | .7 | 2 | 1.0 |
| Davison................... | ..... | ........ | 5 | 2.5 |
| Total............... | 113 | 44.5 | 106 | 53.0 |
| Total Industry.......... | 256 | 100.0 | 200 | 100.0 |

[a] FTC, *Report on the Fertilizer Industry*, 1916; 1950 data computed from information appearing in *Commercial Fertilizer Yearbook*, 1950.

superphosphates in 1913 and in 1950 were the same companies; and, on the basis of number of plants operated, they have experienced little if any change in relative market shares.[8] In 1950 the largest five, and six of the largest eight, superphosphate manufacturers produced phosphate rock. Three of the eight produced concentrated superphosphates, and all of them produced mixed fertilizers.

## B. THE CONCENTRATED SUPERPHOSPHATE INDUSTRY

Concentrated superphosphate is produced by treating phosphate rock with phosphoric acid, which is also made from phosphate rock. Liquid phosphoric acid can be produced by the wet process, in which finely ground phosphate rock is mixed with sulphuric acid, and by the thermal reduction (electric-furnace or blast-furnace) process, in which phosphate rock is reduced to phosphorus and then absorbed in water. A ton of concentrated superphosphate (48 per cent $P_2O_5$) produced by the wet process requires 3,105 pounds of high-grade phosphate rock and 595 pounds of sulphur; a ton produced by the electric-furnace method re-

[8] Measuring concentration in terms of the per cent of total plants is apparently a reasonably satisfactory method. In 1913 the three largest superphosphate manufacturers produced 32 per cent of the total output and operated 32.4 per cent of all the plants, and the seven largest manufacturers produced 46 per cent of the industry's output and operated 44 per cent of all the plants. In 1937 the four largest firms produced 42 per cent of the industry's total output and operated 33 per cent of all the plants. In 1947 the four largest firms produced 35.6 per cent of total output and operated 39.5 per cent of all the plants.

quires 3,210 pounds of rock, 415 pounds of coke, and 690 pounds of silica; and a ton produced by the blast-furnace method requires 3,420 pounds of rock, 2,840 pounds of coke, and 755 pounds of silica.[9] In 1956 only the wet and the electric-furnace processes were in use in the United States. Because of the large rock requirements, concentrated superphosphate plants locate near phosphate-rock fields.[10]

Concentrated superphosphate was first manufactured commercially in the United States in 1890 by the American Phosphate and Chemical Company of Baltimore, Maryland. Because of its high production costs and its tendency to cake by absorbing moisture, and because of initial consumer resistance, American Phosphate discontinued its production. Practically all of American's output went into the manufacture of mixed fertilizers. In 1907 the Virginia-Carolina Chemical Company [11] placed the domestic industry on a permanent basis with a wet (sulphuric-acid) process plant at Charleston, South Carolina. From 1914 to 1916 the Piedmont Electro-Chemical Company produced concentrated superphosphate at Mount Holly, North Carolina, using the electric-furnace process, and in 1924-25 the Federal Phosphorus Company, using the same process, produced concentrated superphosphate at Anniston, Alabama. Federal primarily produced phosphorus products for technical and industrial purposes but also produced small quantities of phosphoric acid for the manufacture of fertilizers. In the meantime the Anaconda Copper Mining Company had begun producing concentrated superphosphate by the wet process in Montana. But early attempts at producing concentrated superphosphate were generally small-scale and short-lived. Even as late as 1930 the industry comprised only five plants, which produced a total annual output of only 95,000 tons of material, or 43,300 tons of available $P_2O_5$ (Table 14).

The federal government, however, generally responsive to agricultural problems, had laid the foundations for what was to become a comprehensive phosphate-fertilizer program.[12] As early as 1894 the Department of Agriculture had pointed out that considerable savings to the farmer might result from the substitution of concentrated for ordinary superphosphate.[13] In 1911 Secretary of Agriculture James Wilson emphasized the need for better preparation and use of fertilizers,[14] and in the same year Congress voted the Department of Agriculture its first funds for fertilizer research. Although World War I focused the government's attention on potash and nitrogen shortages, it began some experimental

[9] Technical and nontechnical descriptions of each process appear frequently in literature on the phosphate-fertilizer industry. I.e., see K. D. Jacob (ed.), *loc. cit.*, n. 2; and A. L Mehring, *Double Superphosphate*, U. S. Dept. of Agric. Circular No. 718 (1944).

[10] See Chap. 8 for an analysis of locational factors in the concentrated-superphosphate industry.

[11] One or two foreign companies attempted concentrated superphosphate production in the U. S. between 1890 and 1900, but their entire output was exported. See Mehring, *loc. cit.*, n. 4, pp. 6-7.

[12] See Chap. 11.

[13] U. S. Dept. of Agric., *Yearbook*, 1894, p. 185.

[14] U. S. Dept. of Agric., *Annual Report*, 1911, p. 108.

work on phosphates. Research increased substantially during the 1920's. By the time Congress passed an act creating the Tennessee Valley Authority (1933), the Department of Agriculture had been operating a

TABLE 14

GOVERNMENT AND COMMERCIAL CONCENTRATED
SUPERPHOSPHATE PRODUCTION, 1907-53 [a]

(Thousands of tons)

| Year | TVA | Commercial | Total |
|------|-----|-----------|-------|
| 1907 | ...... | 1.8 | 1.8 |
| 1908 | ...... | 2.8 | 2.8 |
| 1909 | ...... | 4.9 | 4.9 |
| 1910 | ...... | 6.2 | 6.2 |
| 1911 | ...... | 6.4 | 6.4 |
| 1912 | ...... | 7.1 | 7.1 |
| 1913 | ...... | 8.5 | 8.5 |
| 1914 | ...... | 8.8 | 8.8 |
| 1915 | ...... | 9.0 | 9.0 |
| 1916 | ...... | 9.0 | 9.0 |
| 1917 | ...... | 7.9 | 7.9 |
| 1918 | ...... | 12.6 | 12.6 |
| 1919 | ...... | 14.3 | 14.3 |
| 1920 | ...... | 15.3 | 15.3 |
| 1921 | ...... | 9.2 | 9.2 |
| 1922 | ...... | 8.4 | 8.4 |
| 1923 | ...... | 15.3 | 15.3 |
| 1924 | ...... | 30.4 | 30.4 |
| 1925 | ...... | 36.6 | 36.6 |
| 1926 | ...... | 37.1 | 37.1 |
| 1927 | ...... | 36.9 | 36.9 |
| 1928 | ...... | 68.3 | 68.3 |
| 1929 | ...... | 80.3 | 80.3 |
| 1930 | ...... | 95.2 | 95.2 |
| 1931 | ...... | 48.3 | 48.3 |
| 1932 | ...... | 24.2 | 24.2 |
| 1933 | ...... | 29.5 | 29.5 |
| 1934 | 1.7 | 67.9 | 69.6 |
| 1935 | 25.5 | 65.6 | 91.1 |
| 1936 | 31.9 | 97.9 | 129.8 |
| 1937 | 38.4 | 127.7 | 166.1 |
| 1938 | 58.1 | 128.8 | 186.9 |
| 1939 | 75.7 | 197.0 | 272.7 |
| 1940 | 91.4 | 237.7 | 329.1 |
| 1941 | 59.3 | 258.7 | 318.0 |
| 1942 | 80.0 | 234.5 | 314.5 |
| 1943 | 50.4 | 243.8 | 294.2 |
| 1944 | 28.1 | 253.0 | 281.1 |
| 1945 | 48.2 | 202.8 | 251.0 |
| 1946 | 94.0 | 228.3 | 322.3 |
| 1947 | 148.6 | 235.2 | 383.8 |
| 1948 | 153.9 | 314.8 | 468.7 |
| 1949 | 148.5 | 400.0 | 548.5 |
| 1950 | 134.4 | 552.4 | 686.8 |
| 1951 | 156.4 | 560.1 | 716.5 |
| 1952 | 135.3 | 727.1 | 862.4 |
| 1953 | 135.7 | 880.3 | 1,016.0 |

[a] From The Tennessee Valley Authority.

phosphorus blast-furnace pilot plant for several years, but the federal government did not become an important producer and distributor of concentrated superphosphate and other high-analysis phosphatic materials until TVA got under way (Table 14).

TVA's production and distribution of concentrated phosphatic materials, the Agricultural Adjustment Administration's conservation grants, and more intensified agronomic research were important factors in the growth of the concentrated-superphosphate industry. In the six years following 1934, TVA's first year of operations, annual output increased from 69,600 tons to 329,100 tons. By 1940 TVA's annual output had reached 91,400 tons, and that of commercial producers 237,700 tons. A large proportion of phosphoric-acid plant capacity was diverted to the production of phosphorus for war needs in the years 1942-45, but by 1947 annual production of concentrated superphosphate had passed the prewar peak, and by 1953 had reached 1,016,000 tons.

In 1950 the concentrated superphosphate industry comprised seven commercial firms and the Tennessee Valley Authority. Collectively they operated nine plants having a total annual capacity of about 650,000 tons (Table 15). All plants except the I. P. Thomas plant at Paulsboro, New

TABLE 15

CONCENTRATED SUPERPHOSPHATE PLANT LOCATIONS
AND CAPACITIES, JULY, 1950 [a]

| Company | Location | Annual Capacity (Tons) |
|---|---|---|
| U. S. Phosphoric Products Co. (Tennessee Corp.)[b] | East Tampa, Fla.... | 250,000 |
| Tennessee Valley Authority[c] | Sheffield, Ala....... | 140,000 |
| Anaconda Copper Mining Co.[c] | Anaconda, Montana | 90,000 |
| Armour Fertilizer Works[b],[c] | Bartow, Fla........ | 70,000 |
|  | Columbia, Tenn.... | 5,000 |
| Gates Bro., Inc. (Idaho Farm Bureau)[b] | Wendell, Idaho..... | 40,000 |
| Swift & Co.[b], [c] | Agricola, Fla....... | 30,000 |
| Virginia-Carolina Chemical Corp.[b], [c] | Charleston, S. C.... | 15,000 |
| I. P. Thomas & Son Co.[b] | Paulsboro, N. J..... | 10,000 |
| Total | | 650,000 |

[a] From TVA, Bureau of Mines, and Moody's *Manual of Industrial Investments* 1951.
[b] Large producers of ordinary superphosphate and mixed fertilizers. I. P. Thomas is reported to have had no concentrated superphosphate capacity as such in 1950 but it produced from 5,000 to 10,000 tons per year of concentrated in its superphosphate plants.
[c] Phosphate-rock producers.

Jersey, which was not designed to produce concentrated superphosphate, were located near their sources of phosphate rock. The TVA plant at Wilson Dam, Alabama, and the Armour Fertilizer Works at Sligo, Tennessee, were close to the middle Tennessee phosphate fields. The Gates

Bros., Inc., plant at Wendell, Idaho, and the Anaconda Copper Mining Company plant at Anaconda, Montana, used the western phosphate deposits, principally those in Caribou County, Idaho, and the Idaho-Montana-Wyoming boundary area. The Virginia-Carolina Chemical Corporation plant, when opened in Charleston, used South Carolina phosphate rock. For a number of years, however, it has used Florida rock. The four largest commercial producers—U. S. Phosphoric, Anaconda, Armour, and Gates—accounted for ninety per cent of the industry's capacity in the hands of commercial firms.

The technology of concentrated superphosphate production is more complex and the capital requirements much higher than in superphosphate manufacture.[15] Both factors account in part for the higher concentration of control. Experience with superphosphate technology and fertilizer marketing and an assured source of phosphate rock apparently make entry to the industry easier. Five of the seven commercial firms producing concentrated superphosphate in 1950 had long been established as large superphosphate and mixed fertilizer manufacturers. A sixth, Gates Brothers, was owned by the Idaho Farm Bureau, a farmer co-operative that owned phosphate-rock deposits and distributed fertilizers. Five of the commercial producers and TVA mined phosphate rock.

Between 1950 and 1957 the number of concentrated superphosphate producers increased from seven to fourteen; annual production increased from 687,000 short tons to about 1,265,000 short tons; and concentration declined considerably. Most of the new entrants were integrated phosphate-rock and fertilizer producers: Davison Chemical (W. R. Grace), with plants at Ridgewood, Florida, and Joplin, Missouri; F. S. Royster at Mulberry, Florida; International Minerals at Bonnie, Florida; J. R. Simplot at Pocatello, Idaho; Western Phosphates, Inc., at Fairfield, Utah; American Cyanamid at Brewster, Florida; and Phillips Chemical Company at Adams Terminal, Texas. All seven had previously produced phosphate rock or fertilizers; most had previously produced both. Meanwhile, several established superphosphate producers began manufacturing small quantities of concentrated superphosphate in their normal superphosphate plants, a technically feasible but generally more costly method of production.

## C. The Mixed-Fertilizer Industry

Fertilizer-mixing plants are located near their markets, the average dry-mix plant making approximately seventy per cent of its sales within a radius of fifty miles of the plant site.[16] Some large plants serve larger

---

[15] See Chap. 8.
[16] John H. Lister, *Co-operative Manufacture and Distribution of Fertilizer by Small Regional Dry Mix Plants*, U. S. Dept. of Agric., Circ. No. C-126, June, 1941.

geographical areas, but proximity to the market is the principal consideration in locating plants. The geographical distribution of fertilizer-mixing
plants, like that of superphosphate plants, corresponds closely to the geographical pattern of fertilizer consumption (Table 11).

Mixing plants are classified according to their facilities into: (1)
complete plants producing sulfuric acid, superphosphate, and mixed fertilizers; (2) wet-mix plants producing superphosphate and mixed fertilizers;
and (3) dry-mix plants, which have mixing facilities only. In 1950 about
700 independent firms, including co-operatives, operated 1,043 fertilizer
mixing plants, of which 120 were complete plants, 152 produced superphosphate but no sulphuric acid, and 771 were mixers only.[17]

The number of fertilizer-mixing plants in the United States has varied
from year to year (Table 16), responding to the rise and fall in farmers'

TABLE 16

FERTILIZER MIXING PLANTS IN THE UNITED STATES, 1859-1950 [a]

| Year | Total No. Mixing Plants | Year | Total No. Mixing Plants |
|---|---|---|---|
| 1859 | 47 | 1925 | 587 |
| 1869 | 126 | 1927 | 621 |
| 1879 | 364 | 1929 | 638 |
| 1889 | 390 | 1931 | 599 |
| 1899 | 422 | 1933 | 522 |
| 1904 | 399 | 1935 | 670 |
| 1909 | 550 | 1937 | 743 |
| 1914 | 784 | 1939 | 764 |
| 1919 | 600 | 1947 | 704 |
| 1921 | 588 | 1950 | 1,043 |
| 1923 | 573 | | |

[a] U. S. Dept. of Commerce, Bureau of Census, *Census of Manufactures.* 1950 total computed
from data appearing in *Commercial Fertilizer Yearbook,* 1950.

demand for fertilizers; but ease of entry made possible by a simple technology and low capital requirements has made for a large number of firms.
Despite these structural characteristics a few large producers acquired
a significant share of the industry through merger between the late 1890's
and 1913—the period of merger that also brought under their control
large segments of the phosphate-rock and superphosphate industries—
most of which they still control.

Between its organization in 1895 and 1914 the Virginia-Carolina Chemical Company, the industry's largest producer, acquired a controlling
interest in from forty-five to fifty fertilizer-manufacturing and distributing companies.[18] In 1914 the company controlled directly or through its
subsidiaries 135 active fertilizer plants, and with them virtually the entire

[17] *Commercial Fertilizer Yearbook,* 1950, pp. 74-126.
[18] All company data for 1914 and earlier are from FTC, *Report on the Fertilizer Industry,* 1916,
pp. 173-271.

fertilizer producing capacity in Georgia, South Carolina, and Alabama. The American Agricultural Chemical Corporation was organized in 1899 as a successor to the Agawa Company, incorporated in 1893. Between 1899 and 1902 American Agricultural acquired a controlling interest in forty companies, all but one of which were located along the Atlantic Seaboard north of Baltimore. This plan of acquisition was in keeping with what seems to have been a tacit understanding between Virginia-Carolina and American Agricultural Chemical in the early years to stay out of each other's territory. Between 1902 and 1914, AAC acquired seventeen additional firms, eleven of them in the South. The latter acquisitions broke down the territorial market dominance previously held by V-C and AAC, and by 1910 had precipitated considerable price competition between the two large producers. In 1914 American Agricultural and its subsidiaries operated twenty-nine fertilizer plants, of which eighteen were complete plants, six were complete except for acid chambers, and five were dry-mix plants. The company also owned seventeen distributing firms and controlled additional plants which it did not operate.

By 1914 the Armour Fertilizer Works, incorporated in 1909, had acquired control over twenty-seven operating subsidiaries, principally through joint-stockholding arrangements. Directly and through subsidiaries it controlled forty-one active and several inactive plants scattered over nineteen states, a large number of which were located in Georgia. Twenty-seven of the plants active in 1914 were dry-mix plants; seven were complete plants; and seven were complete except for acid chambers.

The International Agricultural Corporation, on the date of its incorporation in 1909 and immediately thereafter, acquired over forty-eight fertilizer-producing firms and three distributing firms. In 1914 the company operated sixty-three fertilizer plants in the United States and one in Canada. Forty-four of the domestic plants were dry-mix plants, and nineteen were complete except for acid chambers.[19]

Virginia-Carolina, American Agricultural, Armour, International Agricultural, along with the F. S. Royster Guano Company and Swift & Company, constituted the Big Six of the fertilizer industry in 1914, a position they still held in 1950. In contrast with the four largest producers, Royster and Swift grew large principally through internal expansion rather than merger. In 1914 Royster operated nine fertilizer plants it had built and held controlling-stock interests in four subsidiary selling companies and two small fertilizer-producing companies. Swift & Company attained its early position in the fertilizer industry by organizing and financing subsidiaries, of which the Swift Fertilizer Works and the

[19] From 1910 until after 1914 International Agricultural obtained all of its sulphuric-acid requirements from the Tennessee Copper Co. and the Ducktown Sulphur, Copper, and Iron Co., Ltd., under an exclusive contract.

Consolidated Rendering Company were the largest. In 1914 Swift & Company and its subsidiaries operated twenty-nine fertilizer plants and six selling companies. Two of the twenty-nine fertilizer plants were complete plants; seven were complete except for acid chambers; and twenty were dry-mix plants.

The combined fertilizer sales of the Big Six in 1913 amounted to over 3.9 million tons, or 55 per cent of the total tonnage consumed in the United States. The four largest companies accounted for 47.2 per cent, and the two largest, Virginia-Carolina and American Agricultural, accounted for 34.3 per cent. Between 1913 and 1950 the six largest mixed-fertilizer companies' share of total output declined to 33 per cent [20] as the share controlled by farmer co-operatives gradually increased. The co-operative movement got under way in 1932 with a single co-operative association in Kembridge, Virginia. By 1953, sixty co-operatives operated 105 fertilizer plants and distributed from 12 to 22 per cent (estimates varied) of all the fertilizers sold in the United States.[21]

Compared with most manufacturing industries, the mixed-fertilizer industry in 1950 was not characterized by a high degree of concentration. Almost all fertilizer-consuming areas had as alternative sources of supply ten or twelve large firms that sold in all markets, a fairly large number of regional commercial producers and farmers' co-operatives, and one or two local producers. Whatever control the large producers may have had over the mixed-fertilizer industry probably stemmed from their control over superphosphate and phosphate rock—their vertical integration rather than their share of the mixed-fertilizer market.

[20] FTC, *Report on the Fertilizer Industry*, 1950, p. 63. Since most multi-plant producers list a large number of inactive plants, the six largest mixed-fertilizer producers probably controlled about 40 per cent of the industry's mixing capacity in 1950.
[21] Claud L. Scroggs, "Co-operative Fertilizer Production and Distribution—New Facts and Figures," a paper presented at the summer session of the American Institute of Co-operation, Columbia, Missouri, August, 1953. Co-operative distribution varies widely among geographical regions; in four states they account for over one-third of all fertilizers distributed; in ten they account for less than one per cent.

# Part III

## ORGANIZATION, STRUCTURE, AND MARKETING PRACTICES OF COMPLEMENTARY INPUT INDUSTRIES

# CHAPTER 4

# THE SULPHUR INDUSTRY

APPROXIMATELY two thirds of all the phosphate rock mined in the United States is mixed with about equal quantities of sulphur (after it has been converted into sulphuric acid) to produce (1) superphopshate, and (2) phosphoric acid for the manufacture of concentrated superphosphate. Sulphur is therefore an important complementary productive agent for the integrated phosphate-fertilizer industry and for the unintegrated producers of superphosphates.

The principal sources of sulphur are brimstone, or natural sulphur, pyrites, and industrial by-products. Natural sulphur is mined and sold as crude sulphur without further processing. Pyrites and by-products contain sulphur, which can be recovered as sulphur or as sulphur gasses, which can be combined with other elements to produce such compounds as sulphuric acid. The United States produces over seventy-five per cent of the world's supply of natural sulphur, about five per cent of the world's supply of pyrites, or slightly over forty per cent of the world's total sulphur supply.[1] Since 1935 between one-third and one-fifth of the output has been exported; of the remainder about three-fourths has been converted into sulphuric acid and one-fourth consumed in nonacid uses. Slightly over one-third of the sulphuric acid has gone into the manufacture of fertilizers, principally superphosphates and ammonium sulfate.[2]

Whether superphosphate producers buy sulphur in the crude or acid form depends on the extent to which they are vertically integrated. Some superphosphate plants have acid-producing facilities; others do not. The former purchase crude sulphur; the latter purchase sulphuric acid, often from their integrated competitors. Phosphate-fertilizer manufacturers generally produce more acid than they consume; but because of differences in vertical integration and location, they annually purchase about twenty per cent of their acid from producers outside the fertilizer industry and sell nearly twice this quantity to other industries.

*Concentration in Sulphur Production Is High.* Until the turn of the century the United States imported the bulk of its sulphur, most of it from Italy. After 1903, when imports reached a peak of 189,000 long

---

[1] Outside the U. S., pyrites account for about 80 per cent of the total sulphur supply, and natural sulphur for about 20 per cent. In the U. S., ignoring small quantities of industrial by-products, these percentages are reversed.

[2] In 1951, 3,900 short tons of sulphuric acid (100 per cent basis) went into the production of superphosphates, and 1,200 into the production of ammonium sulfate. From G. W. Josephson and Flora B. Mentch, "Sulphur and Pyrites," *Minerals Yearbook 1952*, Bureau of Mines, U. S. Dept. of the Interior.

tons, they declined steadily as domestic production increased from a meager 35,098 long tons to 5.3 million long tons in 1952. Over this fifty-year period natural-sulphur production was concentrated in the hands of about four firms, with the two largest accounting for ninety per cent of total output.

The Union Sulphur Company was the principal producer of sulphur from 1903, when the company was organized, until just before its deposits in Calcasien Parish, Louisiana, were exhausted in 1924. Union was the first large-scale United States producer and the first to perfect the Frasch process for extracting sulphur in liquid form.[3] Union's exact percentage of total sulphur output over its lifetime is not known, but it must have been substantial. Until 1913, when the Freeport Sulphur Company was organized, Union was the only large-scale producer. From 1913 to 1919 Union and Freeport controlled most of the domestic output. In 1919, when Texas Gulf Sulphur Company was organized, Texas Gulf and Freeport together accounted for 55.7 per cent of natural sulphur output. Union presumably accounted for most of the remaining 44.3 per cent. From 1919 to 1924 Texas Gulf and Freeport accounted for from over one-half to nearly three-quarters of total output (Table 17). Union produced a large portion of the rest until, as previously indicated, it ceased operations in 1924. From 1925 to 1932 the industry was virtually a duopoly, with Texas Gulf accounting for approximately two-thirds of total output and Freeport for the remaining third. Duval Texas Sulphur Company started production in 1930, the Jefferson Lake Sulphur Company in 1932.[4] From the early thirties until 1951, these four companies controlled virtually the entire output of natural sulphur, with Texas Gulf and Freeport together accounting for nearly ninety per cent and Duval and Jefferson Lake sharing the remainder. Exact output data by producer since 1951 are not available; but as of 1955 Texas Gulf, Freeport, Duval, and Jefferson Lake still accounted for nearly all the natural sulphur produced in the United States.[5] Only four other producers, all of them small, were either in production or contemplating production.[6]

*Pyrites and Industrial By-products as Substitutes for Natural Sulphur.* Technically the sulphur in pyrites and industrial by-products is a good

---

[3] Dr. Herman Frasch, an American chemist who perfected the process, was for many years president of the Union Sulphur Company. From FTC, *Report on the Sulphur Industry and International Cartels,* 1947, p. 20.

[4] Duval was organized in 1926, but produced no sulphur until 1930.

[5] During the acute sulphur shortage following the outbreak of the Korean conflict in 1950, the federal government assisted in the development of sulphur capacity through the Defense Minerals Exploration Administration, the Defense Minerals Procurement Agency, the Petroleum Administration for Defense, the National Production Authority, the Defense Production Administration, and other agencies. Several small firms, principally in Nevada, Utah, Wyoming, and California took advantage of available government exploration and development loans and accelerated tax amortizations and produced small quantities of sulphur intermittently. Cf. Josephson and Mentch, *op. cit.,* pp. 3-4.

[6] Information supplied by U. S. Department of Agriculture, Bureau of Plant Industry, Soils, and Agricultural Engineering.

## TABLE 17

TOTAL NATURAL SULPHUR PRODUCTION AND PER CENT OF
PRODUCTION ACCOUNTED FOR BY THE FOUR PRINCIPAL
PRODUCERS, 1919-43 AND 1948-51 [a]

| Year | Total U. S. Production (thousands of long tons) | Per Cent of Total | | | | |
|---|---|---|---|---|---|---|
| | | Texas Gulf | Freeport | Duval | Jefferson Lake | Four-Company Total |
| 1919 | 1,191 | 29.26 | 26.44 | ........ | ........ | ........ |
| 1920 | 1,255 | 74.60 | 22.36 | ........ | ........ | ........ |
| 1921 | 1,879 | 54.67 | 2.95 | ........ | ........ | ........ |
| 1922 | 1,831 | 28.53 | 8.82 | ........ | ........ | ........ |
| 1923 | 2,036 | 38.59 | 23.65 | ........ | ........ | ........ |
| 1924 | 1,221 | 56.81 | 16.22 | ........ | ........ | ........ |
| 1925 | 1,409 | 70.97 | 29.03 | ........ | ........ | ........ |
| 1926 | 1,890 | 60.09 | 30.91 | ........ | ........ | ........ |
| 1927 | 2,112 | 62.54 | 37.43 | ........ | ........ | ........ |
| 1928 | 1,982 | 59.56 | 45.81 | ........ | ........ | ........ |
| 1929 | 2,362 | 59.42 | 38.54 | ........ | ........ | ........ |
| 1930 | 2,559 | 67.88 | 30.58 | 1.51 | ........ | ........ |
| 1931 | 2,129 | 60.95 | 37.42 | 1.63 | ........ | ........ |
| 1932 | 890 | 63.79 | 32.04 | 2.54 | 1.50 | 99.87 |
| 1933 | 1,406 | 46.13 | 29.45 | 2.70 | 21.61 | 99.89 |
| 1934 | 1,421 | 59.48 | 31.72 | 3.14 | 5.33 | 99.67 |
| 1935 | 1,633 | 56.55 | 37.54 | 3.94 | 1.50 | 99.53 |
| 1936 | 2,016 | 63.80 | 29.70 | 5.89 | .42 | 99.81 |
| 1937 | 2,742 | 63.60 | 25.95 | 4.82 | 3.44 | 97.81 |
| 1938 | 2,393 | 51.08 | 28.59 | 8.87 | 11.20 | 99.74 |
| 1939 | 2,091 | 39.14 | 37.83 | 12.97 | 9.95 | 99.89 |
| 1940 | 2,732 | 52.28 | 31.49 | 7.96 | 8.04 | 99.77 |
| 1941 | 3,139 | 58.59 | 28.83 | 6.42 | 5.87 | 99.71 |
| 1942 | 3,461 | 62.80 | 29.32 | 5.52 | 2.21 | 99.85 |
| 1943 | 2,539 | 46.75 | 40.49 | 6.88 | 5.88 | 100.00 |
| 1948 | 4,869 | 64.08 | 28.13 | 3.44 | 4.36 | 100.00 |
| 1949 | 4,745 | 58.96 | 31.10 | 4.65 | 5.28 | 99.99 |
| 1950 | 5,192 | 62.09 | 30.11 | ...[b] | 5.35 | 97.57[b] |
| 1951 | 5,278 | 61.48 | 29.56 | ...[b] | 6.74 | 97.78[b] |

[a] 1919-43 data from FTC, *Report on the Sulphur Industry and International Cartels*, 1947, p. 23; 1948-51 data computed from Frasch mine sulphur production as reported in *Minerals Yearbook*, and individual-company production as reported in Moody's *Manual of Industrials*, 1949-52 issues.
[b] Duval's production not available after 1949.

substitute for natural sulphur.[7] From an economic point of view, such sulphur has a distinct competitive disadvantage. The sulphur content of most grades of pyrites is only about forty-two per cent of their gross weight, and that of industrial by-products only about one-third of their gross weight. Transporting a ton of natural sulphur costs much less than shipping a ton of sulphur in pyrites. Natural sulphur is ready for use, but pyrites must be roasted to recover their sulphur content. It is generally more economical to combine roasting with sulphuric-acid pro-

[7] This is not strictly true on a basis of sulphur content per unit. The Federal Trade Commission estimated in 1947 that a given weight of sulphur content in native sulphur produced 30 per cent more sulphuric acid than a like weight in pyrites (*Report on the Sulphur Industry and International Cartels*, 1947, p. 28). This has not always been so. A cost study conducted in 1917 showed native sulphur to be only 5 per cent more productive (cited in Theodore H. Kreps, *The Economics of the Sulphuric Acid Industry* [California: Stanford University Press, 1938], p. 96).

duction than with the production of sulphur. But sulphuric-acid production is a bulk- and weight-gaining process and must be located near its markets.[8] Even if the mining costs per ton of sulphur content were the same, natural sulphur would have a broader geographical market. Since it takes 2.4 tons of pyrites (42 per cent sulphur content) to yield as much sulphur as one ton of natural sulphur, the cost of mining a given quantity of sulphur from most pyritic deposits is higher than the cost of mining the same quantity of native sulphur. Pyrites are the lowest-cost source of sulphuric acid only where such acid is produced as a by-product of copper, lead, or zinc smelting operations and sold in nearby markets. In 1947, of the 940,652 long tons of pyritic ores having a sulphur content of approximately 355,000 tons produced in the United States, over seventy-five per cent was used locally by the companies that produced them.[9] In 1952 the comparable figure was eighty per cent.[10]

Sulphur compounds produced from domestic pyrites and industrial by-products do not compete effectively with natural sulphur. They are produced jointly with other products; their marginal costs are low,[11] and their output is determined by factors other than cost and prevailing natural sulphur prices. Because their marginal costs are low, they supply a demand that native-sulphur producers would scarcely consider a potential market, especially since less than one-fourth of the output of captive by-products plants enters the open market. Domestic pyrites simply set an upper limit beyond which natural-sulphur prices cannot go without inviting competition. This upper limit has been considerably above the competitive price of natural sulphur.

*Sulphur and Sulphuric-Acid Prices Are Rigid.* Since wide differences in costs and joint-product operations insulate the natural and by-product sulphur markets from each other, oligopoly theory would seem to be applicable to the four natural-sulphur producers.[12] That is, the market is such that competition from substitutes does not circumscribe their price and output decisions. With such a high order of oligopoly, it would be expected that in making these decisions each producer considers their indirect as well as their direct effects, and chooses the price and rate of output that maximizes profits for the industry as a whole. In short, sellers will not compete with each other on a price basis. To test the presence of oligopolistic decision making in a given industry is not always easy, but

[8] One ton of sulphur produces from 4.25 to 4.75 tons of acid (Theodore J. Kreps *op., cit.* p. 76).
[9] Henry A. Huschke, "Resources and Processing of Materials Carrying Calcium, Magnesium and Sulphur," a paper presented at the Fertilizer Technology Short Course, University of Maryland, August 25, 1950, p. 5.
[10] Josephson and Mentch, *op. cit.*, p. 5.
[11] Just how low is not known, but in some smelting processes the marginal cost of sulphuric acid has been estimated at less than zero; that is, it would involve additional cost *not* to produce the acid as a by-product.
[12] Cf. Edward H. Chamberlin, *The Theory of Monopolistic Competition* (6th ed.; Cambridge: Harvard University Press, 1948), pp. 46-51.

most economists would agree that price levels substantially above costs and abnormally high profits over a long period of time are convincing evidence of the absence of effective competition. The evidence is more convincing if prices are also rigid. It is unlikely that American business annals contain a price less given to change than that of natural sulphur (Table 18). The quoted price per long ton for bulk shipments of sulphur

### TABLE 18
### NATURAL SULPHUR AND SULPHURIC-ACID PRICES, 1926-53 [a]

Crude Sulphur

| Year | Quoted Price [b] | Average Value | Sulphuric Acid |
|------|------------------|---------------|----------------|
| 1926 | $18.00 | $18.00 | $14.60 |
| 1927 | 18.00 | 18.48 | 15.10 |
| 1928 | 18.00 | 18.00 | 15.50 |
| 1929 | 18.00 | 17.97 | 15.50 |
| 1930 | 18.00 | 17.99 | 15.50 |
| 1931 | 18.00 | 18.02 | 15.50 |
| 1932 | 18.00 | 18.04 | 15.50 |
| 1933 | 18.00 | 18.02 | 15.50 |
| 1934 | 18.00 | 17.91 | 15.50 |
| 1935 | 18.00 | 17.92 | 15.50 |
| 1936 | 18.00 | 17.98 | 15.50 |
| 1937 [c] | 18.00 | 17.96 | ..... |
| 1938 [c] | ..... | 16.76 | 16.50 |
| 1939 | 16.00 | 15.89 | 16.50 |
| 1940 | 16.00 | 15.98 | 16.50 |
| 1941 | 16.00 | 15.99 | 16.50 |
| 1942 | 16.00 | 16.01 | 16.50 |
| 1943 | 16.00 | 16.02 | 16.50 |
| 1943-47 | ..... [d] | 16.42 | 16.50 [d] |
| 1948 | 18.00 | 18.00 | 15.50 [d] |
| 1949 | 18.00 | 18.00 | 17.00 |
| 1950 | ..... [d] | 18.89 | ..... [d] |
| 1951 | $21.00 to $24.00 | 21.51 | ..... [d] |
| 1952 | ..... [d] | 21.57 | 20.00 |
| 1953 | ..... [d] | ..... | ..... [d] |

[a] Quoted sulphur prices from *Oil Paint and Drug Reporter;* average values computed from *Minerals Yearbook.* Sulphuric-acid prices from U. S. Dept. of Commerce, *Survey of Current Business.*
[b] Contract price per long ton, f.o.b. mines.
[c] Quoted price of crude sulphur changed from $18.00 to $16.00 in the fall of 1938. Price of sulphuric acid changed from $15.50 to $16.50 in June, 1937.
[d] Price of natural sulphur changed from $16.00 to $18.00 per ton in October, 1947; from $18.00 to $21.00 and $24.00 in September, 1950; and from $21.00 and $24.00 to $25.50 in April, 1953. Price of sulphuric acid changed from $16.50 to $15.00 per ton in December, 1947; from $15.00 to $17.00 in October, 1948; from $17.00 to $17.75 in April, 1950; and increased to $18.95 in October and to $20.00 in December, where it remained until the end of 1953 except for a $0.10 reduction in October, 1951, which was restored by November.

changed only once between 1926 and late 1947, standing at $18.00 per long ton until 1938, when it was reduced to $16.00 per long ton; it remained there until the fourth quarter of 1947, when it was raised again to $18.00. No further price changes occurred until the fourth quarter of 1950. Net realized prices have been equally as stable, varying only a few cents per ton from official price quotations. Sulphuric-acid prices have reflected the stable prices of sulphur. From 1927 to June, 1937, the price of sulphuric acid remained unchanged at \$15.50 per short ton (66° at works) and remained unchanged at \$16.50 from June, 1937, until December, 1947. Between December, 1947, and December, 1953, sulphuric-acid prices changed four times.

*Sulphur Producers' Profits Have Been High.* Profits (or profits plus rents) in the sulphur industry have been consistently above the competitive level.[13] The annual average rate of return for the four sulphur producers over nearly three decades has been in the neighborhood of twenty per cent, and frequently the rate of return has exceeded thirty per cent (Table 19). A portion of the profits probably has taken the form of a differential rent for superior deposits. The lowest annual average rate of return, earned by Freeport, was a little more than half the rate earned by Texas Gulf. But even Freeport's average for the period was 13.68 per cent—a rate that scarcely suggests a marginal firm.

When considered together, the structure, price behavior, and profits pattern of the sulphur industry add up to convincing evidence that competition has not effectively regulated it. The industry has seldom comprised more than four producers, and at times has been a virtual duopoly. Prices have been uncommonly inflexible and profits have been extraordinarily high. Sulphur prices have doubtless been higher than they would have been under effective competition.

*Cartel Agreements Have Contributed to High Sulphur Prices.* But while the structure, price behavior, and profit history of the sulphur industry have all been consistent with oligopoly theory, these are not the only evidence of noncompetitive pricing. Natural sulphur has competed at home and in international markets with sulphur and pyrites produced elsewere. In their search for market stability, United States sulphur producers have made use of the same instruments of market control employed by producers of phosphate rock, namely, export associations and international cartel agreements.

During World War I the increased output of explosives and food increased the demand for sulphur. When wartime demand disappeared, sulphur stocks accumulated, and competition developed among American producers and between American and Sicilian producers.[14] Domestic and international prices declined. In the domestic market, quoted f.o.b. mine prices declined from \$22.00 per long ton in 1918 to \$16.00 in 1921, and to \$14.00 in 1922. International prices suffered similar declines. To arrest declining prices, Union Sulphur Company, Freeport Sulphur

---

[13] For a comprehensive discussion of the reliability of profits and price and margin flexibility measures as indicia to monopoly power, see *Fritz Machlup, The Political Economy of Monopoly: Business, Labor and Government Policies* (Baltimore: Johns Hopkins University Press, 1952), Chap. 12. See also *Report of the Attorney General's National Committee to Study the Anti-trust Laws* (March 31, 1955), pp. 323-24.

[14] FTC, *Report on the Sulphur Industry and International Cartels*, 1947, pp. 8-9.

### TABLE 19

RATE OF RETURN ON INVESTED CAPITAL AFTER FEDERAL TAXES
FOR THE FOUR NATURAL-SULPHUR PRODUCERS, 1919-51 [a]

| Year | Texas Gulf | Freeport | Jefferson Lake | Duval |
|------|-----------|----------|----------------|-------|
| 1919 | 18.76 | 11.48 | ..... | ..... |
| 1920 | 37.04 | 6.94 | ..... | ..... |
| 1921 | 16.58 | 5.82[b] | ..... | ..... |
| 1922 | 31.24 | 2.53[b] | ..... | ..... |
| 1923 | 36.39 | 6.33 | ..... | ..... |
| 1924 | 36.01 | 2.65[b] | ..... | ..... |
| 1925 | 42.44 | 6.37 | ..... | ..... |
| 1926 | 62.85 | 14.40 | ..... | ..... |
| 1927 | 67.86 | 27.01 | ..... | ..... |
| 1928 | 66.49 | 24.59 | ..... | ..... |
| 1929 | 58.66 | 33.07 | ..... | ..... |
| 1930 | 41.99 | 23.94 | ..... | 20.66 |
| 1931 | 24.99 | 18.51 | ..... | 14.76 |
| 1932 | 16.34 | 21.35 | ..... | 9.98 |
| 1933 | 19.85 | 22.94 | 35.77 | 6.54[b] |
| 1934 | 13.69 | 11.70 | 33.85 | 3.61 |
| 1935 | 12.50 | 12.07 | 5.51 | 6.54 |
| 1936 | 16.66 | 16.73 | ..... | 24.03 |
| 1937 | 19.60 | 17.30 | .51[b] | 14.07 |
| 1938 | 11.75 | 10.87 | 33.27 | 19.69 |
| 1939 | 13.22 | 10.87 | 47.01 | 26.92 |
| 1940 | 15.40 | 12.36 | 28.70 | 20.62 |
| 1941 | 15.34 | 13.63 | 10.46 | 25.13 |
| 1942 | 14.97 | 10.60 | 13.81[b] | 28.99 |
| 1943 | 13.55 | 12.54 | 6.46 | 30.91 |
| 1944 | 16.38 | 11.57 | 16.20 | 31.12 |
| 1945 | 16.91 | 14.40 | 13.40 | 30.00 |
| 1946 | 24.79 | 15.52 | 11.52 | 35.73 |
| 1947 | 34.26 | 11.40 | 11.28 | 34.82 |
| 1948 | 44.77 | 12.68 | 11.55 | 22.48 |
| 1949 | 51.48 | 15.73 | 13.61 | 21.64 |
| 1950 | 47.77 | 16.24 | 28.65 | 18.28 |
| 1951 | 41.38 | 13.39 | 26.12 | 14.05 |
| Annual Average | 25.31 | 13.68 | 18.15 | 22.46 |

[a] 1919-46 from FTC, *Report on the Sulphur Industry and International Cartels*, 1947; 1947-51 computed from company financial statements as they appeared in Moody's *Manual of Industrial Investments*, 1948-52 issues.
[b] Loss.

Company, and Texas Gulf Company, the three leading American producers, on October 4, 1922, formed the Sulphur Export Corporation. The purposes of the export association were to allocate foreign sales (except to Canada, Newfoundland, and Cuba) among United States producers, to handle all such foreign sales, to keep records of all export transactions and make remittances to the several members in accordance with their participation, and to fix the price of sulphur at various ports of export.[15] The export association's agreement was renewed and carried out by Free-

[15] *Ibid.*, 9.

port and Texas Gulf from October 26, 1928, when Union retired from the industry, up to June 20, 1952, when it was voluntarily dissolved. From time to time Sulphur Export Corporation (hereafter called Sulexco) negotiated for sales in foreign markets for Duval and Jefferson Lake, the two nonmember independent domestic producers, and participated in two cartel agreements.

On October 4, 1922, the date Sulexco was formed, it entered into an agreement with Consorzio Obligatorio per l'Industria Solfifera Siciliana, a compulsory association of Sicilian sulphur producers and the principal competitor of American producers in the international sulphur trade. The agreement became inoperative ten years later when the Italian Government dissolved the Consorzio, but it was renewed on August 1, 1934, with the Consorzio's successor organization, the Ufficio per La Vendita dello Zolfo Italiano, and remained effective until the outbreak of World War II in 1939. While effective it established quotas, prices, and terms of sale for sulphur sold anywhere except in Italy and its dependencies and possessions, North America, insular possessions of the United States, Cuba, and islands off the coast of Canada. The agreement also provided in principle that each of the participating parties should maintain the sulphur manufacturing industry in the areas covered "as it at present exists." [16]

On January 23, 1933, Sulexco entered into an agreement with Orkda Grube Aktiebolag of Lokkenverk, Norway, a manufacturer of sulphate from pyrites which was disturbing the Sulexco-Consorzio arrangement by selling in the cartel's territories. The agreement (1) limited Orkda's sales to 70,000 tons per year and to the countries of Norway, Sweden, and Finland, (2) established the prices at which Orkda and Sulexco would sell in these three countries, (3) provided for a payment of $1.00 per ton up to 70,000 tons from Sulexco to Orkda on sales made by the former in the three countries, and (4) provided further that Orkda would not add to its then existing production capacity.[17] The agreement was redrawn on April 1, 1936, to extend the covered market to Europe, Asia, Africa, and adjacent islands, and to provide for control over patents on sulphur production in the two participants' joint territory. Since the Sulexco-Orkda agreement was subject to the approval of the Italian association, it was in effect an integral part of the Sulexco-Ufficio agreement.

---

[16] *Ibid.*, 10. The Sulexco-Consorzio and Sulexco-Ufficio agreements were not the first attempts to control international markets nor the first to involve American producers. Sicilian natural sulphur and British reclaimed sulphur producers had organized a selling syndicate as early as the 1890's. The syndicate's efforts to maintain prices were thwarted by uncontrolled competition from nonaffiliated European sources and, after 1902, from the Union Sulphur Co. From 1908 to 1912 the newly formed Consorzio and Union operated in international markets under a cartel agreement that offered considerable price protection to both parties. The agreement was abrogated by Union in 1913 after Freeport Sulphur became an important competitor in the United States and foreign markets. What may otherwise have developed into intense price competition after 1913 was ameliorated by the great increase in demand for sulphur brought on by World War I.

[17] *Ibid.*, 11.

This agreement became inoperative at the outbreak of World War II, and was officially cancelled by Sulexco on the same date it cancelled its agreement with Ufficio. As stated above, Sulexco was voluntarily dissolved in 1952.

The intent of these agreements was to end what industry representatives called "ruinous" competition in foreign markets.[18] They seem to have attained this end. But when an industry comprising a few producers works in harmony in international markets, it is also likely to work in harmony at home. The extremely rigid domestic prices and the abnormally high profits that prevailed over the lifetime of the agreements suggest that it did. From the end of World War I until Sulexco was formed and negotiated its first international agreement in 1923, foreign and domestic sulphur prices were flexible. As was previously indicated, in less than three years after the agreement was reached, domestic-sulphur prices had been stabilized; and they changed only twice between 1926 and 1950, several months after the outbreak of war in Korea and at a time when the world faced a critical sulphur shortage. This long period of price inflexibility was accompanied by exceedingly high profits, inflexible sulphuric-acid prices, and no discernible undercutting of quoted prices.

The circumstances that have prevailed in the sulphur market since 1950 make it virtually impossible to ascertain whether oligopoly has preserved the pricing practices that were formerly obtained through oligopoly buttressed by export-association activity. In the last quarter of 1950, one of the major producers advanced its domestic price from $18.00 to $21.00 per long ton; another major producer at the same time advanced its price from $18.00 to $22.00. At the time the Office of Price Stabilization froze sulphur prices in 1951 at levels prevailing during the base period (December 19, 1950, to January 25, 1951), domestic prices of major sulphur producers ranged from $21.00 to $24.00 f.o.b. mines, and export prices ranged from $25.00 to $27.00 at the port.[19] While such price behavior suggests greater independence of action among sulphur producers than has been in evidence at any time over the previous quarter century, it occurred in a highly inflated market that gave rise to international prices ranging from $100.00 to $200.00 per long ton, and to rumors of occasional black-market sales in the domestic market ranging up to $100.00 per ton.[20] The price of sulphuric acid, also subject to inflationary pressure, increased from $20.00 per short ton in December, 1950, to $22.35 by May, 1953, where it remained unchanged through December, 1954.

[18] *Ibid.*, p. 89.
[19] Josephson and Mentch, *op. cit.*, p. 10.
[20] *Ibid.*

# CHAPTER 5

# THE POTASH INDUSTRY

ABOUT 94 per cent of the potash consumed in the United States goes into the production of commercial fertilizers; nearly all of it is mixed with superphosphates and nitrogenous materials to produce mixed fertilizers. In spite of recent increases in the amount of potash distributed as a straight material, in the fertilizer year 1952-53, 89.3 per cent of the $K_2O$ (potassium oxide) consumed as fertilizer went into mixtures, and only 10.7 per cent came on the market as a straight material.[1] Fertilizer manufacturers are virtually the potash producers' sole customers; they even buy and distribute most of the potash farmers use as a straight fertilizer material.

The most important domestic potash reserves are the ore fields near Carlsbad, New Mexico, and the lime deposits of Searles Lake, near Trona, California (Table 20). Together the two sources account for

TABLE 20

ESTIMATED WORLD POTASH RESERVES [a]

(THOUSANDS OF SHORT TONS OF POTASH SALTS)

| Country | Department of Commerce Estimate (1940) | Dolbear Estimate, Commercially Recoverable (1946) |
|---|---|---|
| United States: | | |
| New Mexico (ores) | 75,000 | 58,000 |
| Searles Lake (brine) | 10,000—12,000 | 14,000 |
| Utah (brine) | relatively small | 1,000 |
| Total United States | 85,000—87,000 | 73,000 |
| Germany (ores) | 3,000,000 (minimum) | |
| Russia | 3,000,000 | |
| Israel (brines) | 1,000,000 | |
| France (ores) | 300,000 | |
| Spain (ores) | 200,000—300,000 | |
| Poland (ores) | 50,000—55,000 | |
| Total World | 7,550,000—7,657,000 | |

[a] U. S. Dept. of Commerce and Samuel H. Dolbear of Behve Dolbear & Co. for the American Potash Institute. Cited in FTC, *Report on the Fertilizer Industry*, 1950, p. 86.

scarcely over one per cent of the world's total known potash reserves; they are estimated as sufficient to supply United States potash needs for only about forty years at the 1947 rate of production. Nearly all domestic

[1] Walter Scholl, Hilda M. Wallace, and Esther J. Fox, *Commercial Fertilizers Consumption in the United States, 1952-53*, Agricultural Research Service, U. S. Dept. of Agriculture.

reserves are in the public domain and are operated under leases from the federal government.

*Potash Cartels and the United States Market.* Until World War II potash prices and sales in the United States were generally controlled by European cartels. A German cartel, formed in 1870, supplied nearly all the potash consumed in the United States [2] before World War I and had a virtual monopoly over international trade in potash. Under the German Potash Law of 1910, the German Potash Syndicate also obtained complete monopoly control over potash production in Germany.

The terms under which American buyers acquired potash from the syndicate were rigid and uncompromising.[3] Prices in the United States were quoted c.i.f. ports, subject to quantity discounts designed to encourage large orders. Buyers were required to make provision for full payment on all orders, less ocean freight, five weeks in advance of shipment. Title to potash cargoes passed to the buyer at port of shipment, and the buyer paid the freight charges upon the ship's arrival at destination. Before the closing of the booking season each year, United States buyers had to submit to the syndicate a detailed statement of their probable requirements for the forthcoming fertilizer season. Failure to do so before the date designated by the syndicate resulted in the imposition of penalties. Discounts were allowed on orders placed up to the final booking date. Over the period 1897 to January, 1915, when Germany imposed an embargo on potash exports, potash prices in the United States on shipments of 500 tons or over stayed within the narrow range of $34.00—$39.30 per short ton; throughout the entire period prices often remained substantially unchanged for intervals of three to six years. They were the prices of a monopolist; they presumably were monopoly prices.

With the loss of German imports in 1915, the United States was cut off from virtually its entire supply. Imports in 1913 had amounted to over 1,000,000 tons having a $K_2O$ equivalent of 270,720 tons; in 1916 imports totalled only 26,642 tons having a $K_2O$ equivalent of 7,885 tons. The price of 61-per-cent-$K_2O$ muriate of potash jumped from $45.58 per ton in 1914 to the unprecedented level of $483.63 per ton by 1916, and never fell below $208.00 per ton between 1915 and the end of 1919.

Spurred by such high prices, domestic potash production increased from almost nothing just before World War I to 207,686 tons with a $K_2O$ equivalent of 54,803 tons by 1918, most of which was produced from the mines of the Searles Lake, California, and the Great Salt Lake areas. At the end of the war the industry comprised 128 producers, 51 that

---

[2] Bedded potash deposits were first discovered in Germany in 1843; commercial mining operations began in 1861 (Willard L. Thorp and Ernest A. Tupper, *The Potash Industry: A Report Submitted to the Department of Justice by the Department of Commerce*, 1940, p. 5).
[3] *Ibid.*, pp. 52-53.

produced potash from wood ashes and 77 that produced from other sources such as nonsoluble potash ores, industrial wastes, and the brines of Searles Lake.[4] Of these, only the American Trona Corporation (now the American Potash and Chemical Corporation), operating on Searles Lake brines, survived the precipitous price declines that followed the resumption of imports after World War I.

When France acquired Alsace-Lorraine at the end of World War I, it acquired the rich Alsatian potash deposits. The French immediately entered into competition in international markets with the German cartel, undercutting its price in the United States by just enough to obtain the tonnage the French desired.[5] The resumption of imports and the competition between French and German producers drove United States potash prices down from $5.65 to $0.62 per unit of $K_2O$ between 1919 and 1923. The cartel apparently was undisturbed by the small domestic output of the surviving American Trona Corporation, but recognized the new French industry as a real threat. German producers initiated negotiations with the French shortly after the latter began to export, and in 1924 reached an agreement whereby the French would join the German cartel.[6] The outcome of the agreement was the formation of the Potash Importing Company, a New York Corporation, to act as the exclusive agent for the Deutches Kalisyndikat Gesellschaft and the Société Commerciale des Potasse d'Alsace, respectively the German and French producing interests. Potash prices in the United States were again brought under the control of a single organization, and, with the exception of an outbreak of competition between the cartel and Russian and Spanish producers in 1934 and 1935, were largely under its control until World War II.

*The Consent Decree of 1929.* Since the Potash Importing Company was a domestic corporation in control of almost all potash sales in the United States, its operations apparently were in violation of the Sherman Act. The Department of Justice on April 7, 1927, filed a petition in equity, charging the French and German producers with conspiring to restrain trade in the sale of potash in the United States.[7] The French Government filed a motion to dismiss the charges against the Société Commerciale on the grounds that the Societè was an instrument of the sovereign state of France and not subject to the jurisdiction of the United States court. The motion was denied, but on February 28, 1929, the parties consented to a decree whose terms must have been very nearly as satisfactory to the cartel as a dismissal of the charges. The decree simply

---

[4] FTC, *Report on the Fertilizer Industry*, 1950, p. 86.
[5] *Ibid.*, p. 96.
[6] *Ibid.*
[7] *United States v. Deutches Kalisyndikat Gesellschaft*, Equity No. 41-125, U. S. District Court, Southern District of New York, April 7, 1927.

required the defendants to find a new nationality for their joint selling agency.[8]

In May, 1927, one month after the petition in equity had been filed, representatives of the French and German producers notified the Assistant Attorney General that the cartel had incorporated under the laws of the Netherlands the Naamlooze Vennootchap Potash (Kali) Export Maatschappy, with its principal office in Amsterdam and a branch office in New York. The purpose of the corporation was to purchase potash salts from Germany and France and to distribute them in the United States through its New York branch office.[9] Even before the consent decree a large portion of the potash sales previously made in the United States through the Potash Importing Company had been transferred to the N. V. Potash Export My. New York branch office. The German-French cartel complied with the decree simply by dissolving the Potash Importing Company and transferring the rest of its sales there.

At this time the cartel supplied approximately ninety per cent of the potash consumed in the United States; and the remainder was produced domestically, almost entirely by the American Potash and Chemical Corporation. When American Potash was created out of a reorganization of the American Trona Corporation in 1926, stock representing a ninety-per-cent controlling interest in the new corporation was acquired by the New Consolidated Gold Fields of South Africa, Ltd., in exchange for its interests in Trona. In 1929, the year of the German-French cartel consent decree, the stock was transferred to German interests affiliated with the cartel, thereby giving the cartel control over virtually all the potash sold in the United States.[10]

*Competition from Russian and Spanish Potash Producers.* Cartel control over United States potash sales resulted in stable potash prices from 1924 to 1934. Over the ten-year period the c.i.f. port price gradually moved upward from $0.62 per unit of $K_2O$ to $0.70.[11] Prices were unaffected by the Great Depression in spite of a decline in United States potash salts consumption from over 1,000,000 tons in 1930 to less than 450,000 tons in 1932. Imports over the same two-year period fell from nearly 930,000 tons to about 331,000 tons. The cartel evidently preferred to adjust sales to meet the greatly-reduced demand and to leave prices alone.

[8] In the language of the decree the defendants were not to agree on prices, terms of sale, or quantities sold in the United States or to establish a joint sales agency of United States *nationality* to carry out such activities "provided, that no provision of this decree shall be construed to prevent defendants from selling and delivering all or any part of their potash salts outside of the United States to a corporation organized under the laws of *any country other than the United States* [italics mine] . . . or to prevent said corporation from selling and distributing in the United States such potash salts so acquired through usual facilities for sale and distribution, including agents, agencies, branch offices, and other normal channels." *United States v. Deutches Kalisyndikat Gesellschaft,* C. C. H. Trade Reg. Rep. Supp. Vol. IV, par. 4188 (S. D. N. Y. 1929).

[9] Thorp and Tupper, *op. cit.,* p. 21.

[10] FTC, *Report on the Fertilizer Industry,* 1950, pp. 92, 97-98.

[11] Thorp and Tupper, *op. cit.,* p. 18a.

In 1934 a situation developed that apparently caught the cartel off guard. Russian and Spanish potash producers began shipping potash into the United States at prices considerably below the cartel's price. The new competition reduced domestic potash prices from $0.70 to $0.35 per unit of $K_2O$ in a single month (April to May, 1934), and kept the price below $0.40 for the following fifteen months.[12] In the latter half of 1935, when the Spanish joined the cartel and the Russians accepted its price leadership, prices in the United States gradually moved upward. The position of the cartel, except for the effect of developments in the domestic potash industry, remained substantially unchanged until World War II broke up German and French co-operation.

*The Rise of the Domestic Potash Industry.* As pointed out above, the domestic potash industry was founded under the impetus of the cessation of imports and skyrocketing prices during World War I. While many small firms entered the industry then, only the American Potash and Chemical Corporation survived the resumption of imports and the restoration of normal prices after the war, and even this company was later brought under the German-French cartel's financial control.

In 1925 potash deposits were discovered in New Mexico near Carlsbad by prospectors drilling for oil.[13] The Carlsbad deposits comprise only one per cent of the world's potash reserves, but they include over eighty-five per cent of the known reserves of the United States (Table 20) and account for from ninety to ninety-five per cent of total domestic potash output. Most of this has come from only two producers, the United States Potash Company and the Potash Company of America. The former began production in 1931, and the latter in 1934. These two companies and International Minerals and Chemical Corporation,[14] which began operations near Carlsbad in 1940, were the sole producers in the New Mexico fields until December, 1951.

With the development of the Carlsbad deposits, domestic output soon became as important a source of potash as the German-French cartel. After 1935 annual domestic production of $K_2O$, except in the year 1937, exceeded imports (Table 21). With the outbreak of World War II imports were again cut off, and domestic production became almost the sole source of supply. In the postwar period imports increased but in the years 1951-53 they amounted to less than thirteen per cent of total domestic output of $K_2O$.

*Domestic Producers Adopt Cartel's Prices.* But while domestic producers increased from one to four and were absorbing a substantial por-

---

[12] *Ibid.*

[13] Federal Reserve Bank of Dallas, *Monthly Business Review*, Vol. 37, No. 12 (1952), p. 167.

[14] International, one of the largest (See Chaps. 2 and 3) United States producers of phosphate rock, superphosphates, and mixed fertilizers, is the only integrated phosphate fertilizer firm that produces potash or nitrogen.

## TABLE 21

### UNITED STATES POTASH PRODUCTION, IMPORTS, EXPORTS, AND CONSUMPTION, 1924-53 ᵃ
### (THOUSANDS OF TONS OF EQUIVALENT K₂O)

| Year | Domestic Production | Imports | Exports | Domestic Consumption |
|------|---------------------|---------|---------|----------------------|
| 1924 | 22.9 | 200.4 | .... | 222.2 |
| 1925 | 25.4 | 258.2 | .... | 284.0 |
| 1926 | 23.4 | 266.3 | .... | 291.3 |
| 1927 | 43.5 | 225.0 | .... | 274.5 |
| 1928 | 59.9 | 330.5 | .... | 390.9 |
| 1929 | 61.6 | 324.6 | .... | 382.2 |
| 1930 | 61.3 | 342.5 | 9.1 | 390.0 |
| 1931 | 63.9 | 214.8 | 16.6 | 262.0 |
| 1932 | 62.0 | 113.5 | 1.5 | 167.7 |
| 1933 | 143.4 | 171.9 | 17.9 | 293.0 |
| 1934 | 144.3 | 178.5 | 17.7 | 275.0 |
| 1935 | 192.8 | 241.5 | 41.3 | 424.9 |
| 1936 | 247.3 | 211.8 | 38.1 | 396.5 |
| 1937 | 248.5 | 351.4 | 62.0 | 556.4 |
| 1938 | 317.0 | 193.6 | 51.8 | 428.2 |
| 1939 | 307.1 | 99.6 | 83.8 | 382.1 |
| 1940 | 379.7 | 118.7 | 62.8 | 448.9 |
| 1941 | 524.9 | 15.8 | 56.9 | 490.3 |
| 1942 | 679.2 | 4.4 | 57.1 | 628.0 |
| 1943 | 739.1 | 17.1 | 70.0 | 679.3 |
| 1944 | 834.6 | 4.9 | 68.9 | 753.9 |
| 1945 | 874.2 | 6.0 | 67.6 | 808.8 |
| 1946 | 931.8 | 4.4 | 65.6 | 867.1 |
| 1947 | 1,029.9 | 26.0 | 68.1 | 1,011.1 |
| 1948 | 1,139.9 | 27.2 | 65.2 | 1,101.0 |
| 1949 | 1,118.4 | 19.2 | 67.6 | 1,070.0 |
| 1950 | 1,287.7 | 200.5 | 79.2 | 1,409.0 |
| 1951 | 1,420.3 | 313.6 | 68.7 | 1,653.4 |
| 1952 | 1,665.1 | 188.4 | 56.3 | 1,730.5 |
| 1953 | 1,911.9 | 130.4 | 49.1 | 1,812.9 |

ᵃ U. S. Dept. of Interior, Bureau of Mines, *Minerals Yearbook*, various issues.

tion of what had previously been nearly an exclusive market for the German-French cartel, they apparently did so at cartel-established prices. The German-French combine quoted prices c.i.f. Atlantic and Gulf ports. As each new domestic producer entered the industry, including the American Potash and Chemical Corporation operating at Searles Lake, it adopted the port prices quoted by the cartel as basing points.[15] Under the system of multiple basing points, prices established throughout the United States were completely unrelated to production and transportation costs. Fertilizer plants near Carlsbad or Searles Lake paid the port price plus heavy transportation costs, whereas those in the Atlantic and Gulf Coast areas paid only the port price plus a small freight charge. In short, the greater the distance to the point of delivery the lower was the delivered price from domestic mines.

[15] Samuel P. Hayes, Jr., "Potash Prices and Competition," *Quarterly Journal of Economics*, Vol. 56 (November, 1942), esp. pp. 50, 53-55. See also Thorp and Tupper, *op. cit.*, pp. 62-63.

Domestic producers may have adopted the cartel's prices for several reasons, but most of them can probably be reduced to a desire to avoid competition among themselves and with the cartel. As one student of the problem has put it, they could not sell potash in the heavy-consumption areas along the Atlantic and Gulf coasts at prices higher than those quoted by the cartel, and they could not afford to charge less.[16] The ocean-freight charge from European shipping points to United States ports throughout the 1930's was about $5.00 per ton, whereas the rail-water rate from Carlsbad was $8.70 per ton, and from Searles Lake $10.79 and $11.79 to the Gulf and Atlantic ports respectively.[17] Atlantic and Gulf ports were therefore in the cartel's freight-advantage area. With a substantial freight advantage, a long-established dominant market position, and large financial resources, the cartel could have survived a long price war—a longer price war than domestic producers could have endured unless their production costs were considerably lower than those of Europe.[18]

The multiple basing point system of pricing may be said to have arisen spontaneously in the sense that the cartel created it and domestic producers simply adopted it, but it was preserved through formal organizations. On July 1, 1935, the three domestic producers joined with N. V. Potash Export My. to form the American Potash Institute "to promote the use of potash through collective action."[19] The Institute thus brought together into a single organization all the important domestic producers and the German-French cartel's exclusive importing agency. Collectively they accounted for virtually all the potash sales made in the United States and most of those made in world markets. According to the Federal Trade Commission:

> The atmosphere in which the Institute was formed was a thoroughly cooperative one in which representatives of the American producers and N. V. co-operated in the formation of the NRA code for the Potash Industry. In fact it appears that N. V. took a leading part in the formation of the Institute on July 1, 1935, just a little more than 4 weeks after the Schechter Decision invalidated the National Industrial Recovery Act on May 27, 1935.[20]

N. V. Potash's participation in writing the NRA code for potash dates collaboration between the cartel and the three domestic producers almost back to the formation of the Potash Company of America and the United States Potash Company following the discovery of the Carlsbad deposits. Its active role in the organization of the Potash Institute coincided with the invalidation of NRA and the bringing of Spanish and Russian competi-

---

[16] Hayes, *op. cit.*, p. 53.
[17] *Ibid.*, p. 54. The Carlsbad estimates were based on rates prevailing "over a period of years prior to 1940"; the Searles Lake rates on 1939 only.
[18] The profit history of individual potash companies suggests that domestic prices were generally considerably above costs (*infra*, this chapter).
[19] FTC, *Report on the Fertilizer Industry*, 1950, p. 99.
[20] *Ibid.*

tion under control. As early as 1932 the American Potash and Chemical Corporation had entered into an exclusive sales contract with the cartel's Far East sales agent, Dai Nippon Kali, Ltd., in exchange for the privilege of supplying up to thirty per cent of all the potash sold by Dai Nippon in Japan, Korea, and Formosa.[21] When American producers began to look to the European market for sales, they formed an export association, apparently for the express purpose of negotiating with the German-French cartel.[22] An agreement was reached between the two associations that, in exchange for a European quota, the Potash Export Association would sell all potash destined for the markets covered in the agreement to the cartel's subsidiary, United Potash Company, Ltd., of London.[23] Thus from the time the United States potash industry first became significant to the outbreak of World War II, some kind of formal arrangement which could have been instrumental in preserving the basing point system of pricing existed between the cartel and one or all of the three major domestic producers. Such arrangements may not have been necessary for its preservation, but they probably helped. In any case, both before and after the outbreak of competition from Russian and Spanish producers in 1934 the cartel established the base prices, and domestic producers uniformly accepted them.[24]

*The 1940 Consent Decree and Basing Point Pricing.* Late in the 1930's, when the Department of Justice launched an investigation of the entire fertilizer industry, the pricing practices of the potash industry underwent close examination. The facts uncovered by the investigation were presented before a Grand Jury during the March, 1939, term of the United States District Court for the Southern District of New York.[25] On May 26, 1939, the three domestic potash producers and N. V. Potash Export My. and their officers and directors were indicted on criminal charges of conspiracy to: (1) fix and maintain prices and eliminate competition, (2) enhance and maintain prices and prevent the sale of potash at prices lower than the prices so fixed and maintained, (3) dominate and monopolize the production and distribution of potash, and (4) sell potash in commerce

[21] *Ibid.*, p. 106. Prior to 1932 American Potash had sold in the Far East through S. Suzuki & Co., Ltd. Because the Searles Lake Region had a freight advantage over European sources in the Far East, American Potash had exported potash there since the early 1920's.
[22] The Potash Export Association was formed in September, 1938, by American Potash and Chemical Corp., United States Potash Co., and Potash Co. of America. The three charter members accounted for 99 per cent of total domestic potash production. Since World War II broke out soon after its organization, it performed for only one year the functions for which it was organized. For an account of its organization, powers, and activities, see FTC, *Report on the Fertilizer Industry*, 1950, pp. 108-23.
[23] *Ibid.*, p. 113.
[24] For the 1937-38 fertilizer season price leadership worked the other way. Because European prices generally were higher than United States prices during the 1930's, arbitrage developed whereby United States sellers of potash (principally sellers other than the primary producers) bought at United States prices from the cartel and resold in Europe. The cartel attempted to end this traffic by advancing United States prices in the 1935-36 and the 1936-37 seasons. The traffic continued, and the cartel waited for the Potash Company of America to announce a price for the 1937-38 season. Potash responded by raising base prices from $0.50 to $0.535 per unit of $K_2O$. All domestic producers followed each of these advances as they were made (see Thorp and Tupper, *op. cit.*, pp. 59-60).
[25] FTC, *Report on the Fertilizer Industry*, 1950, p. 100.

among the several states only on terms and conditions of sale agreed upon by the defendants and only to purchasers approved by them.[26]

As a result of the indictment, the Department of Commerce at the request of the Department of Justice made an economic investigation of the potash industry.[27] The investigation made the following findings:

1. The United States producers, while generally following the cartel's prices, put their high $K_2O$ content potash on the market at or near prices the cartel quoted for lower grade potash—in effect gradually reducing domestic prices. On May 1, 1934, the American Potash and Chemical Corporation discontinued its method of quoting prices per ton of muriate of potash, a method used throughout the fertilizer industry at that time and still used by most fertilizer producers, and introduced pricing on a per unit of $K_2O$ basis.[28] A month later, American Potash followed its new method of pricing with a price reduction from $0.648 to $0.50 per unit of $K_2O$. Other producers, domestic and foreign, adopted the new price and the new method of pricing.

2. Contrary to the allegations in the government's complaint, Bonneville, Ltd., had commenced producing potash in Utah in 1938; and the Union Potash Company, a newcomer to the industry, had been granted leases in the Carlsbad fields and was conducting explorations in 1940.

3. In 1938 the two New Mexico producers had made Carlsbad a basing point, thereby reducing considerably the freight charges paid by inland fertilizer producers located nearer Carlsbad than port basing points.[29]

On May 15, 1940, two weeks after the Department of Commerce had submitted its report, the Department of Justice substituted a civil complaint for the criminal indictment of May 26, 1939.[30] The complaint charged the defendant companies with violating the anti-trust laws and sought an injunction of the following practices: (1) maintaining and adhering to uniform prices, terms, and discounts; (2) refraining from competing in the sale of potash; (3) quoting prices only on the basis of c.i.f. recognized ports and limiting the number of such ports; and (4) refusing to sell potash to individual farmers, farm co-operatives, or to fertilizer mixers not approved by all defendants. The government moved to dismiss the charges against N. V. Potash Export My. on the ground that it had become inoperative because of the war. The court granted the motion, and on May 21, 1940, American Potash and Chemical Corpora-

---

[26] *Ibid.*

[27] Thorp and Tupper, *op. cit.*

[28] This, as will be shown later, was a much more significant innovation than it may appear. The value of any fertilizer to the farmer obviously derives from its plant-nutrient content and not from its gross weight. The practice of quoting prices on a gross weight basis in other branches of the fertilizer industry has encouraged farmers to buy it on that basis (see Chap. 10).

[29] It is not clear whether the two events were in any way connected, but the addition of the new basing point coincided with the launching of the Department of Justice's investigation that resulted in the March, 1939, grand jury proceedings.

[30] *United States* v. *American Potash and Chemical Corp.,* Civil Action No. 8-498, S. D. N. Y., complaint filed May 15, 1940.

tion, Potash Company of America, and United States Potash Company became subject to a consent decree which permanently enjoined them from agreeing, combining, or conspiring among themselves or with any other potash producer to commit the violations with which they were charged.[31] In compliance with the decree, domestic producers quoted f.o.b. mine prices for Carlsbad and Trona (Searles Lake), and continued to quote prices c.i.f. ports. The f.o.b. mine prices differed from each other and were lower than the quoted c.i.f. port prices. The systematic basing-point pricing which had prevailed for two decades was thereby effectively modified; it was scrapped altogether in 1949 when domestic producers discontinued the practice of quoting port prices and began quoting only f.o.b. mine prices.[32]

During World War II, the Office of Price Administration's ceiling prices for potash were those that had prevailed since May, 1937; and these did not change until March, 1947, when the Carlsbad price was reduced from $0.423 to $0.40 per unit of $K_2O$. In May, 1949, the Carlsbad price was further reduced to $0.375 per unit of $K_2O$. Trona prices remained unchanged until 1950, when they were increased to $0.505. In 1950 the Carlsbad price was increased to $0.42.[33] These were the prevailing prices when the Office of Price Stabilization set ceiling prices in 1951. As nearly as can be determined, all New Mexico producers were charging identical prices on identical grades of potash fertilizer materials when price ceilings were established. Since all were located within a few miles of Carlsbad, such identical pricing cannot be interpreted as a renascence of basing-point pricing. But since the structure of the industry had not changed substantially since the 1930's, it may have been due to the continuation of oligopoly.[34]

*Prices and Profits in the Potash Industry.* Potash prices in the United States obviously have not been determined by competition. Up to the Second World War they were set by a cartel, whose policy presumably was to charge cartel prices. The domestic oligopoly, unwilling to compete, simply adopted the prices the cartel established. As a result potash prices have remained stable over long periods of time (Table 22). They have also been high relative to production costs, especially those on Carlsbad production. From 1936 through 1951 the rates of return after taxes for United States

---

[31] *United States* v. *American Potash and Chemical Corp.,* C. C. H. Trade Reg. Rep., Vol. 3, par. 25461, cited in FTC, *Report on the Fertilizer Industry,* 1950, p. 102.

[32] FTC, *Report on the Fertilizer Industry,* 1950, p. 105.

[33] *Oil Paint and Drug Reporter,* March 24, 1947, *et seq.* (All prices are for bulk shipments of muriate of potash and are subject to seasonal discounts.)

[34] As of 1952 the potash industry comprised, in addition to American Potash and Chemical Corp., Potash Co. of America, and United States Potash Co., six producers: Duval Sulphur and Potash Co. and International Minerals and Chemical Corp. near Carlsbad; Bonneville, Ltd., in Utah; Dow Chemical Co. in Midlands, Michigan (lime wells); and A. M. Blumer Co. of California and North American Cement Corp. of Maryland (by-product potash from cement). The combined output of the six producers is not known but is believed to have been relatively small.

TABLE 22

PRICES [a] OF MURIATE OF POTASH PER UNIT OF $K_2O$, 1922-51 [b]

| Year | C.i.f. Atlantic and Gulf Ports | F.o.b. Carlsbad | F.o.b. Trona |
|------|--------------------------------|-----------------|--------------|
| 1922 | $0.700 | ........ | ........ |
| 1923 | 0.640 | ........ | ........ |
| 1924 | 0.620 | ........ | ........ |
| 1925 | 0.620 | ........ | ........ |
| 1926 | 0.599 | ........ | ........ |
| 1927 | 0.620 | ........ | ........ |
| 1928 | 0.669 | ........ | ........ |
| 1929 | 0.689 | ........ | ........ |
| 1930 | 0.703 | ........ | ........ |
| 1931 | 0.703 | ........ | ........ |
| 1932 | 0.703 | ........ | ........ |
| 1933 | 0.703 | ........ | ........ |
| 1934 | 0.703 | ........ | ........ |
| 1935 | 0.396 | ........ | ........ |
| 1936 | 0.450 | ........ | ........ |
| 1937 | 0.500 | ........ | ........ |
| 1938 | 0.535 | ........ | ........ |
| 1939 | 0.535 | ........ | ........ |
| 1940 | 0.535 | ........ | ........ |
| 1941-46 | 0.535 | $0.423 | $0.455 |
| 1947 | 0.535 | 0.400 | 0.455 |
| 1948 | 0.535 | 0.400 | 0.455 |
| 1949 | 0.535[c] | 0.400 | 0.455 |
| 1950 | ...... | 0.375 | 0.485 |
| 1951 | ...... | 0.420 | 0.505 |

[a] Prices are those prevailing in March of each year for bulk shipments.
[b] 1922-39 prices, Thorp and Tupper, *op. cit.*, p. 18a. 1940-51 prices, various issues of the *Oil Paint and Drug Reporter.*
[c] Discontinued in May, 1949.

Potash Company and Potash Company of America, the two principal Carlsbad producers, averaged 34 per cent and 24.2 per cent respectively (Table 23), and over the sixteen-year period these rates have shown no downward trend. Annual rates of return after taxes for American Potash and Chemical Corporation, the only important producer of potash from Searles Lake brines, have been much more modest but have averaged 9.61 per cent over the sixteen-year period.

The difficulty of distinguishing monopoly profits from rents and profits because of market frictions has been discussed.[35] But abnormally high rates of return have persisted throughout the postwar period, in spite of rising factor prices and the elimination of systematic basing-point pricing through anti-trust action, and notwithstanding the fact that potash was one of the few commodities having a lower base price after the war than throughout the 1930's. This suggests, assuming that investment costs have been proportional to output, that net realized margins have been left largely intact, which in turn suggests that price reductions have just offset

[35] See Chap. 4, n. 13.

TABLE 23

RATES OF RETURN ON INVESTMENT AFTER FEDERAL INCOME
TAXES, FOR THREE POTASH MINING COMPANIES, 1936-51 [a]

| Year | United States Potash Co. Per Cent | Potash Company of America Per Cent | American Potash and Chemical Corporation Per Cent |
|---|---|---|---|
| 1936 | 25.51 | ..... | 11.72 |
| 1937 | 39.51 | 8.60 | 13.84 |
| 1938 | 32.13 | 12.73 | 14.75 |
| 1939 | 28.65 | 13.91 | 16.92 |
| 1940 | 30.89 | 24.30 | 12.20 |
| 1941 | 34.26 | 26.37 | 5.39 |
| 1942 | 30.80 | 25.42 | 8.04 |
| 1943 | 37.32 | 23.72 | 7.43 |
| 1944 | 32.90 | 27.62 | 8.66 |
| 1945 | 41.28 | 28.48 | 6.66 |
| 1946 | 32.91 | 26.66 | 8.34 |
| 1947 | 44.97 | 31.21 | 9.75 |
| 1948 | 38.26 | 33.14 | 6.71 |
| 1949 | 31.26 | 29.67 | 6.81 |
| 1950 | 32.80 | 25.78 | 9.47 |
| 1951 | 30.58 | 25.42 | 7.09 |
| Annual Average | 34.00 | 24.20 | 9.61 |

[a] 1936-46 rates, FTC, *Report on the Fertilizer Industry*, 1950, p. 162. 1947-51 rates computed on comparable basis from financial statements published in Moody's *Manual of Industrial Investments*.

the freight Carlsbad producers formerly absorbed to get into the eastern markets under c.i.f. port basing-point pricing. Thus while anti-trust policy eliminated a geographical pricing system under which prices at destination bore no resemblance to production plus distribution costs, it still may confront the rationalized price of a highly concentrated oligopoly. The only study that has raised the question of remedy for oligopoly in the potash industry has concluded that "existing companies cannot be 'atomized' without serious loss of efficiency and such high costs as to destroy their ability to compete with the importer." [36] However, the evidence offered in support of this conclusion is not convincing, in that all the cost calculations were based on shutdowns of particular units rather than a transfer of their ownership; the study assumed that depreciation and probably certain other costs would remain the same whether the company under consideration operated one, two, or three production units. But the study went on to point out that the facilities were so completely scrambled that "any artificial division [of them] would raise difficult problems." [37] This is not an uncommon problem, and it is one that public policy has rarely solved. Its mere existence makes all the more imperative the government's exercise of circumspection in granting leases in the potash fields in the future.

[36] Thorp and Tupper, *op. cit.*, p. 93.
[37] *Ibid.*, p. 94.

## CHAPTER 6

# THE NITROGEN INDUSTRY

NITROGEN (N) is found abundantly in air, coal, natural nitrate deposits, organic matter, and in the soil. However, in such forms it is not usable as a fertilizer or for industrial purposes. The history of the nitrogen industry is marked by progression from use of the more readily available sources such as the soil, organic matter, and natural nitrate deposits, to the less readily available sources such as coal and air. Oddly enough, while nitrogen's principal peacetime use is as a plant food, its wartime use as an explosive has spurred this development. As wars have interrupted international trade and at the same time added military to civilian demand, nations have had to turn to the less readily available sources of nitrogen.

The increase in the number of exploitable sources of N has had tremendous impact on the quantities and forms of N used in fertilizer manufacture. In 1900 the United States consumed 62,000 net tons of N as fertilizers; in 1920, 227,800; in 1940, 419,100; and in 1953, 1,583,834. In 1900 natural organics such as animal and industrial by-products and wastes supplied 91 per cent of all the N used in commercial fertilizers; in 1948 the same sources supplied only 3.5 per cent, the remainder coming from a variety of chemical products including ammonia and solutions (31.8 per cent) ammonium nitrate (15.3 per cent), ammonium sulphate (27.1 per cent), sodium nitrate (14.7 per cent), and others (7.6 per cent).[1]

N, like potash ($K_2O$) and $P_2O_5$, is one of the three primary plant nutrients. In peacetime fertilizers account for about half the N consumed in the United States; when munitions production is high, especially in wartime, the proportion is much smaller. About forty-five per cent of the N used as fertilizer is applied to crops as a straight material, the rest in mixtures of N, $P_2O_5$ and $K_2O$. A larger proportion of N than of $P_2O_5$ and $K_2O$ is used as a straight material, because N is applied periodically as a side dressing to most row crops at various stages of plant growth, and because recent technological innovations have made it economical to apply ammonia in liquid form. But whether farmers buy their N straight or in mixtures, they generally buy it from fertilizer manufacturers instead of from the chemical companies that pro-

[1] All data in the paragraph in the text come from various reports on fertilizer consumption in the United States, Bureau of Plant Industry, Soils, and Agricultural Engineering, U. S. Dept. of Agriculture.

duce it. Chemical manufacturers, like potash producers, are not integrated with fertilizer manufacturing and do not maintain selling organizations to serve retail markets.[2] They sell nitrogenous chemicals in wholesale lots to fertilizer manufacturers—the largest of which are the integrated phosphate-fertilizer companies—that do sell directly to farmers through their agents and salesmen.

*Nitrate of Soda and the Chilean Cartels.* The sodium nitrate deposits of Chile from which nitrate of soda is made were the most important sources of inorganic nitrogen until 1921.[3] Until the outbreak of World War I the only important alternative source was by-product ammonia, the supply of which was geared more closely to the iron and steel market than to the demand for N. In 1916 imports of Chilean nitrate of soda into the United States amounted to almost 187,000 tons of nitrogen, or about ninety per cent of all the N consumed as fertilizers in the United States that year.[4] Even as late as 1935-39, Chilean nitrate imports accounted for about one-quarter of all the N consumed as fertilizers. Hence, the price of N in the United States and elsewhere for the first two decades of this century was largely dependent upon the pricing policies of Chilean producers.

For a brief period after Chile had established undisputed jurisdiction over the sodium-nitrate deposits that now lie within its borders, it encouraged private producers to exploit them, but levied a tax of approximately $12.00 per ton on all nitrate exports.[5] The greater the volume of exports, the greater the government's revenue. But in spite of steady increases in consumption, supply soon began to exceed demand. Between 1881 and 1884 the price of Chilean nitrate of soda fell from $49.53 to $31.06 per ton. Since the tax remained constant at $12.00 per ton, the entire burden of the price decline fell on the producers.

Chilean producers turned to cartel agreements to control production. Between June, 1884, and August, 1913, they entered into no less than six agreements, all of which differed in details but had the common purpose of regulating output by allocating quotas and imposing penalties on producers who exceeded them.[6] Most of the agreements were short-

---

[2] Mergers and plant acquisitions since World War II have slightly altered the historical pattern of complete independence of ownership and control over N, $P_2O_5$ and $K_2O$ production facilities. The Phillips Chemical Co. acquired a nitrogen plant from the government in 1946 and constructed a concentrated superphosphate plant in 1953. In 1954 W. R. Grace & Co. acquired Davison Chemical Co., an integrated phosphate-fertilizer producer, and constructed a nitrogen plant; and the Smith-Douglass Co., a medium-sized superphosphate and mixed fertilizer manufacturer, acquired a government nitrogen plant and the Coronet Phosphate Co., a phosphate-rock producer.

[3] They are the only commercially-mined nitrate deposits in the world. Exports from them date back to 1830, but the industry did not flourish until about 1880. Before the War of the Pacific (1870-82) Peru and Bolivia shared in their control. By virtue of its victory in the war and through a series of treaties, Chile extended its sovereignty over all the nitrate deposits (George W. Stocking and Myron W. Watkins, *Cartels in Action* [New York: 20th Century Fund, 1946], 120).

[4] Computed from data in Edmund E. Vial, *Prices of Fertilizer Materials and Factors Affecting Fertilizer Tonnage* (Ithaca: Cornell Univ. Press, 1928) p. 31.

[5] Stocking and Watkins, *op. cit.*, p. 120 (the tax remained unchanged for nearly fifty years, and it was the source of 42.8 per cent of the Chilean government's ordinary revenue from 1880 to 1930).

[6] FTC, *Report on The Fertilizer Industry*, 1916, p. 13.

lived. Four of them lasted between nearly two to a little over three years, one lasted five years, and one only five months. In nine of the twenty-nine years between 1884 and 1913 no agreement was in effect. But the producers apparently were able to maintain nitrate-of-soda prices above competitive levels. According to Stocking and Watkins, the organization of each cartel generally resulted in price increases; the lapse of each agreement brought on price declines.[7]

*Development of the Chemical Nitrogen Industry.* World War I demands for munitions and for increased production of food and fibers brought prosperity to the Chilean nitrate industry. Between 1913 and 1918 United States imports of N from Chile increased from a little over 100,000 short tons to nearly 300,000 short tons.[8] In 1917 Chilean nitrogen production reached an all-time high of 511,700 short tons, and prices advanced to $60.13 per short ton. But the war also undermined Chile's dominant position by expanding coke production and hastening the substitution of by-product coke ovens for the wasteful beehive oven,[9] which gradually increased the amount of by-product N available. By-product N (principally sulphate of ammonia) increased throughout the world by more than forty per cent and more than trebled in the United States between 1914 and 1918.[10] But the war's greatest change was the rise of the synthetic-nitrogen industry. In 1913 world production of synthetic nitrogen by all processes accounted for a scant 7.7 per cent of fixed nitrogen output and for less than three per cent of fixed and Chilean nitrogen output combined. By 1918 output had reached 269,700 tons, or twenty-three per cent of fixed nitrogen output and fifteen per cent of fixed and Chilean nitrogen output. Most of the increases occurred in Germany, where allied blockades had cut off the Chilean supply.

*Competition in the 1920's.* With the end of the war German synthetic and by-product nitrogen producers began to export in competition with Chilean nitrates; at the same time world demand for N decreased. Rapid technological advances and national governments' determination to develop their own sources of N spurred expansion in synthetic nitrogen elsewhere. Policies adopted by the Chilean government and the Chilean Nitrate Producers' Association, organized in 1919, greatly stimulated the movement. In the face of generally reduced world demand, the 1920-21 recession, and Germany's new synthetic nitrogen capacity, the Chilean government maintained its export tax, and the association advanced

[7] Stocking and Watkins, *op. cit.*, p. 122.
[8] Nitrate of soda at that time contained 15.65 per cent N. Nitrate of soda imports increased from 600,000 long tons in 1913 to about 1,700,000 long tons in 1918 (Vial, *op. cit.*, p. 31).
[9] Stocking and Watkins, *op. cit.*, p. 125 (For detailed descriptions of various processes for producing nitrogen see Harry A. Curtis [ed.]. *Fixed Nitrogen* [New York: Chemical Catalog Co., 1932], and J. R. Partington and L. H. Parker, *The Nitrogen Industry*, [rev. ed.; London D. Van Nostrand Co., 1940]).
[10] Vial, *op. cit.*, p. 34.

nitrate-of-soda prices from $49.66 to $78.49 per ton between 1920 and 1921.[11]

Scientific research, the drive for national self-sufficiency, and Chilean output restrictions and high prices precipitated in the 1920's what Stocking and Watkins have called the "nitrogen rush." [12] In the five-year period 1924-29, total world synthetic N production increased from 405,085 tons to 1,171,900 tons, cyanamide production more than doubled, and by-product N production increased by nearly forty-five per cent (Table 24). While many countries participated in the rush, Germany, the

TABLE 24

WORLD PRODUCTION OF ALL CHEMICAL NITROGEN, CHILEAN NITROGEN, AND PRODUCTION OF SYNTHETIC PROCESS NITROGEN BY COUNTRY, 1924 AND 1929 [a]

| | (Thousands of short tons of N) | |
|---|---|---|
| | 1924 | 1929 |
| Synthetic Nitrogen: | | |
| Germany................................. | 353.0 | 663.3 |
| United States............................ | 11.1 | 135.9 |
| Japan................................... | 1.8 | 41.2 |
| France.................................. | 4.5 | 56.9 |
| Great Britain............................ | 7.2 | 118.0 |
| Belgium................................. | .... | 24.8 |
| Italy.................................... | 2.4 | 36.6 |
| Netherlands............................. | .... | 4.8 |
| Norway................................. | 25.0 | 61.7 |
| U. S. S. R.............................. | .... | 1.3 |
| Poland.................................. | .... | 11.2 |
| Czechoslovakia.......................... | .... | 7.8 |
| Sweden................................. | .... | 2.3 |
| Spain................................... | 0.2 | 3.3 |
| Switzerland............................. | .... | 3.0 |
| Total Synthetic......................... | 405.1 | 1,172.0 |
| Total By-product........................ | 360.0 | 521.7 |
| Total Cyanamide........................ | 143.0 | 302.6 |
| Total Manufactured...................... | 908.1 | 1,996.2 |
| Chilean Natural......................... | 413.3 | 556.0 |
| Total World............................. | 1,321.4 | 2,552.2 |

[a] U. S. Tariff Commission, *Chemical Nitrogen*, Report No. 114, Series II, 1937, pp. 256-59.

United States, Great Britain, Norway, and France led the pack. In most countries governments played an important role. Nitrogen plants in Russia, Hungary, Poland, and Czechoslovakia were almost entirely state-owned; the state owned some in the Netherlands and France; and in the more important industrial countries the state used tariffs and direct

[11] For an account of the Chilean Nitrate Producer's Association, see Stocking and Watkins, *op. cit.*, pp. 128-29.
[12] *Ibid.*, pp. 129 ff.

subsidies to stimulate synthetic-nitrogen expansion. In the United States the synthetic-nitrogen industry developed without appreciable state aid; but, as will be shown later, the federal government built most of the nitrogen plants constructed during World War II.[13]

Nevertheless, in the main the industry was developed by private businesses, especially the large chemical firms. In Germany, I. G. Farben took the lead; in Great Britain, Imperial Chemical Industries, Ltd., took it;[14] and in the United States, Allied Chemical and Dye Corporation and E. I. du Pont de Nemours & Company were the leaders. But numerous firms entered the industry, and for the best of business reasons: under prevailing prices and estimated production costs the nitrogen industry looked profitable.

The rush resulted in an excess of output over consumption at prevailing prices, and prices declined. They declined precipitously. In the United States the wholesale price per unit (twenty pounds of N) in ammonium sulphate declined from $4.08 in 1920 to $1.02 in 1932; in nitrate of soda from $4.44 to $1.86; and in natural organics from $8.71 to $1.83. In the 1920's nitrogen prices reflected considerable competition.[15]

*The 1930's and the World Nitrogen Cartel.* As early as 1929 Chilean, German, and British producers, the largest exporters and the largest producers outside the United States, had attempted to halt declining prices by cartel agreements.[16] All the early agreements failed, but they laid the groundwork for more successful ones to follow. The Chilean industry was reorganized in 1931 to give Compañía de Salitre de Chile (Cosach) control of about ninety-five per cent of all Chilean nitrate facilities. In Germany the three major producing groups—by-product ammonia, synthetic ammonia, and cyanamide producers—were each highly concentrated through ownership or cartels, and all were further organized together as the German Nitrogen Syndicate (Deutsche Stickstoffsyndikat G. m. b. H.). The British industry was similarly concentrated. Cosach was dissolved by government decree on January 2, 1933; but by January 8, 1934, a state monopoly over Chilean exports, the Chilean Nitrate & Iodine Sales Corporation, had taken its place. Thus in each important

[13] Under the National Defense Act of June, 1916, the U. S. Government constructed a cynamide plant and a small synthetic-ammonia plant at Muscle Shoals during World War I. The plants did not produce on a commerical scale until they were completely remodeled and placed under TVA in World War II. By-product ammonium sulphate was protected by a tariff duty of $5.00 per ton from 1922 to 1930. The U. S. Dept. of Agriculture has maintained a fixed-nitrogen laboratory since 1914.
[14] Before Imperial was created by merger in 1926 it was Brunner, Mond & Co., Ltd.; United Alkali Co., Ltd.; British Dyestuffs Corp., Ltd.; and Nobel Industries, Ltd. (FTC, *Report on the Fertilizer Industry*, 1950).
[15] However, according to Stocking and Watkins (*op. cit.*, p. 163) the early cartels retarded price declines during the first two years of the depression.
[16] For a discussion of the organization and activities of the earlier cartels, especially the 1929 agreement embracing the German Nitrogen Syndicate, Imperial Chemicals and Chilean producers; the Convention Internationale de l'Azote (CIA) embracing producers in Germany, Great Britain, Norway, France, Belgium, the Netherlands, Italy, Poland, Czechoslovakia, and the Irish Free State; and CIA's agreement with Chilean producers, see *ibid.*, pp. 143-44.

producing country except the United States the bargaining units for purposes of forming an international cartel were reduced to one.

Between 1929 and 1938 Germany took the lead in forming a succession of cartels in which important nitrogen producers allocated market shares and determined prices by collective action. The early attempts, as stated above, failed; but with the experience gained by each attempt, as the Great Depression passed, and as United States producers began to co-operate, the cartels gradually became more effective instruments of market control.[17]

*United States Producers and the World Cartel.* Although the United States has always been a large net importer of N,[18] without co-operation from its producers international cartels find it difficult to stabilize international markets. As prices in other markets are raised above United States prices plus transportation costs, United States producers attempt to export to them. The United States is both a large consumer and a large producer of nitrogen. Arbitrage links its nitrogen market with those of other countries. For an international cartel to attain moderate success it must work out a *modus operandi* with United States producers.

For nitrogen this was not so simple as it had been for potash. The two main branches of the United States chemical-nitrogen industry in the 1930's were by-product nitrogen (ammonium sulphate) and synthetic nitrogen. Neither branch comprised so few producers or was so highly concentrated as the potash industry, although synthetic nitrogen was nearly so. Domestic nitrogen producers were located principally in the East and Midwest, close to fertilizer markets and not under the freight handicap that confronted potash producers located at Carlsbad and Searles Lake. In spite of these obstacles and in spite of the anti-trust laws, United States nitrogen producers engaged in restraints of trade during the 1930's that precipitated an investigation by the Department of Justice and five federal grand jury indictments on September 1, 1939.[19] The indictments charged that United States firms participated in the international cartel and that the cartel restrained trade in the United States. The defendants entered pleas of *nolo contendere,* and after payment of fines the cases were disposed of through three civil complaints resulting in consent decrees covering most of the allegations made by the government in the original indictments.[20] While the allegations were

[17] *Ibid.*, pp. 144-68; and FTC, *Report on the Fertilizer Industry*, 1950, pp. 34-53.
[18] See National Planning Association, *Fertilizers in the Postwar National Economy*, Planning Pamphlet No. 42 (Washington, 1945), Fig. G, p. 33.
[19] *U. S. v. Allied Chem. & Dye Corp.*, Crim. Action No. 106-12; *U. S. v. Synthetic Nitrogen Prod., Inc.*, Crim. Action No. 106-16; *U. S. v. E. I. du Pont de Nemours & Co.*, Crim. Action No. 106-15; and *U. S. v. Chilean Nitrate Sales*, Crim. Action No. 106-14, U. S. Dist. Court, So. Dist. of N. Y., Sept. 1, 1939.
[20] *U. S. v. Allied Chem. & Dye Corp.*, Civil Action No. 14-230 (complaint filed May 29, 1941); *U. S. v. Synthetic Nitrogen Products Corp.*, Civil Action No. 15-635 (complaint filed Sept. 5, 1941); and *U. S. v. Imperial Chemical Industries (N. Y.), Ltd.*, Civil Action No. 17-282 (complaint filed Feb. 17, 1942), U. S. Dist. Court, So. Dist. of N. Y.

never adjudicated and established as findings of fact in the court, the defendants' acceptance through three consent decrees of injunctive provisions based upon the initial allegations imparts to them a high order of credibility.

According to the five indictments, United States nitrogen producers and sellers co-operated with the international nitrogen cartel through agreements on: (1) by-product nitrogen, between the Barrett Company, a wholly-owned subsidiary of the Allied Chemical and Dye Corporation, and domestic by-product nitrogen producers; (2) nitrate of soda and indirectly other nitrogenous materials, between Chilean producers and Allied Chemical and Dye and its subsidiaries, the only important producers of nitrate of soda in the United States before World War II; (3) synthetic nitrogen products and indirectly natural nitrates, between German producers and du Pont, Allied Chemical and Dye, and the Barrett Company; and (4) synthetic nitrogen products and indirectly natural nitrates, between Imperial Chemical Industries, Ltd., of England and United States producers of fertilizer nitrogen.[21]

The structure of the nitrogen industry in the United States during the 1930's throws considerable light on the effects of these agreements. As pointed out above, the chemical-nitrogen industry comprises two branches, by-product nitrogen and synthetic nitrogen. The by-product nitrogen industry is a branch of the coal-processing industry; the output of by-product nitrogen (principally sulphate of ammonia) varies directly with the production of pig iron, gas for industrial and residential consumption, and coke for the solid fuel market. Since it is generally more expensive to dispose of ammonia released in coke and coal-gas manufacture as waste than it is to convert it into marketable ammonia, by-product nitrogen forces its way on the market at whatever price it will bring.[22] As in the case of by-product sulphuric acid discussed earlier, the marginal cost of by-product chemical nitrogen is very low—in some cases even negative—and the quantities that reach the market are largely unrelated to demand. The number of by-product producers is large, reflecting the large number of coke and coal-gas manufacturers. In 1934, sixty-five companies operating 108 plants recovered ammonia as a by-product.[23] In contrast, the synthetic-nitrogen industry in the 1930's comprised only a few producers. The Solvay Process Company, a wholly-owned subsidiary of Allied Chemical and Dye, began producing nitrate of soda on a large scale in 1929. Nitrate of soda was not produced on a substantial scale in the United States before Solvay entered the industry.

[21] FTC, *Report on the Fertilizer Industry*, 1950, p. 43.
[22] Stocking and Watkins, *op. cit.*, pp. 148-49.
[23] *Ibid.*, p. 149, quoting U. S. Tariff Commission, *Chemical Nitrogen*, Report No. 114, Series II, 1937.

As of 1934, Solvay and E. I. du Pont de Nemours & Company, which produced both fertilizer and industrial synthetic-nitrogen materials, accounted for almost ninety per cent of the total domestic synthetic-nitrogen capacity. The industry's structure did not change substantially between 1934 and 1940, a year after the five grand jury indictments were returned. In 1940 du Pont and Allied Chemical and its subsidiaries controlled eighty-seven per cent of total domestic capacity, and five small producers controlled the remaining thirteen per cent (Table 25).

TABLE 25

SYNTHETIC NITROGEN CAPACITY BY PRODUCER IN 1940, 1945
(BEFORE AND AFTER DISPOSAL OF GOVERNMENT-OWNED PLANTS),
1951, AND 1955 [a]

(Thousands of Short Tons of N)

| Company | 1940 | 1945 Before disposal of govt. plants | After disposal of govt. plants [b] | 1951 | 1955[c] |
|---|---|---|---|---|---|
| Allied Chemical & Dye Corp......... | 200.0 | 208.0 | 285.0 | 395.0 | over 450.0[f] |
| E. I. duPont de Nemours & Co...... | 138.7 | 168.8 | 168.8 | 188.0 | 188.0 |
| Shell Union Oil Co.................. | 24.3 | 24.0 | 24.0 | 75.0 | 118.0 |
| Hercules Powder Co................ | 10.0 | 10.0 | 42.0 | 55.0 | 55.0 |
| Dow Chemical Co................... | 8.4 | 11.3 | 11.3 | 34.0 | 34.0 |
| Mathieson Chemical Co.[e]........... | 4.9 | 4.0 | 265.0[d] | 271.0 | 233.0[d] |
| Pennsylvania Salt Co.............. | 4.0 | 5.0 | 5.0 | 9.0 | over 9.0[f] |
| Lion Oil Co....................... | ...... | ............ | 100.0 | 160.0 | 298.0 |
| Commercial Solvents Co........... | ...... | ............ | 44.0 | 50.0 | 100.0 |
| Spencer Chemical Co.............. | ...... | ............ | 173.0 | 196.0 | 254.0 |
| Phillips Chemical Co.............. | ...... | ............ | 45.0[d] | 125.0[d] | 253.0[d] |
| Smith-Douglass Co................ | ...... | ............ | 18.0 | 18.0 | 146.0 |
| Midland Ammonia Co.............. | ...... | ............ | ...... | 20.0 | 20.0 |
| Mississippi Chemical Co........... | ...... | ............ | ...... | 24.0 | 89.0 |
| Hooker Electrochemical Co......... | ...... | ............ | ...... | ........ | ....(f) |
| American Cyanamid Co............ | ...... | ............ | ...... | ........ | ....(f) |
| Atlantic Refining Co.............. | ...... | ............ | ...... | ........ | ....(f) |
| Consumers Cooperatives, Inc....... | ...... | ............ | ...... | ........ | 58.0 |
| John Deere Co.................... | ...... | ............ | ...... | ........ | 58.0 |
| Delta Chemical Co................ | ...... | ............ | ...... | ........ | 58.0 |
| W. R. Grace & Co................. | ...... | ............ | ...... | ........ | 72.0 |
| Tennessee Valley Authority........ | ...... | 50.0 | 50.0 | 55.0 | 140.0 |
| Total Private..................... | 390.3 | 431.1 | 1,231.1[d] | 1,675.0[d] | 2,850.0[d] |
| Government Owned (excluding TVA).. | ...... | 800.0 | [261.0][d] | [261.0][d] | [261.0][d] |
| Total......................... | 390.3 | 1,231.1 | 1,231.1 | 1,675,0 | 2,850.0 |

[a] 1940-45 data from FTC, *Report on the Fertilizer Industry,* 1950, pp. 24-25; 1951 data from K. D. Jacob (ed.), *op. cit.;* 1955 data from K. D. Jacob, Bureau of Plant Industry, Soils, and Agricultural Engineering, U. S. Dept. of Agriculture, and *Chemical Week,* Vol. 76, No. 6 (February 5, 1955), pp. 75-76.
[b] The capacities shown are for 1945 before disposal of government plants plus government plants acquired up through 1954; they do not include additional capacity constructed after 1945.
[c] Capacities shown are for 1954 plus plants under construction and scheduled for completion by January, 1955. Capacity for proposed plants not under construction by August, 1953, irrespective of estimated date of completion, is not included.
[d] As of 1955 the government still owned plants having a total capacity of 261,000 short tons: 216,000 short tons of capacity were leased by Olin-Mathieson and 45,000 short tons of capacity by Phillips, and these are included in their capacities.
[e] Merged with Olin to become Olin-Mathieson in 1954.
[f] Exact capacities not known.

The competing interests in the United States nitrogen market during the 1930's, therefore, consisted of a dispersed by-product industry and a highly concentrated synthetic-nitrogen industry. The latter included nitrate-of-soda producers, principally Allied Chemical and Dye, which competed with the Chilean Nitrate Sales Corporation (the exclusive distributor of Chilean nitrate of soda in the United States), and producers of other fertilizer and industrial nitrogen materials, principally du Pont, which competed with imported synthetic nitrogen. These producers faced competition from each other and from by-product nitrogen.

The 1939 indictment of the Barrett Company (as previously indicated, an Allied Chemical subsidiary),[24] charged that its contracts and agreements greatly reduced competition between domestic and Chilean nitrate of soda and between nitrate of soda and by-product nitrogen. Barrett was the sole distributor of nitrate of soda and other synthetic nitrogen produced by another Allied Chemical subsidiary, the Solvay Process Company. The indictment charged that during the 1930's Barrett entered into exclusive agency contracts with producers of by-product nitrogen whereby they would sell their entire sulphate-of-ammonia output through Barrett; and that where Barrett was unable to obtain such contracts, it purchased large quantities of sulphate of ammonia at prices identical with those paid producers for which Barrett acted as exclusive agent. The indictment alleged that Barrett controlled about eighty per cent of total sulphate-of-ammonia sales in the fertilizer year 1938-39,[25] and that it followed a multiple basing-point system of pricing in order to stabilize prices and make them uniform at all delivery points.

Competition between Solvay and the Chilean Nitrate Sales Corporation in the sale of nitrate of soda apparently was brought under control after 1934, when Barrett adopted the Atlantic and Gulf port prices established by the Chilean Nitrate Sales Corporation, even though all of its sales originated at Solvay's Hopewell, Virginia, plant. The 1939 indictment alleged that Barrett and Chilean Nitrate Sales, which together controlled nearly all the nitrate of soda sold in the United States, added identical handling, bagging, storing, and freight charges to the port base prices, required middlemen to adhere to stipulated price schedules, granted them uniform commissions, and permitted them to act as agents for both sellers simultaneously and to add together the sales for both companies in computing their commission rates.

Three of the five indictments returned in 1939 alleged price fixing between German and United States synthetic-nitrogen producers. The indictments returned against Allied Chemical and Dye, du Pont, and Synthetic Nitrogen Products Corporation (the German Stickstoffsyndikat's selling agent in the United States) charged that these three companies and Barrett Company and Solvay Process Company had combined

[24] *U. S.* v. *Barrett Co.,* Crim. Action No. 106-13, U. S. Dist. Court, So. Dist. of N. Y., Sept. 1, 1939.
[25] *Ibid.*

to fix the prices of nitrogenous materials, including Cal-Nitro, calcium nitrate, sulphate of ammonia, and uramon.[26] Each of the companies was charged with quoting identical prices per unit of N, regardless of type of nitrogenous material, at agreed-upon ports and delivery points, and with adjusting freight charges so that prices at all points of delivery were the same for all companies. The du Pont indictment charged du Pont, Solvay, Barrett, and Allied Chemical with having adopted, around 1932, uniform prices and terms of sale on ammonia and other nitrogenous solutions, with having purchased the outputs of such solutions from small industrial producers at arbitrarily fixed prices that discouraged them from expanding, and with having sold substantial quantities of such solutions to large industrial consumers at lower prices than to fertilizer mixers in order to discourage the large purchasers from constructing their own synthetic-ammonia-solution plants. The indictment against Allied Chemical also named Imperial Chemical Industries (New York), Ltd., as one of the defendants, thereby bringing under the five indictments all the principal producers of N in Europe, Chile, and the United States.

As stated earlier, all five indictments were *nolle pros.*, and the three civil complaints subsequently substituted were settled by consent decrees.[27] The injunctive provisions of each decree were voluminous and interwoven with those of the other two, but may all be summarized briefly as having enjoined each of the defendants from entering into agreements with other producers, sellers, or agents to fix prices and other terms of sale, from refusing to sell f.o.b. at any point of production where sellers had nitrogen materials available, and from restricting exports and imports.[28] Put even more briefly, producers of nitrogen materials were to substitute independent for conspiratorial action, at least in so far as the structures of the component parts of the chemical-nitrogen industry permitted.

To have agreed not to conspire in the future does not necessarily mean that the defendants named in the indictments and the civil complaints were guilty of conspiracy in the past. Nevertheless, the evidence presented before the grand jury was sufficiently persuasive to establish a *prima facie* case that the producers and sellers of various nitrogenous materials had restrained trade through price fixing and other agreements. The Department of Justice had conducted an extensive investigation of the entire fertilizer industry before the grand jury returned the five indictments; and the evidence of price fixing, while not conclusive, is highly persuasive. It seems reasonably safe to conclude that nitrogen prices

[26] See n. 19, *supra.*
[27] See n. 20, *supra.*
[28] For a more extended summary of the injunctive provisions, see FTC, *Report on the Fertilizer Industry*, 1950, pp. 46, 48.

during the 1930's, like those of phosphate rock, sulphur, and potash, were higher than those that would have been established by competition.

*Wartime and Postwar Developments in the United States Nitrogen Industry.* The great need for N during World War II resulted in a phenomenal increase in synthetic-nitrogen capacity—most of which was constructed by the federal government. Between 1940 and 1945 capacity increased from 390,000 to 1,231,100 short tons of N, or by 840,800 short tons (Table 25). The government constructed 800,000 and private firms already in the synthetic nitrogen industry constructed the remaining 40,800. At the end of the war nearly seventy per cent of domestic synthetic-nitrogen capacity was government owned, and the future structure of the synthetic-nitrogen industry was greatly dependent on the way in which the War Assets Administration disposed of the government-owned plants.

The disposition brought about considerable deconcentration in the synthetic-nitrogen industry. Except for the sale of the 77,000-ton Buckeye Ordnance Works at South Point, Ohio, to Allied Chemical, the largest producer, the plants were sold to small producers or newcomers. None of the government capacty was sold to du Pont, Shell Unon, Dow Chemical, or Pennsylvania Salt, respectively the second, third, fifth, and seventh (and smallest) ranking producers before the war. A portion of the Missouri Ordnance Works at Louisiana, Missouri, was sold to Hercules, the fourth largest producer; and the 45,000-ton Lake Charles ammonia plant at Lake Charles, Louisiana, was sold to Mathieson, the sixth largest producer. The remaining plants, representing well over half of the total capacity sold, went to Lion Oil, Commercial Solvents, Spencer Chemical, Smith-Douglass, and Phillips Chemical, none of which had produced synthetic nitrogen before World War II. Of the 401,000 short tons of nitrogen capacity still owned by the government as of March, 1955, 216,000 tons and 45,000 tons were leased respectively by Olin-Mathieson and Phillips, and the 140,000-ton plant at Muscle Shoals was operated by the Tennesee Valley Authority.[29] The net effect of the government's construction and subsequent disposal of synthetic-nitrogen plants was to add TVA and five new private firms to the industry, and to reduce the degree of concentration of control by the three largest producers from ninety-two per cent of total capacity to 38.8 per cent.

In the meantime, new plant construction had further increased the number of independent producers and reduced concentration. By January, 1955, the number of synthetic-nitrogen producers in the United States

[29] The TVA plant expanded greatly after 1945, and by 1954 was producing annually 91,500 tons of ammonia and 196,000 tons of ammonium nitrate, or approximately 138,000 tons of N (*TVA: The Use of the Earth for the Good of Man* [Washington, 1954], p. 38).

had increased to twenty-two (Table 25) and eleven additional new firms had synthetic-ammonia plants under construction.[30] The plants already in production had an estimated capacity of 2.85 million tons, more than double the 1945 capacity, and the plants in the planning stage would increase total capacity by an additional 0.72 million tons by mid-1956. While most of this expansion occurred in an inflationary period when the prices of nitrogen materials and solutions were rising, anti-trust, government-plant disposals, and many new postwar entrants had made the domestic nitrogen industry more competitive than it had been in its history.[31]

*A Summary Note on Phosphate Rock and Complementary Inputs.* Large quantities of sulphur are required to produce superphosphates from phosphate rock. Large quantities of nitrogen and potash are mixed with superphosphates to produce the many types of mixed fertilizers American farmers use. The largest purchasers of these complementary inputs are the integrated phosphate-fertilizer producers. Both the buyers and the sellers in these markets have been oligopolists possessing considerable market control, and each oligopoly has had its association and its restrictive agreements designed to circumvent competition. The markets have approximated a state of bilateral oligopoly with collusion on all sides. There is no evidence that the oligopoly powers and association activities of the buyers and sellers have countervailed each other so as to make competition effective.[32] Until after the war sulphur, nitrogen, and potash prices were highly inflexible and unrelated to production and delivery costs, and profits were much higher than in mining and manufacturing generally. Independent superphosphate and mixed-fertilizer producers possessed no opposing power; they were numerous and confronted high concentration buttressed by association activity in their raw-materials markets. The combination of oligopoly structure and restrictive practices unquestionably made fertilizer-resources allocation less efficient and fertilizer prices higher than they would have been under conditions of effective competition.

Anti-trust policy has been applied to the restrictive practices of phosphate rock, sulphur, nitrogen, and potash producers; and, while detailed discussion of the results is reserved for Chapter 9, it appears to have been applied effectively. The sulphur and the pebble-phosphate-rock export associations dissolved themselves voluntarily and the hard-rock export association significantly altered its activities after extended Federal Trade

---

[30] See "Too Much Too Soon?" *Chemical Week,* Vol. 76, No. 6 (February 5, 1955), pp. 75-76.
[31] See various issues of *Prices and Price Relatives for Individual Commodities* (U. S. Dept. of Labor, Bureau of Labor Statistics).
[32] Nor are there any logical grounds for presuming they would. Bilateral oligopoly compounds the uncertainty concerning the way resources will be allocated and goods will be priced (Joe S. Bain, *Price Theory* [New York: H. Holt and Co., 1952], p. 395. Also John K. Galbraith, *American Capitalism: The Concept of Countervailing Power* [Boston: Houghton Mifflin Co., 1952], esp. Chap. 1).

Commission investigations. The sellers of potash have been parties to two consent decrees, the last after a thorough investigation by the Department of Commerce at the request of the Department of Justice had led to a civil complaint charging them with price fixing and refusing to deal. Five federal grand jury indictments have issued against nitrogen producers; they were later replaced by three civil complaints and settled by consent decrees. Thereafter, rapid postwar expansion and the federal government's disposition of its plants substantially reduced concentration in the nitrogen industry. The sulphur and potash industries are still highly concentrated oligopolies, but less so than prior to World War II. The principal imperfections in these markets where fertilizer manufacturers are buyers have been monopoly power and agreements to restrain trade, imperfections with which anti-trust policy is designed to cope. The markets in which they are sellers have had these features and considerable imperfect buyer knowledge. The latter is a market imperfection of a different sort and, as will be demonstrated in Chapter 10, requires a public policy in addition to anti-trust.

# Part IV

## PRICING, PRODUCTION AND DISTRIBUTION PRACTICES IN THE INTEGRATED FERTILIZER INDUSTRIES

# CHAPTER 7

# THE PHOSPHATE-ROCK INDUSTRY

THE vertically-integrated phosphate fertilizer firms mine and beneficiate more rock than they use in their superphosphate manufacturing plants. While they account for seventy-five to eighty per cent of the output of rock, they account for about fifty-five per cent of the output of superphosphates and less than half the output of mixed fertilizers. The integrated firms buy large quantities of sulphur, potash, and nitrogen in competition with each other, their nonintegrated rivals, and other industrial users. They sell the phosphate rock they do not use in their superphospate operations to other superphosphate manufacturers, industrial users, and abroad, in competition with nonintegrated rock miners; the superphosphates they do not use in their mixing operations or sell through their agents and dealers to farmers they sell to nonintegrated mixed-fertilizer manufacturers, in competition with other superphosphate producers. Of the phosphate rock sold in the open market seven vertically-integrated firms supply about one half, and about twenty-four small independents supply the rest. However, because the integrated firms, as pointed out in Chapter 2, export more than the independents, they supply less than half of the domestic open market.

## A. Pricing and Distribution

Phosphate rock is graded according to its bone phosphate of lime (BPL) content. Florida pebble-phosphate rock ranges from sixty-six to seventy-five per cent BPL, Florida hard rock up to eighty-two per cent, Tennessee brown rock from sixty-six to sixty-eight per cent, and western rock averages seventy per cent or more. Rock is sold in lumps or particles of uneven size and uniformity, which contain varying amounts of "impurities" such as silica, alumina, and iron compounds. Prices correspond to these differences in physical properties, and on this basis it is possible to compare the outputs of most producers.

*Base Prices and Price Competition.* Producers sell phosphate rock both under long-term contracts and at spot market, the former accounting for most sales. Before World War II contracts often ran from five to ten years; since the war the contract period is usually one to three years. Sales contracts specify the base price and the BPL content of the rock, provide a method of sampling and analysis and a scale of adjustments should the BPL content of any shipment differ from that stipulated in the

111

contract, and contain an escalator clause providing for specified automatic changes in the base price with changes in costs of labor and fuel.

Although contract prices are less flexible than spot market prices, they are an integral part of a continuous price-making process. Rock producers reserve the right to change the base price provided they notify the buyer prior to certain specified dates within the contract period. For example, one producer's contract states that the base price may be changed on the first day of any January, April, July, or October, provided the producer notifies the buyer ten days in advance of the price change. Unless the buyer rejects the new base price at least three days before it is to become effective, it is incorporated into the contract. If the buyer serves notice of his rejection of the new price within the specified time, the seller reserves the right to continue supplying the buyer at the old price or to terminate the contract. The provision enables the seller to protect himself within limits against substantial changes in the market price, and the escalator clause allows price adjustments in line with changes in costs. Both make the contract price more flexible.[1]

The domestic contracts of all rock producers contained similar provisions from shortly after the formation of the Phosphate Export Association in 1919 until phosphate-rock price ceilings were abandoned in 1946.[2] In the Federal Trade Commission's PEA proceedings, representatives of the export association denied that PEA ever concerned itself with the domestic market. When confronted with frequent references to the uniform provisions of domestic sales contracts in correspondence between officers of individual companies and between company and association officers, they testified that such uniformities were either established practices before PEA or holdovers from the National Recovery Administration days.[3]

The Commission did not determine whether the association standardized the terms of all domestic contracts. But there is evidence that the mere existence of the association was instrumental in doing so. To prevent arbitrage between the domestic market and some of the relatively high-priced foreign markets, domestic contracts uniformly prohibited the resale of rock. All producers operating in the Florida fields used almost identical escalator clauses until about 1946. The integrated companies frequently negotiated exchange and sales agreements with each other to supply their phosphate-fertilizer plants; each company

---

[1] A typical escalator clause for Florida producers throughout the thirties provided that an increase of $0.01 in the hourly wage rate of a certain class of labor automatically increased the price of a ton of phosphate rock by $0.03, and an increase in the price of a barrel of fuel oil by $0.02 automatically increased the price of a ton of rock by $0.01.

[2] In fact, on entering the industry one large producer found the contracts of all the established producers so similar that it devised a contract containing different provisions to avoid, as the company spokesman put it, "a good way to land in jail" (information furnished by an official of one of the large rock producers whose name is withheld by request).

[3] PEA, "Report and Recommendations," 42 FTC 555, 820 (1946).

was therefore acquainted with the contracts used by all the others. Finally, exhibits in the Federal Trade Commission proceedings indicate that PEA members used uniform domestic sales contracts before the passage of the National Industrial Recovery Act.[4]

While similarities in contract provisions may have prevented frequent outbreaks of price competition, they did not wholly eliminate base-price differentials among producers. The base price in any phosphate-rock sales contract is largely a negotiated one. Base prices arrived at on a given date have varied among producers and even among contracts made by a single seller on the same day (Table 26). On November 27, 1935, a large producer negotiated contracts to sell identical grades of phosphate rock to three different buyers at prices ranging from $1.85 to $2.00 per ton. Between November 27 and November 29, 1935, another large producer negotiated six contracts to sell a slightly higher grade of rock, five of which called for a base price of $2.25 per ton and one for a base price of $1.95 per ton. During the first week of March, 1939, a producer negotiated two contracts to sell seventy-seven per cent BPL rock at $2.10 per ton; in the same week another producer contracted to sell the same grade of rock at $2.45 per ton.

Differences in base prices did not always reflect price competition. A few buyers of phosphate rock obtained special price concessions because of superior bargaining position. For example, in 1934, in 1937, and again in 1938, the Virginia-Carolina Chemical Company obtained price concessions from the American Agricultural Corporation by threatening to reopen its Florida mines. Other buyers, either because they were large or because they also owned rock deposits, probably obtained similar concessions. Mining companies often obtained a higher base price for rock sold under one-year contracts than for that sold under longer-term contracts. Most producers also charged different prices to different classes of consumers.[5] In short, the type of buyer, the length of contract, the relative bargaining strength of buyer and seller, the past trade relationships between them, and the amount of market information commanded by each party to the contract are major factors explaining the differences in base prices for a given grade of phosphate rock. Escalator clause price increases showed similar variations among companies between 1935 and 1942, and even among contracts made by the same company on the same day, according to information collected by the Office of Price Administration in March, 1942. Since the same union represented all the mine workers, and since fuel-oil prices were substantially the same for all producers operating in the phosphate fields, such differences in

[4] *Ibid.*, pp. 820 ff. (See especially the contractual relationship among International, Coronet, American Agricultural, Southern Phosphate, Cyanamid, and Metall, and the Grafius letter.
[5] *Infra.*, pp. 129-31.

price increases suggest either that all contracts did not contain identical escalator clauses, or that if they did, they were not uniformly enforced.

TABLE 26

CONTRACT PRICES NEGOTIATED BY THREE FLORIDA MINING COMPANIES ON SELECTED DATES, 1935-42ᵃ

| Producer | A | A | A | A | B | C | C | C | C | C | C | C | C | A | A | A | A | A | A | A | A | A |
|---|---|---|---|---|---|---|---|---|---|---|---|---|---|---|---|---|---|---|---|---|---|---|
| Grade | 68 | 72 | 72 | 72 | 72 | 72/74 | 72/74 | 72/74 | 72/74 | 72/74 | 72/74 | 72/74 | 72/74 | 73 | 74 | 75 | 76 | 76 | 77 | 77 | 77 | 77/76 |
| Nov. 1935 | | $2.00 | $1.85 | $1.85 | $2.865 | $1.85 | $2.25 | $2.25 | $2.25 | $2.25 | $2.25 | $2.25 | $2.25 | $2.00 | | | | | $3.00 | | | |
| Dec. 1935 | | 1.85 | | | | | | | | | | | | | | | | | | | | |
| Oct. 1938 | | 1.95 | | | | | | | | | | | | | | | | | | | | |
| Dec. 1938 | | 2.971 | | | | | | | | | | | | | $2.25 | | | | | | | |
| Jan. 1939 | | | | | | | | | | | | | | | | | | | | | | |
| Mar. 1939 | | | | | | | | | | | | | | | | | | | | | | |
| Apr. 1939 | $2.17 | 2.62 | | | | | | | | | | | | | | $1.90 | 2.352 | 2.425 | 2.10 | 2.10 | $2.46 | |
| June 1939 | | | | | | | | | | | | | | | | 2.85 | | 2.653 | | | | |
| July 1939 | | 2.15 | | | | | | | | | | | | | | 2.70 | | | | | | |
| Sept. 1939 | | 2.008 | | | | | | | | | | | | | | 2.625 | | | | | | |
| June 1940 | | | | | | | | | | | | | 2.30 | | | | | | | | | |
| Aug. 1940 | 2.035 | 2.385 | 2.10 | | | | | | | | | | | | | | | | | | | |
| Dec. 1940 | 2.10 | 2.10 | | | | | | | | | | | | | | | 3.40 | | | | | |
| Feb. 1941 | | | | | | | | | | | | | | | | 3.40 | | | | | | |
| Apr. 1941 | | 2.35 | 2.15 | | | | | | | | | | | | | | | | | | | |
| May 1941 | 2.30 (70%) | 2.45 | | | | | | | | | | | | | | | | | | | | |
| June 1941 | | | | | | | | | | | | | | | | | | | | | | $ 4.15 |
| July 1941 ** | 2.40 (70%) | | | | | | | | | | | | | | | | | | | | | |
| Nov. 1941 | 1.95 (68%) | 2.45 | | | | | | | | | | | | | | | | | | | | 4.20 |
| Dec. 1941 | | 2.41 | | | | | | | | | | | | | | | | | | | | |
| Jan. 1942 | | 2.50 | | | | | | | | | | | | | | | 6.45 | | | | | |
| Feb. 1942 | | | | | | | | | | | | | | | | | | | 4.63 | | | |
| Mar. 1942 | 2.20 (68%) | | | | | | | | | | | | | | | | | | | | | 4.90 |

ᵃ National Archives, OPA Records, *The Phosphate Rock Industry*.

Because of differences in base prices and in the application of escalator clauses, prices on identical grades of phosphate rock varied considerably just before OPA established uniform maximum prices for all producers in each field—in some instances by as much as fifty per cent of the lowest

TABLE 27

RANGE OF F.O.B. MINE CONTRACT PRICES CHARGED CHEMICAL MANUFACTURERS AND ACIDULATORS FOR SPECIFIC GRADES OF PHOSPHATE ROCK PRIOR TO ESTABLISHMENT OF UNIFORM PRICE SCHEDULE IN MARCH, 1942 [a]

| | Number of Producers Included | Range of Approved Prices | Number of Producers Selling at Maximum Price | New Uniform Prices Established in March, 1942 |
|---|---|---|---|---|
| | | Florida Pebble Rock | | |
| (BPL) | | | | |
| 68/66 | 7 | $2.20—2.314 | 5 | $ 2.00 |
| 70/68 | 7 | 2.30—3.239 | 6 | 2.40 |
| 72/70 | 7 | 2.60—3.20 | 1 | 3.00 |
| 75/74 | 7 | 2.618—4.00 | 6 | 4.00 |
| 77/76 | 7 | 2.818—4.75 | 4 | 5.00 |
| | | Tennessee Brown Rock (Underground) | | |
| (BPL) | | | | |
| 68/66 | 2 | $4.50—5.10 | 1 | 4.30 |
| 70/68 | 2 | 4.48—5.00 | 1 | 4.80 |
| 72/70 | 5 | 4.73—5.10 | 1 | 5.30 |
| $P_2O_5$ | | (Finely Ground) | | |
| 29% | 1 | 4.50 | 1 | 4.50 |
| 30% | 3 | 4.00—4.75 | 1 | 4.70 |
| 31% | 1 | 4.65 | 1 | 4.80 |
| 32% | 3 | 4.85—5.00 | 1 | 5.00 |
| 33% | 3 | 5.50—5.75 | 2 | 5.50 |

[a] National Archives, OPA Records, *The Phosphate Rock Industry.*

price (Table 27). Since nearly all producers were selling rock on some contracts at prices lower than their individual ceiling prices,[6] the range of actual prices quoted by the various producers in March, 1942, was greater than most of their individual ceiling prices. Most of the price spread was due to differences in generally prevailing prices on the dates contracts were negotiated, particularly the difference between the price level prevailing from 1935 to mid-1941 and that prevailing toward the end of 1941 (Figure 1), which had not been fully compensated for through renegotiations and escalator clauses. Some of the spread was

[6] OPA records on effective contract prices for each producer at the time uniform price ceilings were established are not complete. They do show that a Florida producer having a price ceiling of $3.00 per ton on 72 per cent BPL rock was selling it under one contract at $2.00, and that a Tennessee producer having a price ceiling of $5.32 per ton on 72 per cent BPL rock was selling it under one contract at $4.25. The records contain many examples of smaller differences between contract and individual ceiling prices.

undoubtedly due to genuine differences in negotiated prices among producers.

With the dissolution of the Phosphate Export Association in 1945 and the removal of OPA controls in 1946, rock producers emerged from the war facing the largest domestic market in their history—and with no formal organization to circumscribe their individual activities at home or abroad. As a consequence, independent pricing has been more in evidence since 1946 than at any time since about 1921, with the possible exception of the domestic price war of 1935.

The evidence supporting this generalization is fragmentary and assumes a variety of forms but, viewed collectively, is fairly persuasive. First, with the demise of PEA the industry had no central agency through which producers could keep informed on prices charged by other producers. Without the benefit of PEA's market-information services, each producer has had to proceed on his own. By 1950 most large rock-mining companies knew less about their rivals' activities than they formerly did. They believed that prices throughout the industry were about the same because all producers dealt with the same union, paid about the same price for fuel, and had started from a common price when price ceilings were removed in 1946; but all were certain that small price differentials existed.[7] Second, technological developments since World War II have altered production costs for all producers, but they have not done so for all producers equally. One producer devised a circular dryer in 1949 that significantly reduced his storage costs. Other companies claim similar innovations in mining, beneficiation, and storage. Rapid technological change is in itself indicative of independent action; it is also likely to encourage independent pricing. Third, the western and southeastern rock producers have been brought into closer competition with each other since 1946.[8] Before the war western producers were small, few in number, and were effectively isolated from the heavy users of fertilizers by high transportation costs. The bulk of the market was supplied by the oligopoly in control of the Florida and Tennessee fields. The rise in fertilizer consumption in the Midwest has created a market accessible to western producers, which by 1950 had increased in number to nineteen. Actual and potential competition from such a large number of new rivals, notwithstanding their small size, has probably made for more competitive pricing within the southeastern oligopoly and throughout the phosphate-rock market generally.

These postwar developments have been conducive to independent

[7] In interviews with them in the summer of 1950 some producers stated that they still used OPA maximum prices and had made their price adjustments since 1946 in accordance with their own prewar escalator clauses; but one producer had adopted an entirely new contract containing an escalator clause radically different from any the industry, to the producer's knowledge, had ever used.
[8] *Infra*, this Chap.

pricing, but by far the most convincing evidence that producers have priced independently is the available price data. Price bids received by TVA from rock producers between December, 1947, and July, 1950 (Table 28), showed slight differences at the end of 1947 and appreciable differences by 1950. For example, out of five bids received on June 24, 1948, two were identical; one differed from these two by only $0.07 a ton; and two others showed differences amounting to $0.485 and $0.71 per ton. On June 6, 1949, only two out of seven bids received were identical, but the difference between the highest and lowest bids was only $0.235 per ton. Out of four bids received on July 24, 1950, no two were identical, and the difference between the highest and lowest bids was $1.185 per ton—the widest range of price options ever received by TVA.

TABLE 28

BIDS RECEIVED BY THE TENNESSEE VALLEY AUTHORITY ON WASHED PHOSPHATE ROCK FROM TENNESSEE AND FLORIDA FIELDS, JUNE, 1947, THROUGH JUNE, 1951 [a]

| Date Bids Opened | Bids Received in Price Per Long Ton | | | | | | Price Spread per Ton |
|---|---|---|---|---|---|---|---|
| | A | B | C | D | E | F | |
| 12-31-47 | $5.12 | $4.23 | ........ | ........ | ........ | ........ | $.89 |
| 6-24-48 | 5.01 | 5.08 | $4.30 | $4.525 | $5.01 | ........ | 0.78 |
| 11- 1-48 | 7.81 | ........ | ........ | 7.125 | 7.30 | ........ | 0.685 |
| 6-29-49 | 6.75 | 6.55 | 6.60 | 6.60 | 6.785 | $7.50 | 0.90 |
| 2- 9-50 | 5.26 | ........ | ........ | 5.12 | ........ | ........ | 0.14 |
| 3- 6-50 | 6.975 | ........ | ........ | ........ | 6.905 | ........ | 0.07 |
| 6- 9-50 | 7.065 | ........ | ........ | ........ | 6.995 | ........ | 0.07 |
| 7-24-50 | 6.925 | 5.86 | ........ | 6.91 | 7.045 | ........ | 1.185 |

NOTE:

Prices are for wet crushed rock of comparable grades at mines. Where producers submitted prices for different grades of rock prices were adjusted to a comparable basis by applying market price differentials between the grades as of the dates bids were opened. It should be noted that the lowest converted f.o.b. mine price on each date bids were opened is not necessarily the cheapest delivered price to TVA's Sheffield plant.

[a] TVA files, Wilson Dam, Alabama.

*Price Stabilization and Price Discrimination Under PEA.* PEA's activities clearly tended to stabilize domestic Florida pebble prices (Figure 1). Although the two pebble-rock export associations were formed in 1919 immediately after the passage of the Webb-Pomerene Act, several years elapsed before they controlled a significant percentage of total rock exports. From 1901 until 1926, when PEA had gained control of nearly eighty-two per cent of total rock exports, Florida pebble prices were relatively flexible. Over the twenty-three-year period, average monthly prices changed eighty-five times, an average of 3.5 times per year. In only three out of the twenty-three years, 1912, 1914, and 1919, did the average monthly price remain unchanged throughout the year. Over the four-year period, 1947-1950, average monthly prices changed fourteen times,

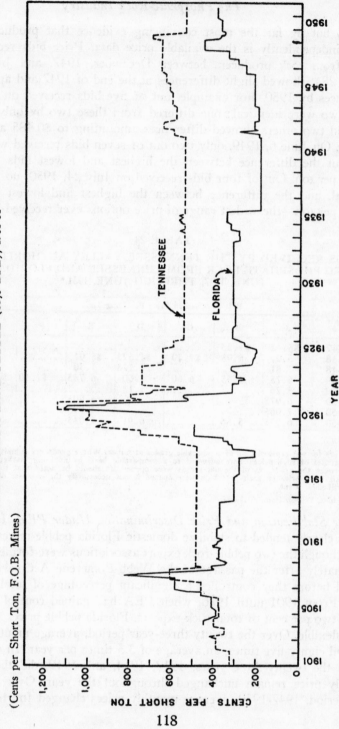

FIGURE 1

MONTHLY PRICES OF TENNESSEE PHOSPHATE ROCK (75% BPL)
AND FLORIDA LAND PEBBLE (68% BPL), 1901-51 [a]

(Cents per Short Ton, F.O.B. Mines)

[a] 1901-28 prices from E. E. Vial, *Prices of Fertilizer Materials and Factors Affecting Fertilizer Tonnage*, 1928. 1928-51 prices from data furnished by the American Potash Institute.

again an average of 3.5 times per year. Pebble-rock prices were not in-sensitive to postwar "disinflationary" pressures and decreased from $4.61 to $3.60 per ton between February and July, 1949.

In contrast, Florida pebble-rock prices were remarkably stable from 1927 to 1941, when PEA members controlled nearly the entire output of phosphate rock. Over this fourteen-year period, average monthly prices changed only eleven times, an average of less than one change per year. Except for the two-week period of intense price cutting in December, 1935, domestic pebble-rock prices remained virtually un-changed for the entire period. From September, 1928, through the Great Depression and until August, 1933, pebble rock sold for $3.16 per ton. Between August, 1933, and December, 1935, pebble rock experienced seven price changes, five of which were increases made possible in part by the NRA and in part by the first cartel agreement with the French.[9] In December, 1935, however, much to the alarm of the export associa-tion,[10] several producers cut domestic prices on low and standard grades of pebble rock. In the short span of about two weeks contract prices on sixty-eight per cent BPL rock fell from $3.47 to $1.88 per ton.[11] In January, 1936, prices were again stabilized and, except for insignificant changes of $0.02 and $0.10 per ton in January, 1939, and August, 1941, remained unchanged until price ceilings were established by OPA. Such evidence indicates that PEA, while stabilizing its members' position in foreign markets through price and quota agreements, also stabilized prices at home. Evidently phosphate-rock prices for the fourteen-year period preceding World War II were not set by the unhampered forces of a competitive market.

In the Federal Trade Commission proceedings, PEA members con-tended that their export market subsidized the domestic market during the period PEA was operative. To support this contention they presented data showing that while the average f.o.b. mine price on exported rock for the 1919-40 period was $3.80 per ton, the average domestic price

---

[9] Through the French Agreement of December, 1933, Florida pebble producers were given 16 per cent of the European market; in the ten-year period preceding the cartel agreement they had actually supplied only 12.4 per cent. The increase in shipments to Europe was probably conducive to price increases at home.

[10] On December 30, 1935, President Grace wrote as follows to the Phosphate Export Association's Council: "It is regrettable to observe, as even we in the export business cannot help but note, that domestic prices some sixty days or less ago were at a level 100% higher than those of which we hear today. I believe that without the continuation of fair play which has animated us in 1935, 1936 will witness similar recessions in export prices" (42 FTC 798).

[11] The brief but effective outbreak of competition in December, 1935, was probably a result of several market forces. Throughout the depression producers had attempted to balance supply and demand by maintaining prices and curtailing output. Florida producers operated at only 63.6 per cent of capacity in 1931 and at only 51.6 per cent in 1932. In spite of such drastic reductions in output, stocks in the hands of Florida producers increased from 800,000 tons to 1.1 million tons between December 31, 1930, and December 31, 1935. Throughout 1935 Coronet threatened to unload its accumulated stocks on the foreign or the domestic market if its contract with International Minerals and Chemical Corporation was not renewed at the end of 1935 (42 FTC 776-802). The Coronet-International contract was not renewed in 1935. Since the contract involved five of the seven pebble-rock producers, virtually the entire pebble-rock industry knew beforehand what the outcome of the Coronet-International negotiations would be. The December, 1935, price resulted in part from the threat of Coronet's accumulated stocks.

TABLE 29

PHOSPHATE ROCK
EXPORT AND DOMESTIC PRICES
1919-40 [a]

| | Export Price | Domestic Price 68% BPL | Export Price Minus Domestic Price |
|---|---|---|---|
| 1919 | $7.63 | $3.54 | $4.09 |
| 1920 | 7.61 | 4.32 | 3.29 |
| 1921 | 6.74 | 4.28 | 2.46 |
| 1922 | 5.63 | 3.13 | 2.50 |
| 1923 | 3.91 | 3.09 | 0.82 |
| 1924 | 3.46 | 2.93 | 0.53 |
| 1925 | 3.34 | 2.64 | 0.70 |
| 1926 | 3.74 | 2.89 | 0.85 |
| 1927 | 3.66 | 2.92 | 0.74 |
| 1928 | 3.42 | 3.01 | 0.41 |
| 1929 | 3.31 | 2.95 | 0.36 |
| 1930 | 3.24 | 3.07 | 0.17 |
| 1931 | 3.19 | 3.39 | —0.20 |
| 1932 | 3.07 | 2.97 | 0.10 |
| 1933 | 2.81 | 2.77 | 0.04 |
| 1934 | 3.77 | 2.93 | 0.84 |
| 1935 | 3.98 | 2.85 | 1.13 |
| 1936 | 4.37 | 2.31 | 2.06 |
| 1937 | 4.45 | 2.14 | 2.31 |
| 1938 | 4.72 | 2.21 | 2.51 |
| 1939 | 4.26 | 2.20 | 2.06 |
| 1940 | 3.70 | 2.32 | 1.38 |

[a] FTC, *Report on International Phosphate Cartels*, 1946.

over the same period was only $2.70 (Table 29). The inference to be drawn was that domestic prices would necessarily have been higher had rock producers charged the same price in both markets. The Federal Trade Commission apparently accepted this line of reasoning:

Since World War I, . . . export prices for phosphate have been consistently higher than domestic prices, the latter having at times been very nearly the cost of production. Presumably, the higher export prices aided American producers, in part, at least, in maintaining the lower domestic prices, and a deprivation of the profitable export markets might have, and probably would have, resulted in higher prices in this country.[12]

This interpretation is consistent with the theory that a monopolist confronted with different elasticities of demand in separate markets will charge different prices in them. But if the lower domestic price was a direct result of the higher export price, the lower price was no less a monopoly price—a point that the Federal Trade Commission overlooked.

The price data presented by PEA before the Federal Trade Commission permits only a crude comparison between foreign and domestic prices. The average annual domestic and foreign prices computed by PEA do not relate to identical grades of rock. The association computed the two

[12] 42 FTC 834.

average annual price series by dividing total tons sold in each market into total revenue received from each market. No allowance was made for differences in average grades of rock or for differences in the dates contract prices were negotiated. The only clue to differences between the average grade of rock exported and the average grade sold in the domestic market is a single sentence appearing in the testimony of the president of PEA before the Joint Committee on Agriculture in 1938: "I might say here that the average grade of pebble phosphate exported is about 72 per cent, which is 1 per cent lower than the average grade used in the domestic market." [13] This passing reference hardly provides a common basis for comparing foreign and domestic prices.

To make comparison even less accurate, the average annual prices computed by PEA did not relate to the same time period. Domestic contracts, particularly those negotiated between 1935 and 1940, were long-term contracts, frequently covering periods of from five to ten years. Sales to foreign consumers, on the other hand, in accordance with terms of the several cartel agreements, were not booked for more than one year in advance. The computed average export price for any given year during the period 1919-40 represented the average price quoted during the year of shipment, or at most during the year immediately preceding, whereas the computed average domestic price was actually a weighted average of prices established over the preceding one to ten years. Moreover, an average export price concealed whatever price differentials may have prevailed among shipments to the various foreign countries.

To overcome some of these ambiguities in PEA's two derived annual price series, Table 30 compares the average annual export prices f.o.b. mine realized for various foreign countries and the average annual domestic prices quoted for identical grades of rock for the years 1933-39. Quoted domestic prices may sometimes have been slightly higher than realized prices, but the comparison is more relevant than one based upon average values per ton.

When put on a comparable basis with respect to time and grade of rock, and when differences among foreign countries are allowed for, the price data suggest a more complex price policy than one of simple discrimination between foreign and domestic consumers. Average export prices did not exceed average domestic prices on the same grades of rock until 1936, just after the December, 1935, domestic price war. From 1933 through 1935 nearly all rock, particularly the high-grade seventy-

[13] U. S., Congress, Joint Committee to Investigate the Adequacy and Use of Phosphate Resources of the U. S., *Hearings,* 75th Cong., 3rd Sess., 1938, p. 975.

TABLE 30

EXPORT AND DOMESTIC PRICES FOR SPECIFIC GRADES
OF ROCK, 1933-39 [a]

(Average base price per long ton at mines)

| Destination | 1933 | 1934 | 1935 | 1936 | 1937 | 1938 | 1939 |
|---|---|---|---|---|---|---|---|
| Export | Grade 75/74 Per Cent BPL | | | | | | |
| Austria.............. | $5.25 | $4.04 | $4.54 | $4.27 | $4.18 | $4.51 | $4.35 |
| Belgium............. | 2.51 | 4.93 | ...... | ...... | ...... | 5.63 | ...... |
| Czechoslovakia....... | 3.70 | 3.89 | 3.62 | 3.70 | 4.39 | 4.11 | 5.27 |
| Denmark............ | 3.29 | 3.78 | 3.28 | ...... | ...... | ...... | ...... |
| Germany............ | 2.45 | 3.59 | 4.93 | 5.51 | 5.32 | 5.44 | 5.40 |
| Holland............. | 3.26 | 3.79 | 3.77 | 5.05 | 5.71 | 5.26 | ...... |
| Hungary............. | ...... | ...... | 3.85 | 3.70 | 3.75 | 3.66 | 3.64 |
| Italy................ | 3.07 | 3.87 | 4.84 | 4.76 | 5.03 | 4.87 | 4.96 |
| Latvia.............. | 4.42 | ...... | ...... | ...... | ...... | ...... | ...... |
| Poland.............. | 3.42 | 5.61 | 5.62 | ...... | ...... | 4.53 | ...... |
| Spain............... | 2.96 | 3.40 | 3.52 | 4.10 | ...... | ...... | ...... |
| Sweden............. | 3.92 | 3.39 | 4.88 | 5.10 | 5.25 | 5.20 | 4.98 |
| Switzerland.......... | 3.72 | 5.52 | 5.63 | 5.67 | 5.71 | 5.63 | 5.61 |
| United Kingdom...... | 2.94 | 3.42 | 4.28 | 5.55 | 5.11 | 4.14 | 5.61 |
| Yugoslavia.......... | 3.72 | 4.36 | 4.86 | ...... | 4.18 | ...... | 5.37 |
| Canada............. | 2.41 | 4.61 | 4.97 | 5.09 | 2.92 | ...... | ...... |
| Unweighted avg. export price............ | $3.40 | $4.16 | $4.47 | $4.77 | $4.69 | $4.82 | $5.02 |
| Average domestic price. | 5.37 | 5.10 | 5.40 | 3.85 | 3.85 | 3.85 | 2.90 |
| | Grade 70 Per Cent BPL | | | | | | |
| Austria.............. | $2.79 | ...... | ...... | ...... | ...... | ...... | ...... |
| Denmark............ | 2.44 | $2.17 | $3.66 | ...... | $4.13 | $4.15 | ...... |
| Germany............ | 2.37 | 2.96 | 3.94 | $4.32 | 4.52 | 4.36 | $4.32 |
| Holland............. | ...... | ...... | ...... | ...... | 4.75 | ...... | ...... |
| Italy................ | 2.30 | ...... | ...... | ...... | ...... | ...... | ...... |
| United Kingdom...... | 5.87[b] | 6.68[b] | ...... | ...... | ...... | ...... | ...... |
| Canada............. | ...... | ...... | 3.48 | ...... | ...... | ...... | ...... |
| Unweighted avg. export price............ | $3.15 | $3.94 | $3.69 | $4.32 | $4.47 | $4.25 | $4.32 |
| Average domestic price. | 3.82 | 3.52 | 3.90 | 2.35 | 2.35 | 2.35 | 2.15 |
| | Grade 68 Per Cent BPL | | | | | | |
| Austria.............. | ...... | ...... | $3.27 | ...... | ...... | ...... | ...... |
| France.............. | 1.31 | ...... | ...... | ...... | ...... | ...... | ...... |
| Germany............ | 2.82 | ...... | 3.91 | ...... | ...... | ...... | ...... |
| Canada............. | ...... | $3.13 | 2.99 | ...... | ...... | ...... | ...... |
| Unweighted avg. export price............ | $2.07 | $3.13 | $3.39 | ...... | ...... | ...... | ...... |
| Average domestic price. | 3.11 | 3.14 | 3.15 | $1.85 | $1.85 | $1.85 | $1.90 |

[a] Export prices from FTC, *Report on International Phosphate Cartels,* 1946; domestic prices from Bureau of Mines, U. S. Dept. of the Interior, *Minerals Yearbook,* 1933-41.
[b] Apparently typographical errors in the table from which this table was compiled. It will be noted that higher grades of rock sold in the United Kingdom during the same time at considerably lower prices.

five/seventy-four per cent BPL rock,[14] sold at considerably higher prices
in the United States than in most foreign countries. For this three-year

[14] The grade designation "75/74 per cent BPL" means the shipment of rock must average 75 per cent BPL, and no portion of the shipment contains rock graded lower than 74 per cent BPL.

period the average f.o.b. mine export price for seventy-five/seventy-four per cent BPL rock was $4.01 per ton, the average domestic price, $5.29; for seventy per cent BPL rock the average export price was $3.59, the average domestic price, $3.75; and for sixty-eight per cent BPL rock the average export price was $2.86, the average domestic price, $3.13. To the extent that PEA subsidized domestic consumers at all by engaging in price discrimination, the subsidy was limited to the period after 1935.

The price data for each country to which rock was exported suggest that PEA followed a multiple-market price discrimination policy, setting different prices in each of a large number of markets as demand varied. As a result, many countries obtained Florida rock at much lower prices than others, and frequently at prices lower than United States prices. In 1933, fourteen European countries and Canada, all the countries for which prices are available, obtained seventy-five/seventy-four per cent BPL rock at lower prices than domestic consumers paid; prices for Belgium, Germany, Spain, Canada, and the United Kingdom were only one-half the domestic price. For the three-year period 1933-35 only Poland and Switzerland paid higher f.o.b. mine prices for high-grade rock than the United States.

From 1936 to 1939 the range of prices on high-grade rock narrowed considerably, and export prices were generally higher than those quoted in the domestic market. Only in 1939, however, was the average f.o.b. mine price in the United States lower than all f.o.b. mine export prices. Prices on other grades of rock followed a similar pattern. If receiving lower prices because of a discriminatory pricing policy is a "subsidy," consumers in some countries received greater subsidies than consumers in the United States.

The price spreads between various grades of rock differed considerably between the domestic market and most foreign markets throughout PEA's lifetime, and these spreads were altered substantially after PEA entered the international phosphate cartel. From 1927 to 1933, the only pre-cartel years for which data are available, the domestic market price of seventy per cent BPL rock was nineteen per cent higher than that of sixty-eight per cent BPL rock, and the price of seventy-five/seventy-four per cent BPL rock was sixty-nine per cent higher; the average export price of seventy per cent BPL rock was twenty per cent higher than that of sixty-eight per cent BPL rock and the price of seventy-five/seventy-four per cent BPL rock was fifty-one per cent higher.[15] But from 1934 through 1938, while the cartel was in operation, the f.o.b. mine domestic price for high-grade-rock was sixty-six per cent higher than the price of seventy per cent

[15] The price spreads between grades varied widely among countries (see Table 30).

BPL rock; the high-grade f.o.b. mine export price was only twenty-nine per cent higher than the price of the lower grade.

The large difference between prices for high-grade and for low-grade rock in the domestic market between 1934 and 1939 encouraged the use of greater quantities of low-grade rock at home; the small difference between these prices in foreign markets encouraged the use of greater quantities of high-grade rock in export markets. Since the available $P_2O_5$ content of superphosphates is in part determined by the grade of rock used, this price policy may have contributed to the production of more low-analysis phosphate fertilizer materials in the United States than would otherwise have been produced.

In January, 1939, Florida pebble producers raised the domestic price on sixty-eight per cent BPL rock by $0.05 per ton and lowered the price on seventy per cent and seventy-five/seventy-four per cent BPL rock by $0.20 and $0.95 per ton respectively, thereby bringing the spread between high and low grades more in line with that of export prices. Whether any significance can be attached to the timing of this readjustment in prices is not altogether clear. But it is worth pointing out that it occurred just after the Joint Congressional Committee had concluded its hearings on phosphate resources of the United States [16] and about one month before the Department of Justice began its investigation of the fertilizer industry.

The multi-market discriminatory-pricing policy pursued by PEA apparently proved profitable. In 1937, six Florida companies, all members of PEA, earned a rate of return on investment of 15.21 per cent (Table 31); in comparison, four Tennessee companies earned 4.53 per cent. Profits declined as World War II spread after 1938, interrupting trade with European countries. By 1940 profits rates had declined to 10.26 per cent, and by 1941, in spite of rising rock sales (Figure 2), to 8.67 per cent.

## B. Pricing and Distribution Within the Domestic Market

The principal purchasers of phosphate rock in the United States are superphosphate and chemical manufacturers. Of the 10.8 million tons of phosphate rock sold in the United States in 1954, about fifty-nine per cent went into the production of superphosphates, twenty-two per cent into the production of chemicals, seven per cent was applied directly to the soil, and two per cent was used for such miscellaneous purposes as research and the production of stock and poultry feed, parting compounds, defluorinated rock, refractories, and other products. Approximately sixty-seven per cent of the total was ultimately used as fertilizer in one form or another.

[16] *Supra*, n. 13.

TABLE 31

PER CENT PROFITS OF INVESTMENT IN MINING OPERATIONS
FOR SIX FLORIDA AND FOUR TENNESSEE PHOSPHATE-ROCK
PRODUCERS, 1937-46 [a]

| Year | Six Florida Companies | Four Tennessee Companies |
|---|---|---|
| 1937 | 15.21 | 4.53 |
| 1938 | 12.40 | 3.60 |
| 1939 | 11.23 | 3.48 |
| 1940 | 10.26 | 4.18 |
| 1941 | 8.67 | 4.26 |
| 1942 | 14.88 | 9.10 |
| 1943 | 5.98 | 5.42 |
| 1944 | 8.16 | 5.35 |
| 1945 | 10.09 | 7.90 |
| 1946 | 15.61 | 13.47 |
| 1937-46 Average. | 11.25 | 6.13 |

[a] FTC, *Report on The Fertilizer Industry*, 1950, p. 59.

*General Method of Distribution.* Phosphate-mining companies, to minimize mining, drying, and storage costs, stabilize their rates of output by specifying in contracts with their customers the maximum tonnage deliverable in any one month. For example, a superphosphate producer contracting to purchase 12,000 tons of rock per year for three years may be limited by contract to a maximum monthly shipment of 1,000 tons. Since the stipulated maximum monthly shipment does not usually vary greatly from one-twelfth of the total annual shipment, it also tends to be the *minimum* monthly shipment. With deliveries thus scheduled throughout the year, mining companies can maintain fairly uniform monthly rates of output and at the same time avoid serious inventory fluctuations. The highly seasonal demand for phosphate fertilizers [17] would make the stabilization of output and inventories impossible in the absence of such contracts unless buyers were offered sufficient off-season discounts to induce them to level out their monthly purchases. And long-term sales contracts permit gearing annual production to annual sales (Figure 2). The yearly production of Florida and Tennessee rock has rarely varied from yearly sales by more than two or three per cent. Even in the depression years 1930-32, when annual sales dropped from 3.93 million to 1.76 million tons, year-end inventories increased only from 0.97 million to 1.13 million tons.[18]

Inflexible prices and the close correspondence between annual output and sales suggest that the phosphate-rock industry, at least for the period

[17] See Chap. 8.
[18] Year-end inventories are published annually by the Bureau of Mines in *Minerals Yearbook*.

FIGURE 2

ANNUAL PRODUCTION, MARKETED PRODUCTION, AND PRICES
FOR FLORIDA AND TENNESSEE ROCK, 1901-52ᵃ

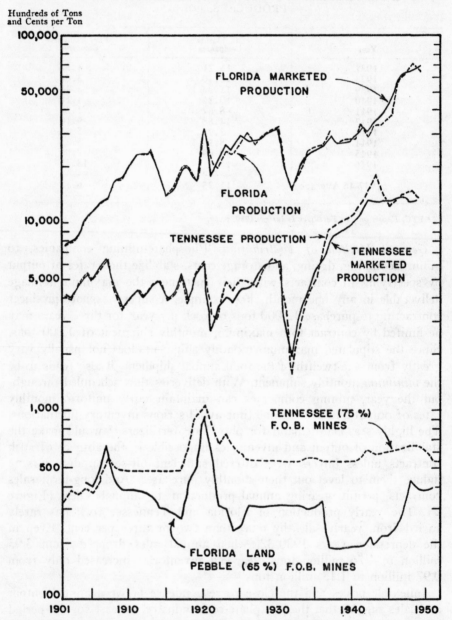

ᵃ Semi-log scale; 1901-28, E. E. Vial, *Prices of Fertilizer Materials and Factors Affecting the Fertilizer Tonnage*, 1928; 1928-52, data furnished by the American Potash Institute.

1925-42, generally met shifts in demand by changing only its rate of output. Except for the two-week domestic price war in 1935, Florida and Tennessee producers apparently followed this policy. Although suggesting collusion, price inflexibility is partially due to the slight effect changes in base prices have on delivered prices. In 1938 the f.o.b. mine price for sixty-eight per cent BPL Florida rock was $1.85, while the rail freight per ton to such fairly nearby points as Montgomery, Alabama, and Columbia, South Carolina, was $4.71 and $4.83 respectively.[19] In addition to the base price and rail change, the buyer paid a $2.00 boarding charge and a $0.75 liner charge for each car door. With the average cost of transport comprising about seventy-five per cent of the delivered price, a ten per cent reduction in the base price would have resulted in only a three per cent reduction in delivered prices. A producer had little incentive to lower base prices, and producers collectively had less.

*Differences in Distribution Policies Toward Types of Consumers.* Because of vertical integration, about thirty-five to fifty per cent of all phosphate rock mined is consumed in the fertilizer and chemical operations of the mining companies,[20] but the proportion of rock output transferred to subsequent operations varies widely among firms. At least two integrated firms use all the rock they mine and frequently purchase additional rock; other large-scale mining companies such as International, American Agricultural, and Swift use only between twenty and forty per cent of their rock in subsequent operations; and several of the small-scale producers use little or none of their own rock.

The Federal Trade Commission in its investigation of the Phosphate Export Association [21] attached much significance to the phosphate industry's partial vertical integration. As was previously indicated, the Commission concluded that vertical integration increased the effectiveness of the export cartel in raising prices and profits on exported rock, enabling producers to charge lower domestic prices. In reaching this conclusion the Commission reasoned that vertically integrated companies, which bought phosphate rock for fertilizer manufacture whenever their own rock was insufficient or did not meet their grade requirements, had an interest in keeping down the domestic price of rock and chose to take their profits on fertilizer sales rather than phosphate-rock sales.

This explanation has two defects: the logic is faulty, and the empirical data do not support it. Rock producers would scarcely have been acting in their own best interests if they subsidized a branch of an industry only

---

[19] FTC, *Report on International Phosphate Cartels,* 1946, p. 55.
[20] The exact tonnage transferred annually by rock producers to their subsequent operations is difficult to ascertain. On the basis of phosphate rock required to produce their annual outputs of superphosphate, phosphoric acid, and other materials, companies engaged in rock mining consumed about 50 per cent of all the rock sold in the United States in 1949.
[21] PEA, "Report and Recommendations," 42 FTC 555 (1946).

thirty-five per cent controlled by them at the expense of a branch they almost wholly controlled. Since the variation among companies in sales of rock to integrated operations ranged from none to substantially all of a company's total rock output, such a price policy could not have won approval by all rock-producing firms. If integrated producers had charged independent fertilizer producers higher prices for rock than they charged their own fertilizer departments,[22] they would have enjoyed no particular cost advantage in the fertilizer market unless the total cost per unit of output within the integrated firms was less than that for unintegrated firms. And even if vertical integration resulted in lower unit costs for the final product, the integrated producer had no economic incentive to transfer rock from mining operations to fertilizer departments at any price other than that consistent with good cost accounting. There is no logical support, therefore, for the argument that their fertilizer operations provided the integrated firms with a profits incentive for suppressing phosphate-rock prices in the domestic market.

What is perhaps more important, the Federal Trade Commission's explanation is not supported by the empirical data. Profits in phosphate-rock mining generally have been considerably higher than those in fertilizer production.[23] By itself this scarcely proves the existence of any type of pricing policy, but it is evidence that rock producers have not subsidized fertilizer operations by selling phosphate rock at uneconomically low prices. The average export price has generally exceeded domestic price; but as was previously pointed out, in no year have domestic prices been lower than all foreign prices. In the absence of convincing evidence to the contrary, it can be concluded that vertical integration in itself has probably had no appreciable effect upon the general level of phosphate-rock prices in the United States.

Throughout the Thirties, rock prices were stable, and rates of return were higher in phosphate mining than in fertilizer production and other mining industries generally; in large measure this reflected the effectiveness of international price discrimination made possible by the cartel agreements. The best evidence of this is the noticeable drop in profits on Florida rock-mining operations for the years following 1938, when war in Europe ended the international pricing and quota arrangements, although domestic sales increased more than enough to offset the decrease in shipments abroad.[24] In the Thirties, monopolistic organization, not vertical integration, governed the price of phosphate rock.

[22] Price data furnished OPA by one large rock producer show that average annual prices to outside customers were higher than those charged "owned and affiliated companies" in eight years during the period 1932-41; in two years they were lower. The average differential for the ten-year period, however, was only $0.21 per ton. The slight difference in average price each year is probably due to other terms of sale rather than to a policy of charging higher prices to outside customers, e.g., differences in grade of rock, length of contract, purchasers' buying status, etc.

[23] Cf. Tables 31 and 43, pp. 125 and 163.

[24] See FTC, *Report on International Phosphate Cartels*, 1946, pp. 59-60, and Table 31, *supra*.

It does not follow from this conclusion that vertical integration has had no effect on resource allocation in the phosphate-fertilizer industry. But such effects as the vertically-integrated firms may have had has probably stemmed more from the market power they possessed than from the fact that they were vertically integrated. A high degree of market power *and* vertical integration may very well have retarded the introduction of new products and processes that competed with old ones. Given a commodity passing through three states of production, *A, B* and *C* (corresponding for example to phosphate rock, superphosphate, and mixed fertilizers), no two of which are controlled by a single entrepreneur, in a competitive market a new commodity, *B'* or *C'*, would be introduced if its expected rate of return per unit of capital were greater than that for the old commodity. But if two or three stages of production are integrated and are controlled by a few firms, the expected rate of return must be high enough on the new investment to compensate entrepreneurs for the obsolescence of the old. As a case in point, phosphate-rock producers manufacturing ordinary superphosphate must expect a sufficiently high rate of return on investment in a new concentrated superphosphate plant to cover the obsolescence on their ordinary superphosphate plants before the new commodity will be introduced. Moreover, if the basic raw material *A* is controlled by a few producers, all of which produce *B* or *C,* or both, a nonintegrated producer may be deterred from producing *B'* since he cannot be sure of his source of supply. But in each case the basic cause of the failure to innovate is, not vertical integration, but market power.

For most of the interwar period integrated and nonintegrated producers controlling a large share of total rock output were bound together in the Phosphate Export Association. The integrated producers had large capital investments in ordinary superphosphate and fertilizer plants that took a high proportion of their domestic rock sales. With the industry so organized it is not surprising that the large entrenched producers were slow to introduce new phosphatic fertilizers and frequently registered complaints against government agencies, particularly the Tennessee Valley Authority, for producing and distributing them.[25] According to the Federal Trade Commission, "Representatives of farmer organizations, land-grant colleges and state and federal organizations who have appeared before congressional committees since 1938 have repeatedly emphasized that the phosphatic fertilizer industry is set up to produce 20 to 25 per cent superphosphate rather than the higher double and triple superphos-

---

[25] U. S., Congress, Joint Committee to Investigate the Adequacy and Use of Phosphate Resources of the U. S., *Hearings*, 75th Cong., 3rd Sess., 1938, *passim*, especially pp. 49, 790-91, 811 ff, and 1,119 ff. See also the testimony of various phosphate fertilizer producers (U. S. Cong., Senate, Committee on Agriculture and Forestry, *Hearings on S.1251, National Fertilizer Program*, 80th Cong., 1st Sess., 1947; U. S. Cong., House, Subcommittee of House Committee on Agriculture, *Hearings, 1948 Fertilizer Supplies*, 80th Cong., 1st Sess., 1948; *1949 Fertilizer Supplies*, 81st Cong., 1st Sess., 1949.

phates both of which require additional processing and cost more to manufacture."[26]

Market power and vertical integration probably have also been partly responsible for the use of tying sales, which have made it difficult for farmers to obtain separate fertilizer materials. Integrated firms with a large share of the phosphate-rock market are the largest purchasers of the two other principal ingredients of mixed fertilizers, potash and nitrogen. A considerable portion of their total investment is in superphosphate and fertilizer-mixing plants. Mixing potash and nitrogen with phosphatic materials, thus tying the sale of one plant nutrient to the other two, assures the sale of certain quantities of phosphatic materials each year.

It has frequently been alleged that these factors fostered an uneconomical pattern of phosphate-fertilizer distribution which, in spite of changing demand, remained virtually unchanged for the forty years preceding the Korean conflict.[27] Various farm groups, particularly those in the Midwest, have charged that integrated producers will not sell high-analysis fertilizer materials separately to independent and co-operative mixers or to farmers, but instead put them into their mixed fertilizers. In 1949, Benton J. Strong of the National Farmers Union told a subcommittee:

In phosphate, sale of high concentrates direct to farmers is discouraged if not forbidden by primary producers. In some areas, at least, there is a stiff differential to mixers or dealers for high-analysis phosphate which is to be sold direct to farmers as compared to that to be used for mixing.[28]

Many similar allegations made by spokesmen for farmers, farmers' co-operatives, and other interested groups appear in various hearings before Congress since 1938.

Evidence to establish the validity of such charges, however, is not so abundant. Those who have criticized the industry have usually failed to differentiate between material shortages resulting from distribution practices and those caused by market forces beyond the industry's control, such as postwar dislocations and lend-lease commitments. On the other hand, industry spokesmen have rested their case on such inconclusive and irrelevant evidence as moderate profits and increases in both fertilizer production and mixed fertilizers' average plant-nutrient content. These defenses hardly stand up against evidence such as the letter read before a congressional committee in 1949; it came from Commercial Solvents Corporation and read in part as follows:

[26] FTC, *Report on the Fertilizer Industry*, 1950, p. 64.
[27] *Ibid.*
[28] U. S., Cong., House, Subcommittee of Committee on Agric., *Hearings, 1949 Fertilizer Supplies*, 81st Cong., 1st Sess., 1949, p. 54.

As you may have noticed from various publications, we are one of the few companies offering anhydrous ammonia to manipulators or distributors who made it available to farmers for direct application to the soil. We are told that by this method (direct application) the cost of applying fertilizers is reduced from approximately $2 an acre to 50 cents an acre.[29]

Phosphate-rock producers' pricing policy has no doubt tended to preserve the traditional pattern of fertilizer production and distribution. When phosphate-rock price ceilings were established in 1942, maximum prices to chemical manufacturers and acidulators were about twenty-five per cent less than maximum prices to other buyers of rock.[30] Since additional charges were made in all cases for purchases in less than carload lots, the f.o.b. mine price differentials obviously could not have been justified on the basis of economies of scale in distribution. With no other satisfactory explanation available, it seems likely that the differentials were designed to encourage a particular pattern of phosphatic-fertilizer production and distribution.

It is clear, however, that partial vertical integration of an industry alone cannot explain the maintenance of a system of fertilizer production and distribution consistent with the commercial interests of integrated producers. It may satisfactorily explain why some manufacturers would prefer to innovate slowly and to pursue pricing and distribution policies which would discourage innovation by others. The realization of such preferences requires considerable market power and collusive action on the part of those who hold them. As has already been demonstrated, Florida pebble-rock producers possessed sufficient power through PEA to stabilize domestic prices. They uniformly placed certain contractual restrictions on their domestic customers in the resale of phosphate rock, and through their control of the flotation process and the Fernandina terminal facilities they restricted entry in the Florida pebble and hard-rock fields. But it does not follow from this that they had the power to prevent others from introducing new and more efficient phosphatic fertilizers and from selling straight fertilizer materials to farmers. It does follow that at times they probably have not competed vigorously among themselves in the manufacture and distribution of more efficient fertilizers, and that their strategic market position has made it possible for them to refrain from quickly imitating their independent rivals who competed in these terms. But as will be shown later, uneconomical resource allocation

[29] *Ibid.*

[30] The maximum price for sixty-eight/sixty-six per cent BPL Florida rock to chemical manufacturers and acidulators was $2.00 per *gross* ton. An additional charge of $0.60 was made for grinding (sixty-two per cent through 200 mesh). The maximum price for ground rock (eighty-five per cent through 200 mesh) of the same grade to buyers "other than chemical manufacturers and acidulators" was $3.00 per *net* ton (National Archives, OPA records). Anaconda's price schedules on western rock filed with OPA called for a maximum price of $5.90 per ton to superphosphate manufacturers, $6.75 per ton to fertilizer mixers and dealers, and $7.75 per ton to other consumers (*Minerals Yearbook,* 1945).

in the fertilizer industry is in large measure due to irrational demand. So long as such irrational demand exists, the effects of market power are difficult to identify and assess. In recent years interregional competition in phosphate rock has begun to mitigate the market power once possessed by the large integrated Florida-rock producers, thereby making a public policy designed to lessen the social costs of irrational demand one of high priority.[31]

## C. INTERREGIONAL COMPETITION

In the interwar period the relatively high cost of recovering Tennessee rock and the long distances separating western deposits from the fertilizer-consuming centers of the South left most of the market to the handful of Florida producers banded together in PEA. In recent years, however, the geographical center of the fertilizer market has gradually shifted toward the West. Between 1930 and 1953 fertilizer consumption in the Midwest and the West increased from 13.2 per cent to 38.4 per cent of total domestic consumption, the greater part of the increase occurring in the war and postwar years (Table 32). This shift has put a significant share of total effective demand for rock within reach of the western mining companies, thereby more than doubling the number of firms competing to supply it.

TABLE 32

FERTILIZER CONSUMPTION BY REGIONS

1910-53 [a]

(In Thousands of tons)

| Region | 1910 | | 1920 | | 1930 | | 1941 | | 1949 | | 1953 | |
|---|---|---|---|---|---|---|---|---|---|---|---|---|
| | Tons | Per Cent | Tons | Per Cent | Tons | Per Cent | Tons | Per Cent | Tons | Per Cent | Tons | Per Cent |
| New England.......... | 208 | 3.8 | 351 | 4.9 | 372 | 4.5 | 444 | 4.9 | 521 | 2.9 | 486 | 2.2 |
| Middle Atlantic........ | 853 | 15.6 | 1,017 | 14.2 | 1,086 | 13.2 | 1,344 | 14.9 | 1,856 | 10.2 | 2,044 | 9.3 |
| East North Central.... | 339 | 6.2 | 672 | 9.4 | 788 | 9.6 | 1,109 | 12.3 | 3,595 | 19.7 | 4,552 | 20.7 |
| West North Central... | 34 | 0.6 | 115 | 1.6 | 110 | 1.3 | 155 | 1.7 | 1,191 | 6.5 | 1,750 | 7.9 |
| South Atlantic......... | 3,146 | 57.7 | 3,999 | 55.7 | 3,857 | 47.0 | 3,650 | 40.5 | 5,536 | 30.4 | 6,180 | 28.0 |
| South Central......... | 827 | 15.2 | 942 | 13.1 | 1,812 | 22.1 | 1,936 | 21.5 | 4,090 | 22.5 | 4,878 | 22.1 |
| West................. | 45 | 0.8 | 80 | 1.1 | 187 | 2.3 | 380 | 4.2 | 1,412 | 7.8 | 2,162 | 9.8 |
| TOTAL............ | 5,452 | 100.0 | 7,176 | 100.0 | 8,212 | 100.0 | 9,018 | 100.0 | 18,201 | 100.0 | 22,052 | 100.0 |

[a] Various annual reports on fertilizer consumption published by the Bureau of Plant Industry, Soils, and Agricultural Engineering, U. S. Dept. of Agriculture.

*Causes of the Geographical Shift in Demand for Rock.* Factors contributing to increased fertilizer consumption in the West and Midwest include the price-support program for agriculture, the past low ratio of plant-nutrient applications to removals, the extension of TVA's test-demonstration farm program to these regions, and the development of high-analysis

[31] See Chap. 11.

phosphate fertilizers which can be more economically transported. Because price supports have increased farm income generally, they have increased fertilizer consumption in all regions.[32] But price supports have increased the incomes of the large-scale commercial farms, relatively numerous in the Midwest, more than the incomes of the small-scale and part-time farms, most of which are in the South.[33] In the past, farmers in the Midwest and the West removed the primary plant nutrients from their soils much more rapidly than they replaced them; in the South and East the opposite was true (Table 33). They reached a point where more fertilizer was required to maintain soil fertility and crop yields. For this reason the geographical center of the fertilizer market will very likely continue to shift westward for some time to come. Through its research and test-demonstration farm programs[34] TVA makes concentrated superphosphate available to farmers. After World War II it made concentrated superphosphate available to midwestern and western farmers through farmers' co-operatives and commercial firms. Some farms are so far removed from sources of phosphate that they can economically use only high-analysis phosphate materials such as TVA distributes. TVA's fertilizer-distribution program probably stimulated considerable demand in the West and Midwest for commercially produced high-analysis phosphate fertilizers.

The recent shift of the fertilizer market toward the West led to increased activity in the western phosphate fields. In 1950 the western industry comprised eighteen commercial mining companies and two co-operatives.[35] Ten were in commercial production, and the rest were engaged primarily in prospecting. The annual output of western producers before World War II was a scant one-tenth of Tennessee's and less than two per cent of the national total. In 1954 it exceeded Tennessee's and amounted to thirteen per cent of the national total. Since the West is potentially the greatest source of phosphate rock in the United States and the most likely source of competition to Florida pebble producers, the recent increase in western output has important implications for future competition.

*Freight Advantage Areas.* Over fifty per cent of the total cost per ton of phosphate rock delivered in most areas is transportation costs. The rail-freight charge per ton of phosphate rock shipped from Florida exceeds the f.o.b. mine price on shipments going into the neighboring states of Georgia and Alabama. The rail-freight charge to Missouri, Wisconsin,

---

[32] See text at n. 5, Chap. 8.
[33] Cf. William H. Nicholls, "America's Biggest Farm Surplus—Too Many Farmers," from lectures given at the Tennessee Workshop on Economic Education, June 20, 1951; *Readings in Economics*, Paul A. Samuelson, *et al.*, ed. (New York: McGraw Hill, 1952), p. 172.
[34] See Chap. 11 for a detailed account of TVA's fertilizer program.
[35] U. S. Dept. of the Interior, Bureau of Mines, *Minerals Yearbook, 1950*.

## TABLE 33

PER CENT OF THE PHOSPHORUS, NITROGEN, AND POTASH
REMOVED FROM THE SOIL BY HARVESTED CROPS THAT WAS
REPLACED IN FERTILIZERS AND MANURES; BY STATE, 1949 [a]

|  | Phosphorus | Nitrogen | Potash |
|---|---|---|---|
| **East and Southeast** | | | |
| Alabama | 448 | 122 | 163 |
| Connecticut | 424 | 240 | 142 |
| Delaware | 352 | 147 | 221 |
| Florida | 1057 | 349 | 354 |
| Georgia | 418 | 139 | 188 |
| Louisiana | 169 | 87 | 46 |
| Maine | 419 | 102 | 126 |
| Maryland | 382 | 132 | 169 |
| Massachusetts | 382 | 197 | 126 |
| Mississippi | 134 | 120 | 54 |
| New Hampshire | 152 | 55 | 42 |
| New Jersey | 604 | 163 | 176 |
| New York | 287 | 144 | 82 |
| North Carolina | 527 | 131 | 157 |
| Pennsylvania | 325 | 161 | 146 |
| Rhode Island | 705 | 333 | 280 |
| South Carolina | 512 | 143 | 221 |
| Tennessee | 196 | 76 | 54 |
| Vermont | 241 | 151 | 87 |
| Virginia | 382 | 86 | 97 |
| West Virginia | 208 | 87 | 69 |
| **Midwest, Southwest, and West** | | | |
| Arizona | 122 | 56 | 1 |
| Arkansas | 99 | 59 | 39 |
| California | 110 | 120 | 25 |
| Colorado | 54 | 41 | 33 |
| Idaho | 83 | 63 | 30 |
| Illinois | 217 | 76 | 99 |
| Indiana | 176 | 57 | 112 |
| Iowa | 71 | 37 | 45 |
| Kansas | 17 | 5 | 6 |
| Kentucky | 159 | 33 | 29 |
| Michigan | 204 | 111 | 87 |
| Minnesota | 104 | 63 | 75 |
| Missouri | 118 | 49 | 40 |
| Montana | 43 | 30 | 27 |
| Nebraska | 16 | 11 | 11 |
| Nevada | 6 | 1 | 0 |
| New Mexico | 57 | 4 | 0 |
| North Dakota | 14 | 7 | 14 |
| Ohio | 228 | 91 | 125 |
| Oklahoma | 23 | 4 | 6 |
| Oregon | 61 | 28 | 14 |
| South Dakota | 19 | 11 | 17 |
| Texas | 45 | 10 | 9 |
| Utah | 85 | 59 | 25 |
| Washington | 42 | 28 | 22 |
| Wisconsin | 225 | 145 | 110 |
| Wyoming | 92 | 77 | 44 |

[a] Furnished by Dr. F. W. Parker of the Bureau of Plant Industry, Soils, and Agricultural Engineering, U. S. Dept. of Agriculture.

and Michigan is nearly twice the f.o.b. mine price.[36] The cost of western rock delivered in Utah is nearly fifty per cent transportation charges; in California it is over fifty per cent.

Before World War II the area in which each of the phosphate-rock producing centers had a freight advantage was determined largely by the cost of transporting the rock itself. The lowest-cost method for getting $P_2O_5$ from the mine to all but the most distant markets was to ship phosphate rock and sulphur, or sulphuric acid, to the consuming market and then to process them into ordinary superphosphate. Under freight rates prevailing since 1945, however, the cheapest means is to ship concentrated phosphate produced near its source of phosphate rock.[37] If farmers always purchased $P_2O_5$ in its cheapest available form,[38] competition between western and Florida phosphate rock would depend, not on relative production and transportation costs of rock, but on relative production and transportation costs of concentrated phosphatic materials. Producers in either center could take over large portions of the phosphate-fertilizer market by producing concentrated phosphates, as long as producers in the other center sold only low-analysis phosphates.

Under 1946 freight rates the freight-advantage areas for concentrated superphosphate produced in the West and South were approximately as shown in Figure 3. The areas were computed on the basis of prevailing rates on concentrated superphosphate moving from plants located at Montpelier, Idaho, Houston, Texas, and Tampa, Florida. Shipments of phosphatic materials have moved from Anaconda, Montana, in sufficient volume to obtain a commodity rate. If shipments from Montpelier justify the same commodity rate when large-scale production is reached, the freight advantage areas for western and southern concentrated superphosphate would be approximately as shown in Figure 4. Under June, 1946, Montpelier rates, fifteen per cent of the phosphate-fertilizer market fell within the freight advantage area of western producers; under the Anaconda commodity rates applied to a production site at Montpelier, the freight advantage area of western producers includes twenty-two per cent of the total phosphate-fertilizer market.[39]

[36] The ratio of freight charges to f.o.b. mine price does not increase in direct proportion to the distance for two reasons: freight rates are established on the tapering principle, with long hauls bearing a lower ton-mile rate than short hauls; and the more distant consumers buy higher-grade rock than nearby consumers in order to reduce the delivered cost per unit of BPL; the higher the BPL content the higher the f.o.b. mine price.

[37] See text at n. 23, Chap. 8. With rising transportation costs, the area where $P_2O_5$ can reach the farmer more cheaply in ordinary superphosphate (a process which requires shipping the rock itself to the consuming area) than in concentrated materials produced near phosphate-rock mines has been greatly reduced.

[38] They do not always do so (see Chap. 8).

[39] See Roscoe E. Bell and Donald T. Griffith, *Transportation Costs as They Affect New Phosphorus Industries in the West*, studies made by the Division of Industrial Resources and Development, Bonneville Power Administration, 1947, pp. 19-25. In all cases the cheapest published water, rail, or water and rail rates were used. Because rail increases in both regions since 1946 have been approximately the same, they did not substantially alter the areas shown.

FIGURE 3

APPROXIMATE FREIGHT ADVANTAGE AREAS FOR WESTERN-
PRODUCED AND SOUTHERN-PRODUCED CONCENTRATED
SUPERPHOSPHATE (Under June, 1946, Montpelier, Rates)[a]

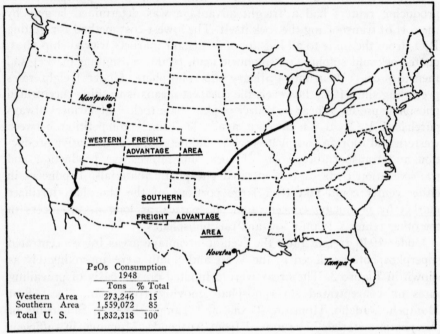

| P₂O₅ Consumption 1948 | | |
| --- | --- | --- |
| | Tons | % Total |
| Western Area | 273,246 | 15 |
| Southern Area | 1,559,072 | 85 |
| Total U. S. | 1,832,318 | 100 |

[a] Economic studies by Bonneville Power Administration.

While the percentages show that most of the phosphate market still lies beyond the reach of western producers, the increase in the western freight-advantage area from fifteen per cent to twenty-two per cent of the domestic market accompanying the small reduction in freight rates has important implications for future competition and for public policy. Producers in the West and Florida will be under considerable competitive pressure to introduce high-analysis phosphate materials that can reach intermediate areas at the lowest total cost per unit of $P_2O_5$. Should producers in either region fail to keep pace with technological developments in the other, they will lose a significant percentage of the market, so long as producers in both regions are not in collusion on price and production policy. Interregional competition has not been vigorous in the past because: (1) the periphery of both freight-advantage areas consumed too little phosphate to stimulate spatial competition. (2) Farmers who bought superphosphates in mixed fertilizers and as straight materials did not always buy the most economical grade. This deadened both interregional and intraregional competition to offer phosphates having the lowest price

FIGURE 4

APPROXIMATE FREIGHT ADVANTAGE AREAS FOR WESTERN-
PRODUCED AND SOUTHERN-PRODUCED CONCENTRATED
SUPERPHOSPHATE (Under June, 1946, Anaconda Rates
Applied to Montpelier)[a]

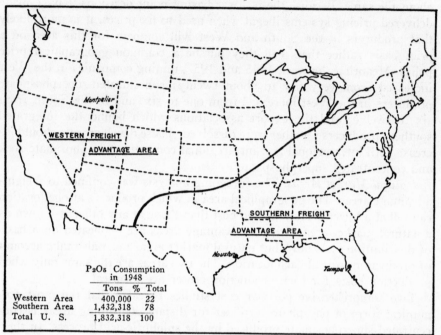

| P₂O₅ Consumption in 1948 | | |
|---|---|---|
| | Tons | % Total |
| Western Area | 400,000 | 22 |
| Southern Area | 1,432,318 | 78 |
| Total U. S. | 1,832,318 | 100 |

[a] Economic studies by Bonneville Power Administration.

per unit of $P_2O_5$. (3) Anaconda was the only concentrated-superphosphate producer in the West, and its output was tied to its by-product sulphuric acid production. Most of the half-dozen or so concentrated-superphosphate producers in the South were either members of the Phosphate Export Association or dependent on them for their phosphate-rock supplies. (4) Most of the concentrated-superphosphate producers in the Florida freight-advantage area also produced large quantities of ordinary superphosphate; since their newer concentrated superphosphates competed with their own more established ordinary superphosphate, they probably had no incentive to push their concentrated product.[40]

While some of these barriers still exist, they are not nearly so strong. The intermediate territory has clearly become a sufficiently important part of the total market to stimulate rock and concentrated-superphosphate producers in both the South and West to compete for it. Between 1930 and 1953 fertilizer consumption in the North Central states increased

[40] *Supra,* p. 130.

from eleven per cent to twenty-nine per cent of the nation's total; the consumption of $P_2O_5$ increased from twenty per cent to nearly thirty-nine per cent of total United States consumption between 1943 and 1953. Transportation costs to this region from both rock-producing centers are about the same. Because the postwar basing point decisions [41] have made delivered pricing systems illegal when used to fix prices, it is more likely that producers in the South and West will compete for this area on a price basis rather than will they pursue a common geographical price policy. Meantime, between 1945 and 1957, mining companies in the West increased from very few to about twenty; concentrated-superphosphate producers in the West increased from one to six, and in the South from six to twelve; and the export associations which bound the integrated southern producers together were dissolved. These developments should increase both interregional and intraregional competition in phosphate rock and concentrated superphosphate.

*Natural Market Areas.* The foregoing analysis was confined to freight-advantage areas. The geographical area in which producers at one location can sell at a lower total delivered cost than those at any other is known as a natural market area. Freight-advantage areas are delineated on a basis of distribution costs only, but natural market areas must also take account of production costs at each location. The two areas are the same only when production costs for each production center are identical.

Two comprehensive postwar cost studies revealed that the most economical form of phosphate fertilizer for distant consuming areas is concentrated superphosphate produced by the sulphuric-acid process. In their 1950 study, Waggaman and Bell presented detailed cost analyses for various phosphatic materials produced in the West from western phosphate rock.[42] In 1947 Swift & Company [43] made similar analyses for proposed plants in the Florida and Tennessee [44] fields. Each study found that concentrated superphosphate produced by the sulphuric-acid process yielded the lowest-cost $P_2O_5$ (Table 34). These two studies also indicated that the cost of producing concentrated superphosphate was approximately the same for both regions. The estimated cost of producing one ton of $P_2O_5$ in the form of concentrated superphosphate by the sulphuric-acid process in Florida in 1947 was $50.00; in the West it was $52.21, or only 3.4 per cent higher. The costs of producing elemental phosphorus,

[41] *Corn Products Refining Co. v. FTC,* 324 U. S. 726 (1945); *FTC v. A. E. Staley Mfg. Co. and Staley Sales Corp.,* 324 U. S. 746 (1945); *FTC v. The Cement Institute,* 33 U. S. 683 (1948).
[42] Roscoe E. Bell and William H. Waggaman, "Western Phosphates—Comparison of Sulfuric Acid and Thermal Reduction Processing," *Industrial and Engineering Chemistry,* February, 1950, pp. 269, 276, 286.
[43] See Chap. 8. Since both cost studies were based largely on data for the postwar years, their results are fairly comparable. Swift & Company adjusted its data to 1947 costs; the Waggaman and Bell study used data for 1947 and 1948.
[44] Swift & Company's study showed a Tennessee plant to be uneconomical because of higher rock costs and factors which virtually prohibited the use of the sulphuric acid process. For this reason data in Table 34 and the discussion in the text are confined to Florida and the West.

TABLE 34

PRODUCTION COSTS OF SPECIFIC HIGH-ANALYSIS PHOSPHATE
MATERIALS IN FLORIDA AND THE WEST AND DELIVERED COSTS
OF WESTERN MATERIALS 800 AND 1,400 [a] MILES FROM
PRODUCTION SITE[b]

| | Production Costs Per Ton of $P_2O_5$ | | Total Delivered Costs Per Ton of $P_2O_5$ for the West | | | |
|---|---|---|---|---|---|---|
| | | | 800 Miles | | 1,400 Miles | |
| | Florida | West | Freight | Delivered Costs | Freight | Delivered Costs |
| Elemental Phosphorus: | | | | | | |
| Electric-furnace process.... | $ 70.78 | $ 66.32 | $7.49 | $73.81 | $10.27 | $76.59 |
| Blast-furnace process..... | ....... | 71.70 | 7.49 | 79.19 | 10.27 | 81.97 |
| Phosphoric Acid: | | | | | | |
| Sulphuric-acid process..... | 52.56 | 57.28 | 22.15 | 79.43 | 28.21 | 85.49 |
| Electric-furnace process.... | 78.05 | 73.74 | 22.15 | 95.89 | 28.21 | 101.95 |
| Blast-furnace process...... | ....... | 79.19 | 22.15 | 101.34 | 28.21 | 107.40 |
| Concentrated Superphosphate from High-Grade Rock and Phosphoric Acid: | | | | | | |
| Wet-process phosphoric acid.................. | 50.21 | 52.21 | 13.92 | 66.13 | 15.42 | 67.63 |
| Electric-furnace phosphoric acid.................. | | 62.61 | 13.92 | 76.53 | 15.42 | 78.03 |
| Blast-furnace phosphoric acid.................. { | ..... | 66.47[c] | 13.92 | 80.39 | 15.42 | 81.89 |
| } | ..... | 61.00[d] | 13.92 | 74.92 | 15.42 | 76.42 |

[a] 1946 rates on east-bound freight increased abruptly beyond 1,400 miles.
[b] Western costs from Waggaman and Bell, *Industrial and Engineering Chemistry*, February, 1950. Florida costs from cost study by Swift & Co. Freight charges from Bell and Griffith, "Transportation Costs as They Affect New Phosphorous Industries in the West," 1947 (unpublished).
[c] As estimated by Waggaman and Bell.
[d] As estimated by TVA.

phosphoric acid, and concentrated superphosphate by the electric-furnace process were lower in the West than in Florida. No comparable cost data on blast-furnace operations in Florida are available.

These data suggest that cost differences within the freight-advantage areas of western and southern phosphate producers are negligible, and therefore that their respective natural markets and freight-advantage areas coincide. But the data need elaborating. They ignore some of the more recently developed phosphatic materials such as calcium metaphosphate and the nitrophosphates.[45] Reported mining costs for the West vary more widely than those for the Florida pebble fields, partly because in the West both established firms and firms scarcely beyond the prospecting or early developmental stage report their costs, while Florida's mining companies are well established. A more important reason for the greater variation in mining costs in the West than in Florida is geological. Florida pebble rock is produced by strip-mining. Most of the phosphate matrix (the mass in which the rock is embedded) lies below a relatively shallow overburden which can be stripped off by large draglines. The matrix

[45] See Chap. 11. However, there are no a priori grounds for supposing that the two natural market areas for these materials would differ significantly from those for concentrated superphosphate.

is put through a beneficiation plant where a large part of the rock is recovered. A special flotation process recovers much of the remainder.[46] All these operations take place above ground. Variations in mining costs are due to differences in the ratios of overburden to matrix, of matrix to phosphate rock recovered, and of flotation to washer recovery.[47] These ratios are fairly uniform throughout the Florida pebble-rock field. The difference between the highest and lowest mining and drying costs for five Florida pebble producers was only $0.64 per ton in 1945 and only $0.20 per ton in 1946 (Table 35). In both years mining and drying costs for three producers varied by only a few cents. In the western fields, on the other hand, costs vary widely. In some areas phosphate-rock outcroppings surface the sides of mountains, and here production costs in 1947 ran as low as from $0.70 to $1.25 per ton. In most areas the rich phosphate deposits are located well below the surface and must be recovered by underground mining, with different excavation methods for different locations where the rock formations have undergone intense folding and faulting. In 1947 underground mining costs varied from $3.50 to $5.00 per ton. They averaged $4.25. These costs compare with estimated costs of $5.23 per ton for Tennessee rock and $4.00 per ton for Florida pebble rock. The natural market area of western producers at any given time therefore depends largely on which deposits are being exploited.

Nevertheless, on the basis of average mining costs, from fifteen per cent to twenty-two per cent of the phosphate-fertilizer market falls in the natural market area of western producers, a much larger share than they had before the war. As the center of the fertilizer market moves further westward and as each western recovery problem fosters its own technology, this share should increase. Western and Florida rock producers should therefore compete more vigorously in the future than they have in the past. All the evidence supports this conclusion; but again the necessary caveat: it assumes rational demand and no collusion among sellers.

---

[46] Chap. 2, n. 23, and text following n. 23.

[47] Data supplied by two large producers showed that in 1948 the ratio of overburden to matrix was about 2 to 1; the ratio of matrix to phosphate rock recovered was about 4 to 1; and the ratio of flotation rock to washer rock ranged from 1 to 1 to 6 to 1. The ratio of overburden to matrix in Florida mines increased considerably between 1940 and 1950.

TABLE 35

PER TON COST OF PRODUCTION OF REGULAR DRIED PHOSPHATE ROCK IN FLORIDA, TENNESSEE, AND THE WEST, 1945-47 [a]

| | 1945 | | | | | | 1946 | | | | | 1947 |
|---|---|---|---|---|---|---|---|---|---|---|---|---|
| | Co. #1 | Co. #2 | Co. #3 | Co. #4 | Co. #5 | Average | Co. #1 | Co. #2 | Co. #3 | Co. #4 | Average | Average |
| **Tennessee Mines** | | | | | | | | | | | | |
| Mining, wash, & recovery | $2.866 | $3.248 | | | | $3.076 | $2.945 | $2.772 | | | $2.845 | |
| Drying | .501 | 1.001 | | | | .802 | .492 | 1.034 | | | .830 | |
| Loading & shipping | .304 | .364 | | | | .344 | .245 | .373 | | | .334 | |
| Other prod. exp. | | .431 | | | | .208 | | .047 | | | .024 | |
| Selling, gen. & adm. exp. | .226 | .153 | | | | .177 | .219 | .189 | | | .198 | |
| Total | $3.897 | $5.197 | | | | $4.607 | $3.901 | $4.415 | | | $4.231 | $5.23 |
| **Florida Mines:** | | | | | | | | | | | | |
| Mining, wash, & recovery | $2.080 | $1.762 | $1.930 | $2.530 | $1.679 | $1.978 | $2.248 | $1.644 | $1.965 | $2.280 | $2.050 | |
| Trans. & storage, wet rock | .448 | .317 | .283 | .360 | .240 | .176 | .531 | .299 | .311 | .350 | .172 | |
| Drying | .087 | .340 | .317 | .030 | .277 | .349 | .081 | .368 | .303 | .027 | .376 | |
| Loading & shipping | | .071 | .277 | | .053 | .139 | | .085 | .248 | | .142 | |
| Depn. insurance & taxes | | .235 | | | .261 | .078 | | .376 | | | .050 | |
| Gen. mine expense | | .106 | .034 | | .743 | .162 | | .090 | .023 | | .022 | |
| Total to mine & dry | $2.615 | $2.831 | $2.841 | $2.920 | $3.253 | $2.882 | $2.860 | $2.862 | $2.850 | $2.657 | $2.812 | |
| Selling, gen. & adm. exp. | .510 | .238 | .129 | .660 | .186 | .301 | .692 | .393 | .227 | .560 | .425 | |
| Total | $3.125 | $3.069 | $2.970 | $3.580 | $3.439 | $3.183 | $3.552 | $3.255 | $3.077 | $3.217 | $3.237 | 4.00 [b] |
| Western Mines (Total) | | | | | | n. a. | | | | | n. a. | 4.25 [c] |

[a] Florida and Tennessee 1945 and 1946 costs from National Archives, OPA Records; 1947 costs computed from indexes supplied by producers; western costs from Bureau of Mines, U. S. Dept. of the Interior, in letter dated September 28, 1951.
[b] Estimated. The average production cost in the Florida pebble fields in 1946 was $3.24 per ton. Cost indexes made available by two large pebble-rock producers show that mining costs increased by 23.5 per cent between 1946 and 1947. The estimated cost per ton in 1947 is $3.24 × 1.235, or $4.00.
[c] A weighted average of costs ranging from a low of $0.70 to a high of $5.00 per ton.

# CHAPTER 8

# THE SUPERPHOSPHATE AND MIXED-FERTILIZER INDUSTRIES

A MERICAN farmers spend over one billion dollars annually on fertilizers, the manufacture of which requires about two thirds of the phosphate rock, one fifth of the sulphur, over ninety per cent of the potash, and, in peacetime, half the nitrogen consumed in the United States. In 1951, fertilizer expenditures amounted to about seven per cent of total farm cash income, but farmers in some regions and in certain types of agriculture spend much more. For example, those in the Middle Atlantic states average fourteen per cent, and grain farmers throughout the United States average eleven per cent. The financial success of many farmers depends on the fertilizers they buy and how they use them.

## A. Special Features of Fertilizer Demand

Efficient fertilizer usage requires technical skills (and possibly entrepreneural abilities) few farmers possess. The optimum combination and amount of N, $P_2O_5$, and $K_2$ for a given farm depends on the composition of its soil, the type of crop, the amount of rainfall,[1] crop and fertilizer prices, and the prices and quantities of other farm inputs. It takes years of training in the agronomic sciences to ascertain the nutrients particular crops require when grown on particular soils, and knowledge of the chemical composition of fertilizers to buy them wisely after the plant-nutrient requirements have been ascertained. Public policy has long recognized that most farmers do not possess these skills. Scientists in the land-grant college system, agricultural experiment stations, the agricultural extension services, and in other public agencies stand ready to analyze the farmer's soil and advise him on his fertilizer needs. Access to a tax-supported expert, i.e., the soil scientist,[2] differentiates the farm operator from most entrepreneurs.

As an intermediary between sellers and buyers the soil scientist can exert considerable influence on the types and quantities of fertilizers demanded and supplied, but his influence is limited. He can neither coerce nor command; some farmers do not have ready access to him; some who

---

[1] Fertilizers, especially phosphate, compete with plants for the soil's moisture. The optimum fertilizer application for a damp season is therefore not the same as that for a dry season.

[2] The term is used collectively to cover agronomists, soil scientists, and others whose combined influence shapes the recommendations on fertilizers to farmers. In point of fact, the farmers' principal source of such advice, excluding the advice received from other farmers, is the state extension service's county agent, who advises him not only on fertilizers but on other farm inputs as well.

have access neither seek nor heed his advice; and prevailing practices, the availability of various fertilizers, and the state of scientific knowledge condition his recommendations. For these reasons soil scientists' fertilizer recommendations may not accord with maximum efficiency in the purchase and use of fertilizers. Farmers who do not seek the soil scientists' services and who lack the necessary technical skills to use fertilizers efficiently may rely on their experience, adopt the practices of successful neighbors or local test-demonstration farmers, or rely on their fertilizer dealer, whose general familiarity with fertilizers and local conditions make him helpful, but who consciously or unconsciously may tailor his advice to fit the fertilizers he sells. The fertilizer practices of these farmers probably fall short of maximum efficiency in the purchase and use of fertilizers by an even wider margin.

Public policy has also made the fertilizer market a quasi-public utility. In all the forty-eight states fertilizer control laws regulate the kinds of fertilizers sold.[3] In 1950 over half of the states set minimum plant-nutrient requirements on fertilizers sold within their borders; some limited the number of grades that could be sold; all required registration of brands and analyses. Although decisions on production techniques are left to management, the types of fertilizers produced are greatly influenced by the recommendations of soil scientists and the actions of control boards. Decisions on what fertilizers should be used, although made by the farmer, are also greatly influenced by them. In these ways public agencies assume a part of the entrepreneural functions in farming and in the fertilizer industry.

The demand for fertilizers, aside from the effect of public policy, is highly seasonal and appears to be a function of farm income. Agriculture is a seasonal business. According to the monthly tag sales reported by the various state control officials,[4] about forty-five per cent of all commercial fertilizers sold each year are sold in the first quarter, twenty-two per cent in the second quarter, twelve per cent in the third quarter, and twenty-one per cent in the fourth quarter. In some regions the seasonality of demand is even more pronounced. For example, in the Southeast nearly seventy per cent of total annual fertilizer sales are made in February, March, and April, and eighty-three per cent are made in the five-month period of January to May inclusive. Although there is a lag between the purchase of tags and the actual sale of the tagged fertilizer, tag sales indicate roughly the wide seasonal variation in fertilizer sales. Similar seasonal variations characterize the sales of nitrogen, phosphates, and potash, the materials that go into manufactured fertilizers.

[3] See Chap. 11.
[4] See National Fertilizer Association, *Monthly Service Letter,* 1948-51 issues.

Demand for fertilizers also appears to vary directly with farm cash income. Actual annual expenditures on fertilizers usually conform to those estimated by an equation using gross cash income for the current year and gross and net cash income for the preceding year. In the entire period 1910-49, except for the years 1944-48 when farm income increased more rapidly than available fertilizer supplies, actual and estimated fertilizer expenditures were almost identical (Figure 5). While the relationship between annual expenditures on fertilizers and cash farm income varies among regions,[5] the estimating equation has a high predictive value for all regions except those where year-to-year changes in fertilizer consumption are large, notably the Midwest and the Far West.

Several factors explain the historical relationship between fertilizer expenditures and cash farm income.[6] Over much of the period 1910-49, data for the South greatly influenced the data for the United States as a whole. Most cash income on southern farms was derived from crops, and dealers sold most southern farmers their fertilizers on credit. Southern farmers sought to buy all the fertilizer they could because of the heavy removal of nutrients through leaching and cropping. How much they could buy was probably determined by fertilizer dealers on the basis of how last year's debts were paid, which in turn would vary directly with last year's farm cash income. This tended to link the current year's fertilizer sales with last year's farm cash income. And since farmers regard last year's farm prices as the best estimates of prices for the current year, a fairly high degree of correlation should also exist between the current year's expected farm cash income and total fertilizer expenditures.

This explanation has become less satisfactory as fertilizer consumption has increased in other regions, as the South has shifted resources out of crop farming into livestock and pastures, and as the Secretary of Agriculture has followed the practice (required by the 1949 Agricultural Act) of announcing price supports in advance of planting. Nevertheless, the past and present relationship between farm cash income and fertilizer expenditures has important implications for anti-trust policy. If total fertilizer expenditures can be explained altogether in terms of farm income, it follows that they are independent of fertilizer prices. That is, the amount farmers spend on fertilizers, and therefore the combined total revenues fertilizer manufacturers receive, will be the same at all prices. In short, the coefficient of price elasticity of demand confronting the fertilizer industry as a whole is equal approximately to unity.[7] Under such

[5] See A. L. Mehring, "Relationship between Farm Income and Farmers' Expenditures for Fertilizer and a Forecast of the Commercial Demand for Fertilizer in 1944 and 1945 by States," *The American Fertilizer*, April 8, 1944, pp. 832 ff.

[6] I am indebted to Dr. Allen B. Paul, staff economist of the Brookings Institution, for having brought to my attention most of factors identified in the text.

[7] See B. T. Shaw, F. W. Parker, and Mordecai J. B. Ezekiel, "Price Factors in Plant-Food Consumption," *Industrial and Engineering Chemistry*, March 1945, p. 282.

FIGURE 5

ACTUAL AND ESTIMATED EXPENDITURES ON FERTILIZER
IN THE UNITED STATES, 1910-49 [a]

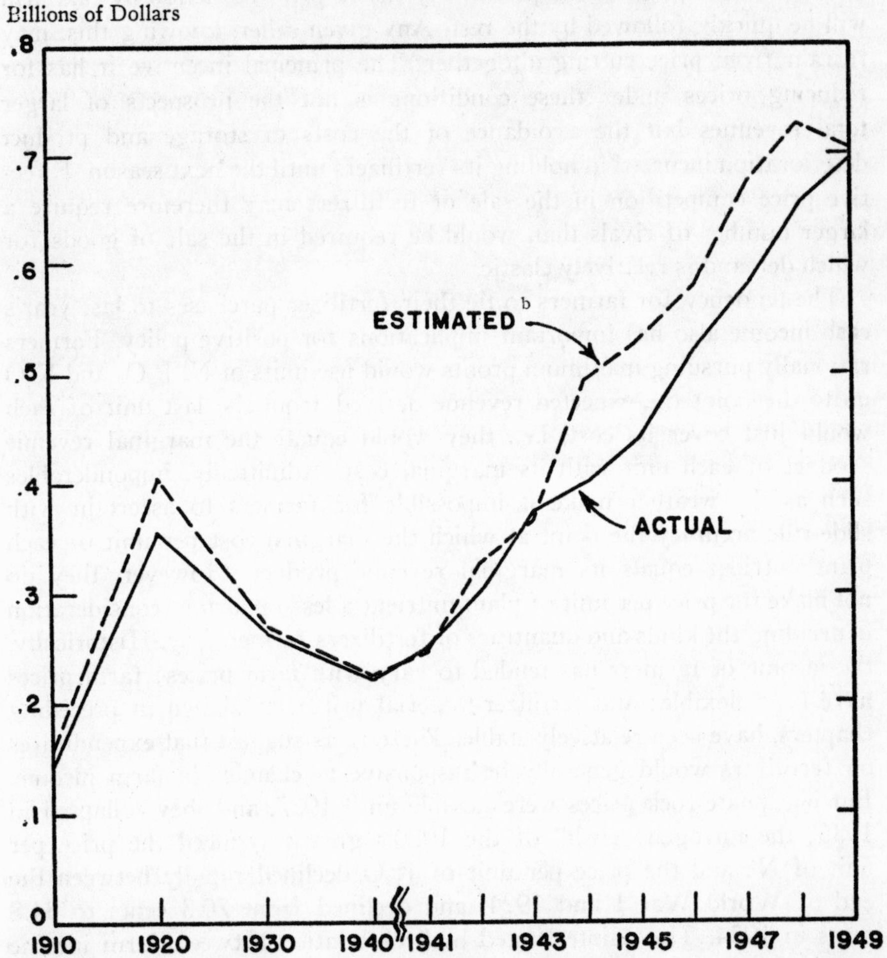

[a] A. L. Mehring, Bureau of Plant Industry, Soils, and Agricultural Engineering, U. S. Dept. of Agriculture.
[b] Mehring used the equation:

$$X_0 = .03293Y_{-1} + .01766Y_0 + 1.159 \frac{P_{-1}}{Y_{-1}} - 18.84$$

where

$X_0$ = fertilizer expenditures in the given year;

$Y_{-1}$ = cash income of farmers in the previous year;

$Y_0$ = cash income of farmers in the given year; and

$P_{-1}$ = cash income of farmers in the previous year after production costs are paid, i.e., farmers' profits on operations (cash income is defined as cash income from crops and government payments).

demand conditions a seller can increase total revenue through price changes only at the expense of its rivals. In fertilizer markets where sellers are few, this fact increases the probability that a price reduction by one firm will be quickly followed by the rest. Any given seller, knowing this, may refrain from price cutting altogether. The principal incentive it has for reducing prices under these conditions is not the prospects of larger total revenues but the avoidance of the costs of storage and product deterioration incurred in holding its fertilizers until the next season. Effective price competition in the sale of fertilizers may therefore require a larger number of rivals than would be required in the sale of goods for which demand is relatively elastic.

The tendency for farmers to tie their fertilizer purchases to last year's cash income also has important implications for positive policy. Farmers rationally pursuing maximum profits would use units of N, $P_2O_5$ and $K_2O$ up to the point the expected revenue derived from the last unit of each would just cover its cost, i.e., they would equate the marginal revenue product of each unit with its marginal cost. Admittedly, imponderables such as the weather make it impossible for farmers to ascertain with slide-rule accuracy the point at which the marginal cost per unit of each plant nutrient equals its marginal revenue product. However, they do not make the price per unit of plant nutrient a less important consideration in deciding the kinds and quantities of fertilizers farmers buy. Historically, the income of farmers has tended to vary with farm prices; farm prices have been flexible; and fertilizer-material prices, as shown in preceding chapters, have been relatively stable. These facts suggest that expenditures on fertilizers would generally be responsive to changes in farm income. But phosphate-rock prices were flexible until 1927, and they collapsed in 1935; the nitrogen "rush" of the 1920's greatly reduced the price per unit of N; and the price per unit of $K_2O$ declined rapidly between the end of World War I and 1924, and declined from 70.3 cents to 34.8 cents in 1934. The uninterrupted high correlation between farm income and fertilizer expenditures from 1910 to 1943, in spite of such sudden and appreciable changes in plant-nutrient unit costs, establishes a reasonable presumption that farmers' decisions on the use of fertilizers are not guided by plant-nutrient prices as much as rational demand would dictate.

## B. Fertilizer Production and Distribution

*Superphosphate.* Since superphosphate is the principal ingredient of mixed fertilizers and one of the principal fertilizers applied as a straight material, its consumption is as seasonal as that for the fertilizer industry as a whole. Between 1934 and 1940, about forty-three per cent of annual superphosphate sales were made in March, April, and May, while only twelve per cent to fifteen per cent were made in June, July, and August.[8] Seasonal demand causes seasonal swings in production and inventories. For the period 1934-40, monthly production rates and monthly inventories in the peak months of December and January were twice those for the rough months of May and June.[9] Superphosphate producers try to spread production more evenly throughout the year by specifying maximum shipments per month in their sales contracts with mixers, and thus set a lower limit on monthly shipments. Their efforts have been successful only in periods of critical superphosphate shortages such as 1943-47.

Ordinary superphosphate plants are located near their markets. According to data furnished by twenty superphosphate producers [10] located in twelve states, the average shipping distance per ton of ordinary superphosphate is 110 miles. Nine of the companies reported an average shipping distance of 75 miles or less; five reported a maximum shipping distance of 400 miles; five, a maximum of 300 miles; five, a maximum of 200 miles; and four, maximum shipping distances ranging from 60 to 150 miles. The only western firm in the sample reported a maximum shipping distance of 1,000 miles, although its average shipping distance was only 100 miles, or 10 miles less than the average for all the twenty reporting companies. Ordinary superphosphate (and mixing) plants are concentrated in the principal fertilizer-consuming areas (Table 36).

For three reasons the market orientation of the ordinary superphosphate industry can be explained largely in terms of relative costs of transport. First, the conversion of phosphate rock into ordinary superphosphate, principally because of the large quantities of sulphuric acid used, is a bulk-gaining process. To produce a ton of ordinary superphosphate carrying twenty per cent of available $P_2O_5$ requires approximately 1,200 pounds of high-grade phosphate rock (thirty-four per cent $P_2O_5$ and 1.5 per cent $CO_2$) and about 1,110 pounds of sulphuric acid of strength 50° Be' (62.18 per cent $H_2SO_4$). To produce the acid would require approximately 230 pounds of elemental sulphur. Hence, it would be necessary to assemble only 1,200 pounds of phosphate rock and 230 pounds of sulphur in order to produce a ton of ordinary superphosphate; i.e., the superphosphate would weigh about 570 pounds more than the initial raw materials (exclusive

---

[8] U. S. Dept. of Commerce, *Facts For Industry*, 1934-40, monthly reports on superphosphate.

[9] *Ibid.*

[10] The data were obtained from questionnaire returns from approximately 25 per cent of all firms engaged in producing ordinary superphosphate. Several multi-plant firms reported the average for all their plants in a single state on the same questionnaire, so the number of plants represented by the twenty returns is not known; but since the largest five or six fertilizer producers did not respond, the returns probably represent less than 25 per cent of all the plants in the industry.

TABLE 36

COMPLETE PLANTS, SUPERPHOSPHATE PLANTS, MIXING
PLANTS, AND P₂O₅ CONSUMPTION; BY STATE, 1949 [a]

| | Complete Plants[b] | Superphosphate Plants | Fertilizer Mixing Plants | Total Plants | Total P₂O₅ Consumption[c] (Tons) |
|---|---|---|---|---|---|
| United States......... | 120 | 152 | 771 | 1043 | 2,267,668 |
| New England.......... | 2 | 4 | 27 | 33 | 62,368 |
| Maine............... | 1 | 0 | 15 | 16 | 25,933 |
| New Hampshire...... | 0 | 0 | 0 | 0 | 3,775 |
| Vermont............ | 0 | 1 | 0 | 1 | 11,693 |
| Massachusetts........ | 1 | 3 | 7 | 11 | 10,958 |
| Rhode Island......... | 0 | 0 | 1 | 1 | 2,212 |
| Connecticut.......... | 0 | 0 | 4 | 4 | 7,797 |
| Middle Atlantic........ | 14 | 9 | 128 | 151 | 246,686 |
| New York........... | 3 | 2 | 23 | 28 | 79,114 |
| New Jersey.......... | 2 | 3 | 24 | 29 | 31,159 |
| Pennsylvania......... | 0 | 2 | 32 | 34 | 82,132 |
| Delaware............ | 0 | 0 | 9 | 9 | 6,723 |
| Maryland............ | 9 | 2 | 37 | 48 | 30,638 |
| District of Columbia.. | 0 | 0 | 1 | 1 | 203 |
| West Virginia........ | 0 | 0 | 2 | 2 | 16,717 |
| East North Central..... | 17 | 39 | 51 | 107 | 594,775 |
| Ohio................ | 11 | 11 | 17 | 39 | 125,968 |
| Indiana............. | 1 | 11 | 10 | 22 | 121,413 |
| Illinois............. | 3 | 8 | 9 | 20 | 224,090 |
| Michigan............ | 1 | 4 | 6 | 11 | 67,274 |
| Wisconsin........... | 1 | 5 | 9 | 15 | 56,030 |
| West North Central..... | 1 | 11 | 31 | 43 | 222,271 |
| Minnesota........... | 0 | 1 | 9 | 10 | 55,985 |
| Iowa................ | 0 | 3 | 6 | 9 | 63,677 |
| Missouri............ | 1 | 6 | 5 | 12 | 66,641 |
| North Dakota........ | 0 | 0 | 2 | 2 | 5,352 |
| South Dakota........ | 0 | 0 | 0 | 0 | 1,835 |
| Nebraska............ | 0 | 1 | 5 | 6 | 4,717 |
| Kansas.............. | 0 | 0 | 4 | 4 | 24,064 |
| South Atlantic........ | 55 | 30 | 304 | 389 | 532,014 |
| Virginia............. | 9 | 4 | 28 | 41 | 86,235 |
| North Carolina....... | 11 | 7 | 53 | 71 | 170,136 |
| South Carolina....... | 10 | 2 | 66 | 78 | 91,284 |
| Georgia............. | 17 | 17 | 97 | 131 | 115,769 |
| Florida............. | 8 | 0 | 60 | 68 | 68,590 |
| East South Central..... | 11 | 28 | 65 | 104 | 337,611 |
| Kentucky........... | 0 | 3 | 9 | 12 | 85,145 |
| Tennessee........... | 3 | 9 | 4 | 16 | 67,098 |
| Alabama............ | 6 | 8 | 34 | 48 | 121,916 |
| Mississippi.......... | 2 | 8 | 18 | 28 | 63,452 |

TABLE 36—*Continued*

| | Complete Plants[b] | Superphosphate Plants | Fertilizer Mixing Plants | Total Plants | Total P₂O₅ Consumption[c] (Tons) |
|---|---|---|---|---|---|
| West South Central..... | 10 | 11 | 43 | 64 | 158,209 |
| Arkansas............ | 2 | 2 | 11 | 15 | 34,978 |
| Louisiana............ | 4 | 4 | 6 | 14 | 27,963 |
| Oklahoma............ | 0 | 1 | 3 | 4 | 18,841 |
| Texas............... | 4 | 4 | 23 | 31 | 76,427 |
| Mountain............. | 1 | 7 | 23 | 31 | 34,778 |
| Montana............. | 1 | 0 | 0 | 1 | 2,913 |
| Idaho............... | 0 | 3 | 4 | 7 | 8,383 |
| Wyoming............ | 0 | 0 | 1 | 1 | 1,387 |
| Colorado............ | 0 | 1 | 5 | 6 | 8,051 |
| New Mexico......... | 0 | 2 | 2 | 4 | 3,522 |
| Arizona............. | 0 | 0 | 5 | 5 | 8,317 |
| Utah................ | 0 | 1 | 5 | 6 | 2,012 |
| Nevada............. | 0 | 0 | 1 | 1 | 193 |
| Pacific.............. | 9 | 13 | 99 | 121 | 78,956 |
| Washington.......... | 2 | 2 | 9 | 13 | 10,348 |
| Oregon............. | 2 | 5 | 9 | 16 | 10,812 |
| California........... | 5 | 6 | 81 | 92 | 57,796 |

[a] Plants by state from 1950 *Commercial Fertilizer Yearbook;* P₂O₅ consumption by states from A. L. Mehring, *1949 Fertilizer Consumption,* Bureau of Plant Industry, Soils, and Agricultural Engineering, U. S. Dept. of Agriculture.
[b] Complete plants produce sulphuric acid, superphosphate and mixed fertilizers. Superphosphate plants acidulate and mix but do not produce their own supply of acid; mixing plants perform mixing operations only.
[c] P₂O₅ consumed in all straight materials and mixed fertilizers. The data are for total as distinct from available, P₂O₅.

of air and water) that went into its manufacture.[11] Even if the transportation costs per ton for superphosphate and for the initial raw materials were the same, it would obviously be economical to assemble the raw materials near the market for superphosphate. Second, no single geographical area produces both sulphur and phosphate rock. Elemental sulphur deposits are concentrated in Texas and Louisiana; phosphate-rock deposits are concentrated in Florida, Tennessee, and the West. To locate close to either phosphate-rock or sulphur supplies would necessitate getting supplies of the other product from distant sources.[12] Finally, relative freight rates have encouraged location near consuming markets. The freight

[11] The weights of rock, acid, etc., used here are only typical. The actual weights to be used in a plant depend on grade of rock and strength of acid, on the relative cost of rock and of acid, and on the grade of superphosphate desired. The above data are near enough to practice to illustrate the point under discussion, namely, that superphosphate weighs nearly 40 per cent more than the sulphur and rock used. If, however, the superphosphate manufacturer had no acid plant and had to bring in sulphuric acid of, say, 60° Be' strength (77.67% H₂SO₄), the weight of rock and acid for a ton of superphosphate would be about 2,090 pounds, i.e., a little more than the weight of the resultant superphosphate. If higher-strength commercially marketed sulphuric acid, i.e., 66 Be' (93.18% H₂SO₄), were available to him, the combined weights of rock and acid required for a ton of superphosphate would be about 1,940 pounds. These calculations emphasize the advantage of shipping sulphur rather than sulphuric acid to the point of manufacture of superphosphate.
[12] Except, of course, where by-product sulphuric acid happens to be produced close to phosphate-rock fields, as is the case in some western localities.

charge per ton-mile for sulphur and phosphate rock, particularly the latter, is lower than for manufactured fertilizers. For example, in October, 1951, the shipping costs per ton of manufactured fertilizers, which includes ordinary and concentrated superphosphate and all kinds of mixed fertilizers, from Nashville, Tennessee, to Chicago, Illinois, was $8.36; this was approximately the cost of transporting a ton of phosphate rock by rail a distance twice as great, from Florida to Chicago.

Because ordinary superphosphate plants are located near their markets, raw-material freight charges account for a large portion of manufacturers' total costs.[13] Cost data for 1950 furnished by six midwestern superphosphate producers (Table 37) indicate that transportation costs on raw

TABLE 37

PRODUCTION COSTS PER TON OF ORDINARY
SUPERPHOSPHATE FOR THE MIDWEST, 1950 [a]

|  | Per Ton Superphosphate | Per Cent of Total Price |
|---|---|---|
| Phosphate rock costs at mine.......................... | $   3.08 | .......... |
| Sulphur costs at mine............................... | 3.22 | .......... |
| Total material costs............................ | 6.30 | 16.4 |
| Transportation costs, phosphate rock................. | 4.92 | .......... |
| Transportation costs, sulphur....................... | 3.54[b] | .......... |
| Total transportation costs, raw materials........... | 8.46 | 22.1 |
| Other sulphuric acid manufacturing costs............. | 2.94 | 7.7 |
| Acidulation costs: | | |
| Labor......................................... | .49 | 1.3 |
| Plant overhead................................ | 2.43 | 6.3 |
| Average costs per ton superphosphate................. | 20.62 | .......... |
| Average handling and delivery charge................. | 9.56 | 25.0 |
| Total costs, delivered to dealer.................... | 30.18 | 78.8 |
| Average price paid by farmers...................... | 38.30 | 100.0 |
| Manufacturer's profits, dealer's margin, and delivery charge........................................ | 8.12 | 21.2 |

[a] Acidulation costs from M A. Abrahamsen, *Manufacturing Costs as Reported for Cooperative Fertilizer Plants in the North Central States, 1949,* Farm Credit Administration, U. S. Dept. of Agriculture Special Report 218, 1951; all other costs computed from data supplied by six large midwestern superphosphate producers.

[b] Computed from transportation costs on the quantity of sulphur required to produce one-half ton of sulphuric acid, which is approximately the quantity of sulphuric acid required to produce one ton of ordinary superphosphate.

materials alone amount to nearly twenty-seven per cent of total production costs and to twenty-two per cent of the average delivered sales price.

[13] As was already indicated, however, the total transportation charge per unit of $P_2O_5$ delivered to the farmer would be even greater if ordinary superphosphate plants were located near either phosphate-rock or sulphur deposits.

When a ton of ordinary superphosphate reaches the mixing plant, the dealer, or the farmer, it has incurred transportation charges of $18.02; in 1950 this amounted to forty-seven per cent of the average selling price and to sixty per cent of the total cost of production and delivery excluding manufacturers' profits and dealers' margins.

The other principal elements of the price of superphosphate are raw-material costs f.o.b. mine, sulphuric-acid manufacturing costs,[14] plant overhead (including all indirect labor), and manufacturers' profits and dealers' margins. Once the phosphate rock and sulphuric acid are ready for blending, direct labor costs are relatively small, accounting for about 2.4 per cent of total manufacturing costs and only 1.3 per cent of the final delivered price.

With transportation charges on phosphate rock and sulphur accounting for such a significant proportion of the total cost, superphosphate production costs vary greatly from state to state. In 1943 and 1950 (Table 38),

TABLE 38

COSTS OF PRODUCING ONE TON OF ORDINARY SUPERPHOSPHATE
IN TWENTY-FOUR STATES, 1943 AND 1950 [a]

| State | 1943 | | | | 1950 | | | | |
|---|---|---|---|---|---|---|---|---|---|
| | Material | Direct Labor | Other Processing | Total | Material | Material Transport | Labor | Other Processing | Total |
| Alabama....... | $ 7.83 | $ 0.31 | $ 0.88 | $ 9.02 | | | | | |
| California..... | | | | | $ 12.93 | $ 3.60c | n. a. | n. a. | n. a. |
| Connecticut.... | | | | | | | | | |
| Florida........ | 7.61 | 0.20 | 0.97 | 8.78 | | | | | |
| Georgia....... | 8.11 | 0.38 | 1.01 | 9.50 | 6.70 | 5.58c | $ 0.46 | $ 1.13 | $ 13.87 |
| Illinois........ | 8.79 | 0.65 | 0.82 | 10.26 | | | | | |
| Indiana....... | 10.24 | 0.61 | 1.08 | 11.93 | | | | | |
| Kentucky..... | | | | | 7.03 | 6.61c | 0.53 | 2.58 | 16.75 |
| Louisiana..... | 8.93 | 0.30 | 0.83 | 10.06 | | | | | |
| Maryland..... | 8.57 | 0.36 | 1.07 | 10.00 | | | | | |
| Massachusetts.. | 11.92 | 0.38 | 1.29 | 13.59 | | | | | |
| Michigan...... | | | | | 8.80 | 7.95c | 0.53 | 2.83 | 20.11 |
| Mississippi..... | 8.90 | 0.28 | 0.93 | 10.11 | 10.41 | 7.54 | 1.22 | 1.30 | 20.47 |
| Missouri...... | | | | | 8.20 | 2.60c | .93 | 1.47 | 13.20 |
| New Jersey..... | 9.36 | 0.59 | 0.71 | 10.66 | | | | | |
| New York...... | 10.66 | 0.43 | 0.91 | 12.00 | | | | | |
| North Carolina.. | 7.38 | 0.32 | 0.87 | 8.57 | | | | | |
| Ohio.......... | 9.59 | 0.60 | 1.03 | 11.22 | 8.29 | 7.01 | 0.78 | 0.92 | 17.00 |
| South Carolina.. | 7.63 | 0.46 | 1.15 | 9.24 | 5.50b | 5.62b,c | 0.51 | 1.90 | 13.53 |
| Tennessee..... | 6.76 | 0.34 | 0.70 | 7.80 | 7.75 | 5.55c | 0.45 | 1.75 | 15.50 |
| Texas......... | 7.56 | 0.65 | 0.79 | 9.00 | 9.35 | 7.75c | 0.50 | 0.33 | 17.93 |
| Utah.......... | | | | | 6.55 | 2.75c | 3.00d | | 12.30 |
| Virginia....... | 9.42 | 0.35 | 0.79 | 10.56 | | | | | |
| Wisconsin..... | | | | | 11.62 | 7.42 | 0.30 | 2.20 | 21.54 |
| Average........ | $ 8.78 | $ 0.424 | $ 0.931 | $ 10.14 | $ 8.59 | $ 5.83 | $0.837 | $ 1.64 | $ 16.56 |

[a] 1943 data from U. S. Office of Price Administration Records, National Archives; 1950 data furnished by superphosphate companies in response to questionnaire.
[b] Partially estimated.
[c] Does not include sulphur freight costs included in f.o.b. producing plant selling price for $H_2SO_4$.
[d] Includes overhead.

[14] Less than half of all the superphosphate plants produce their own sulphuric acid. The sulphuric acid manufacturing costs in Table 37 are based on data furnished by two of the six reporting midwestern firms and are probably representative of such costs for the industry as a whole.

they were relatively low in the South and along the Atlantic seaboard, where plants were located in general proximity to the Florida and Tennessee phosphate-rock deposits or the Louisiana and Texas sulphur deposits, and where they could be supplied by cheap water transportation. In the Midwest and East, where sulphur and phosphate rock reach superphosphate plants after long rail or water hauls, superphosphate production costs were considerably higher.[15]

The long distances separating phosphate rock and sulphur from superphosphate users and a simple technology requiring little labor explain why most of the delivered price per unit of $P_2O_5$ to the farmer represents the costs of distribution. The cost f.o.b. mine of the phosphate rock and sulphur to produce one ton of ordinary superphosphate in 1950 was $6.30 (Table 37). The labor, overhead, manufacturer's profits, and other costs involved in converting the sulphur to sulphuric acid and blending the acid with phosphate rock to produce one ton of ordinary superphosphate amounted to $7.86. This gives a total mining and manufacturing cost of only $14.16. In contrast, the price of a ton of superphosphate delivered to farmers in the Midwest was $38.30. The difference of $24.14 represented distribution costs; of this, $8.46 represented the cost of transporting the phosphate rock and sulphur (or sulphuric acid) to the superphosphate plant; $9.56, the handling and delivery charges incurred between the superphosphate plant and the dealer's or agent's warehouse; and about $6.12, the dealer's or agent's commission [16] and the cost of delivering the superphosphate from his warehouse to the farmer. Distribution costs accounted for about sixty-three per cent of the final price to the farmer; raw-material production costs, seventeen per cent; and fabrication costs, twenty per cent.

While future technological change may reduce mining and in-transit fabrication costs somewhat, significant reductions in the cost of $P_2O_5$ to the farmer lie in improved distribution techniques. If technological change should reduce in-transit fabrication costs by fifty per cent, which seems unlikely, and the total reduction were passed on to the farmer, the price would be reduced by no more than $2.50. In 1950 a price reduction nearly this great could have been effected by substituting paper for cotton bags, and a greater price reduction by substituting bulk for bagged superphosphate. But the most promising source of economy in $P_2O_5$ distribution lies in substituting concentrated for ordinary superphosphate.

---

[15] Regional wage differentials accounted for a small portion of the regional differences in cost. In 1949 the prevailing straight-time average hourly earnings in the fertilizer industry for the South were $0.74, while those for the United States as a whole were $0.92. Hourly earnings for other regions were as follows: New England, $1.01; Middle Atlantic $1.09; Border States, $1.00; Great Lakes, $1.20; Middle West, $1.03; Southwest, $0.79; and Pacific, $1.28 (U. S. Bureau of Labor Statistics, *Wage Structure, Fertilizer, 1949 and 1950*, Bulletin No. 77, Series 2).

[16] The dealer's cash price per ton to the farmer in 1950, based on approximately 100 published price lists, averaged 13 per cent higher than the producer's delivered price to the dealer. Dealers' and agents' margins ranged from 11 to 15 per cent over delivered prices to them.

*Concentrated Superphosphate.* Concentrated superphosphate is so named because it usually contains from forty to fifty per cent available $P_2O_5$, or between two and two-and-one-half times as much $P_2O_5$ as ordinary super-phosphate.[17] Although manufacturing costs per unit of $P_2O_5$ are slightly higher for concentrated than for ordinary superphosphate, total distribution costs per unit of $P_2O_5$ for the concentrated material are considerably lower.

Concentrated superphosphate is made from phosphate rock and phosphoric acid, which also comes from phosphate rock, and generally is made at lower costs near phosphate-rock deposits.[18] Twelve of the fourteen plants producing concentrated superphosphate in 1957 were located at their sources of phosphate rock. The phosphoric acid used in making concentrated superphosphate can be produced by any one of three processes: (1) the electric-furnace process, (2) the blast-furnace process, and (3) the sulphuric acid or wet process.[19] In all three processes the weight of a unit of $P_2O_5$ is substantially reduced (Table 39) as phosphate rock is

TABLE 39

PRINCIPAL RAW MATERIALS REQUIRED TO PRODUCE
A TON OF CONCENTRATED SUPERPHOSPHATE
(48% $P_2O_5$) BY VARIOUS METHODS [a]

| | Sulphuric-Acid or "Wet" Method | Electric-Furnace Method | Blast-Furnace Method |
|---|---|---|---|
| Phosphate rock (34% $P_2O_5$)...... | 3,105 lb.[b] | 3,210 lb.[c] | 3,420 lb.[d] |
| Sulphur........................ | 595 lb.[b] | | |
| Coke (85% carbon)............. | | 415 lb.[e] | 2,840 lb.[g] |
| Silica (96% silicon dioxide)....... | | 690 lb.[f] | 755 lb.[h] |
| Total................... | 3,700 lb. | 4,315 lb. | 7,015 lb. |

[a] Data furnished by Tennessee Valley Authority.
[b] Assumes 92% overall recovery of $P_2O_5$ in making phosphoric acid from rock, 90% conversion of $P_2O_5$ in rock to available form on acidulation, and 97.5% conversion of sulphur to sulphuric acid.
[c] Assumes 97.4% overall recovery of $P_2O_5$ as elemental phosphorus, 99.8% recovery of $P_2O_5$ from phosphorus, and 90% conversion of $P_2O_5$ in rock to available form.
[d] Assumes 80% recovery of $P_2O_5$ as elemental phosphorus, 99.8% recovery of $P_2O_5$ from phosphorus, and 90% conversion of $P_2O_5$ in rock to available form.
[e] Assumes 34% $P_2O_5$ and 2% ferric oxide in rock and 3% excess coke. In practice it is seldom economical to use rock of this grade in an electric furnace.
[f] Assumes 34% $P_2O_5$ rock carries 10% silicon dioxide and 49% calcium oxide.
[g] Assumes 360 lbs. coke for reduction, 3 tons of coke to furnish necessary heat per ton of $P_2O_5$ volatilized, and 95% volatilization.
[h] Assumes silicon dioxide to calcium oxide weight ratio of 0.8 as in electric furnace.

transformed into concentrated superphosphate or into a highly concentrated intermediate product such as elemental phosphorus. The weight per unit of $P_2O_5$ in concentrated superphosphate is only sixty per cent of

[17] However, as pointed out earlier, all superphosphate containing over 29 per cent available $P_2O_5$ is generally called concentrated.
[18] See Chap. 2.
[19] For detailed descriptions of the three processes and their applicability to the western phosphate-rock deposits, see William H. Waggaman and Roscoe E. Bell, "Western Phosphates—Comparison of Sulfuric Acid and Thermal Reduction Processing," *Industrial and Engineering Chemistry*, Feb. 1950, pp. 276, 286.

the weight of the principal materials required to produce a unit of $P_2O_5$ by the sulphuric-acid process, only fifty-three per cent of that required in the electric-furnace process, and only thirty-four per cent of that required in the blast-furnace process. The advantage of locating a concentrated superphosphate plant near its phosphate-rock supply may obviously be great.

*Swift & Company: A Case Study in Plant-Site and Process Selection.* Swift & Company concluded in 1947, on the basis of a detailed study of cost-price relationships,[20] that $P_2O_5$ could be produced and delivered throughout the West and most of the Midwest at a lower cost in concentrated than in ordinary superphosphate. "Multiple-grade"[21] mixed fertilizers, the production of which required a more highly concentrated phosphatic material than ordinary superphosphate, held a distinct cost advantage over corresponding simple grades throughout the United States. Preliminary cost estimates showed that concentrated superphosphate had a cost advantage of from $0.05 to $0.12 per unit of $P_2O_5$ in the Midwest, and that multiple grades held at a cost advantage over simple grades of $0.055 per unit of plant nutrient east of the Mississippi, and of $0.10 per unit west of the Mississippi.

Selection of the type of product, process, and plant site determined the exact cost advantages and required a comparison of costs at various locations for alternative methods of processing phosphate rock for the manufacture of concentrated superphosphate and multiple-grade (high-analysis) mixed fertilizers. Swift could use any of three processes to produce phosphoric acid. Since an intermediate product of both the electric- and blast-furnace processes is elemental phosphorus,[22] these two processes permitted several alternative methods of production and distribution: (1) Furnaces for producing elemental phosphorus could be constructed near the source of rock; the elemental phosphorus could be shipped to a plant near the market and there reduced to phosphoric acid; and rock could be shipped from the nearest mine and blended with the phosphoric acid to produce concentrated superphosphate. (2) Or the elemental phosphorus could be converted to phosphoric acid at the plant near the rock mine and the acid and rock shipped to a point near the market, where they could be blended to produce concentrated super-

---

[20] I am indebted to C. T. Prindeville, vice-president in charge of the Plant Food Division of Swift & Co., for the materials on the Swift & Co. study.

[21] This is a term the company uses to designate fertilizers of over 40 per cent plant-nutrient content. Fertilizers containing less are designated "simple" grades.

[22] Elemental phosphorous is used in the production of munitions and certain foods and industrial products. Electric- and blast-furnace plants therefore have a wider potential market than those using the sulphuric acid process. Because Swift's preliminary studies showed the elemental phosphorus market to be small, and profitable only if supplied by plants located near Tennessee rock and purchasing electric current at rates comparable to those TVA charged its own plant at Wilson Dam, the Company ignored this potential advantage of the two furnace processes in the later stages of its study. The elemental phosphorus market expanded after 1947, and current studies might lead to different conclusions.

phosphate—an option also open to Swift if it used the sulphuric-acid process. (3) Or all facilities for producing concentrated superphosphate, whether Swift used the electric-furnace, blast-furnace, or sulphuric-acid process, could be located near the source of rock. The history of the two furnace methods revealed that the electric furnace had displaced the blast furnace in commercial operations in the United States. Even producers most advantageously located for blast-furnace operations had converted to electric furnaces.[23] Swift therefore limited its detailed cost calculations to the electric-furnace and sulphuric-acid processes.

The company calculated the cheapest combination of production and distribution costs for phosphoric acid made by each of the two processes for plants located at Agricola and Tampa, Florida, Harvey, Illinois, Sheffield, Alabama, Mt. Pleasant, Tennessee,[24] Hammond, Indiana, and National Stock Yards area, East St. Louis, Missouri, and the delivered costs at all major points of consumption (Table 40). A sulphuric-acid or "wet-process" plant located at Agricola, Florida, gave the cheapest combination of production and distribution costs on phosphoric acid for the market

TABLE 40

DELIVERED COSTS OF ELECTRIC-FURNACE AND
WET-PROCESS PHOSPHORIC ACID AT SELECTED
DESTINATIONS FROM SELECTED PLACES OF
MANUFACTURE, 1947 [a]

| Cost at Destination | Place of Manufacture | Phosphoric Acid | | | |
|---|---|---|---|---|---|
| | | 55% elec. furn. | | 50% wet process | |
| | | Fla. rock | Tenn. rock | Fla. rock | Tenn. rock |
| Agricola | Agricola | $54.23 | ....... | $27.16 | ....... |
| Tampa | Tampa | 42.93 | | 28.56 | ....... |
| Harvey | Harvey | 70.43 | ....... | 30.65 | ....... |
| TVA | Sheffield | 44.93 | $41.23 | ....... | ....... |
| Sheffield area | Sheffield | 58.11 | 54.41 | ....... | ....... |
| Mt. Pleasant | Mt. Pleasant | | 51.33 | ....... | ....... |
| Hammond | Hammond | 65.33 | 64.13 | 39.23 | $38.23 |
| Hammond | Tampa | 57.53 | | | |
| Hammond | Agricola | | | 41.76 | |
| Hammond | TVA, Sheffield | 58.53 | 54.80 | ....... | ....... |
| Hammond | Sheffield area | 71.71 | 67.98 | ....... | ....... |
| Hammond | Mt. Pleasant | | 62.93 | ....... | ....... |
| Hammond | Hammond (from phosphorus made at Tampa) | 49.93 | ....... | ....... | ....... |
| Hammond | Hammond (from phosphorus made at Sheffield area) | 62.55 | 58.85 | ....... | ....... |
| Hammond | Hammond (from phosphorus made at Mt. Pleasant) | | 55.55 | ....... | ....... |
| N. S. Yards[b] | N. S. Yards | 69.93 | 68.23 | 36.03 | 34.43 |
| N. S. Yards | Tampa | 56.13 | ....... | | |
| N. S. Yards | Agricola | | | 40.36 | ....... |
| N. S. Yards | TVA, Sheffield | 53.93 | 50.23 | ....... | ....... |
| N. S. Yards | Sheffield area | 67.11 | 63.41 | ....... | ....... |
| N. S. Yards | Mt. Pleasant | | 60.13 | ....... | ....... |
| N. S. Yards | N. S. Yards (from phosphorus made at Agricola) | 49.43 | ....... | ....... | ....... |
| N. S. Yards | N. S. Yards (from phosphorus made at Sheffield area) | 61.88 | 58.18 | ....... | ....... |
| N. S. Yards | N. S. Yards (from phosphorus made at Mt. Pleasant) | | 55.00 | ....... | ....... |

[a] Swift & Co.
[b] East St. Louis, Mo.

[23] Notably, Victor Chemical Company in Tennessee.
[24] Cost data showed that an electric-furnace process was the most economical method of production for a plant located in Tennessee. Hence, no cost data appear in Table 40 for a "wet-process" plant located in Tennessee.

as a whole. For two destinations, the National Stock Yards area and Hammond, total production costs for phosphoric acid were slightly less than total production costs at Agricola plus transportation charges, but a plant at either site would not serve the rest of the market so cheaply as a plant at Agricola.

Swift then computed the cost of producing concentrated superphosphate at Agricola, Hammond, and National Stock Yards and found that it could be produced at Agricola and shipped to both Hammond and National Stock Yards at a lower total cost per unit of $P_2O_5$ than it could be produced at either site (Table 41). The company constructed a sulphuric-acid-process plant near its Agricola phosphate desposits and in 1949 began producing concentrated superphosphate on a commercial scale.

TABLE 41

COST OF PRODUCING CONCENTRATED SUPERPHOSPHATE
AT THREE PLANT SITES, 1947 [a]

|  | Agricola | Hammond | N. S. Yards [b] |
|---|---|---|---|
| Phosphate rock.................. | $0.026 | $0.086 | $0.081 |
| Phosphoric acid.................. | 0.402 | 0.581 | 0.535 |
| Factory expense................. | 0.047 | 0.052 | 0.052 |
| Total cost per unit at plant....... | $0.475 | $0.719 | $0.668 |
| Freight: Agricola to Hammond..... | $0.163 | .......... | .......... |
| Delivered cost at Hammond..... | .......... | $0.638 | .......... |
| Agricola to N. S. Yards.......... | $0.151 | .......... | .......... |
| Delivered cost at N. S. Yards..... | .......... | .......... | $0.626 |

[a] Swift & Co.
[b] East St. Louis, Mo.

The experience of Swift & Company undoubtedly parallels that of other producers. The Armour Fertilizer Works constructed a wet-process concentrated-superphosphate plant at Bartow, Florida, at about the same time Swift constructed its plant at Agricola. Since 1949 Davison Chemical has closed down its concentrated-superphosphate plant at Baltimore, Maryland, and built one at Bartow, Florida; Gates Brothers has built one at Wendell, Idaho; Simplot Fertilizer Company, one at Pocatello, Idaho; F. S. Royster and International Minerals, one each at Mullberry, Florida; Western Phosphates, one at Garfield, Utah; American Cyanamid, one at Brewster, Florida; and Virginia-Carolina, one at Nichols, Florida. The Thurston Chemical Company and Missouri Farmers Association have built a plant each at Joplin, Missouri; and Phillips Chemical has built one at Pasadena, Texas. All except the last three are near phosphate mines, and all use the sulphuric-acid process.

## C. PRICING PRACTICES IN FERTILIZER DISTRIBUTION

Mixed fertilizers and fertilizer materials are distributed to farmers principally through mixed-fertilizer manufacturers' agents and dealers, but some mixers sell a portion of their output directly to farmers from their own plants and warehouses through company salesmen. Mixers and their agents, as shown earlier, distribute fertilizer nitrogen and potash as well as mixed fertilizers and superphosphates. Nitrogen and potash producers generally do not maintain distribution organizations to sell to farmers.[25] They sell in wholesale quantities to integrated and noninte-grated mixers, who in turn sell N, $P_2O_5$, and $K_2O$ as mixtures or as straight materials to farmers, principally through their agents and dealers. The larger agents and dealers generally serve more than one fertilizer manufacturer, and when they do they are known as "joint" or "split" agents or dealers. Most large manufacturers also maintain several so-called "exclusive agents." Such agents are usually subsidiary selling companies, but they frequently distribute fertilizers under their own local brand and that of their parent company even when both are manufactured by the parent company.

Agents and dealers operate under contracts negotiated with fertilizer manufacturers from season to season.[26] Although the contracts vary among regions and producers in minor details, all contain essentially the same provisions covering the method and rate of compensation. Usually the agent is paid five per cent of what is known as consumer's-basis-time price or cash price per ton. When he guarantees the payment of all notes taken by him as security on time sales, he is paid an additional five per cent. Agents receive additional compensation for furnishing transportation and warehouse facilities when the quoted price to the dealer provides that the manufacturer furnish these services, and they also receive graduated bonuses on fertilizer sales exceeding a specified tonnage. In 1942 bonuses ranged from one per cent on yearly rates in excess of 250 tons but less than 500 tons up to three per cent on sales exceeding 1,000 tons.

*Division of Sales Territories.* Since the National Fertilizer Association was formed in 1925,[27] fertilizer and fertilizer materials have been dis-tributed under a "zone" or "district" pricing system. Under the associa-tion's by-laws adopted in June, 1925, the United States was divided into nine districts. Under the National Industrial Recovery Act, the associa-tion, acting as the Code Authority, redistricted the United States into

[25] *Supra,* Chap. 7, at n. 39.
[26] For a detailed description of distribution methods and agent and dealer arrangements, see *The Fertilizer Industry* (U. S. OPA Records, National Archives, pp. 188 ff).
[27] The association formed in 1925 merged two older regional associations, the Southern Fertilizer and the National Fertilizer associations.

twelve zones and many sub-zones, which producers have continued to use.

Zone pricing in the fertilizer industry has sometimes been attributed to a combination of strong competition and high freight costs.[28] Whether it has actually reflected competition or has served as a convenient means for stabilizing prices depends largely on the period under consideration. Price schedules in the Federal Trade Commission's files show that in 1928 most producers quoted prices on a zone-delivered basis, but the number of non-comformists was large. Many firms quoted f.o.b. plant prices, and at least one large producer used zone pricing in some districts and f.o.b. plant pricing in others.[29] Under NRA, however, a uniform system of cost accounting and a zone-delivered price system became the chief means for controlling price competition.

Under the NRA Fertilizer Code of Fair Competition producers subscribed to a delivered-to-the-consumer price system for all zones, and an open price system whereby each producer filed with all other producers and with the Code Authority copies of new price lists issued in each zone. In eighteen months under the Code fertilizer prices increased about ten per cent and showed greater stability than they did for the eighteen-month periods preceding and following NRA. Immediately after the Supreme Court declared the NRA unconstitutional in the Schecter case, fertilizer prices fell by about fifteen per cent. Such price behavior may not demonstrate the effectiveness of zone pricing in stabilizing competition (zone pricing continued after the NRA was declared unconstitutional), but it strongly suggests that a compulsory open price system, which is greatly facilitated by zone pricing, prevents competitive price cutting. In fact it did this under NRA.

Zone pricing in the fertilizer industry, when rigidly followed by all producers, leads to freight absorption and "phantom" freight, but to considerably less of each than the more familiar cases of basing-point pricing. Within each zone or sub-zone, dealers (and farmers) pay the same price per ton of fertilizer regardless of the location of the supplying plants. The delivered-to-the-consumer cash price for each sub-zone is computed by adding to the f.o.b. plant price the average rail-freight charge for the sub-zone, the average trucking charge from dealer's railhead or warehouse to the farmer, and the dealer's margin. Consumers located nearer the producing plant than the average distance pay a "phantom" freight, while those located farther from the plant have a portion of their freight absorbed.

---

[28] U. S. OPA, *The Fertilizer Industry*. National Archives, p. 188.
[29] This diversity is believed to have occurred after the Department of Justice declared in 1926 that a delivered price system, when achieved by agreement, was to be construed as price fixing (see *infra*, this chapter).

Even during and immediately after NRA, however, when delivered prices within each zone were more uniform than at any other time in the industry's history, the pattern of distribution did not depart significantly from that to be expected under unrestricted competition. The reasons are fairly obvious. Consumers generally had the option of taking their fertilizer either at the quoted delivered price or at the f.o.b. plant price. Consumers located near the plant could avoid paying phantom freight by hiring their own trucks; and fixed costs are so small and delivery charges so high that there is little room for either phantom freight or freight absorption.[29] Delivered prices are therefore generally equal to the sum of production costs, dealers' margins, and transportation charges.

In recent years, while continuing to quote delivered prices by zone, producers have provided for freight allowances which virtually make such prices equal to f.o.b. plant price plus transportation at all destinations. Nearly all producers publish price lists giving the dealer's price and the suggested consumer's price based on the average delivery charge for the zone in which the price list is applicable. The lists usually contain detailed schedules of freight allowances granted the dealer or consumer if either takes delivery at the producer's plant or warehouse. If the dealer takes delivery at his own warehouse or nearest railhead, he is instructed to adjust his prices by the difference between the average freight charge included in the price and the actual freight charge incurred by the producer. The final price to the farmer, whether he buys at the delivered price or at the f.o.b. plant price, should be the sum of the f.o.b. plant price and the cost of delivery to his own farm.[30]

*Competition in Fertilizer Pricing.* Except for the monopolistic element included in N, $P_2O_5$, and $K_2O$ prices to mixers and their distributors,[31] fertilizer prices paid by farmers are regulated by strong competitive forces. That is, gross margins between raw-material costs and the prices of mixed fertilizers and straight materials to farmers—the portion of the retail price of fertilizers equated with value added in fertilizer manufacturing and distribution—are generally set by effective competition. Competitive pricing can be explained largely in terms of the industry's structure. In almost all localities, but particularly in the important consuming areas of the South, the Middle Atlantic states, and the Midwest, each farmer has a large number of alternative sources of supply (Table 36). But the

---

[29] The American Trucking Association protested the scale of trucking allowances given dealers and farmers under the NRA code, stating that in some zones they were too low to induce farmers to hire trucks and deliver their own fertilizer. In some zones, however, railroads had reduced freight rates on fertilizer to the level of the trucking allowances, thereby rendering the protest largely inapplicable (NRA Records G, *The Fertilizer Industry,* National Archives, pp. 188 ff.).

[30] Whether farmers buy directly from the producer or from the dealer they buy at retail prices. Since the difference between the wholesale and suggested retail price is the dealer's commission, they pay for dealer's services in either case.

[31] See Chaps. 2, 4, 5, and 6.

nature of the market itself, aside from its structural features, also encourages competitive pricing.[32] As already pointed out, a high percentage of total annual fertilizer sales occurs in the short fertilizer season comprising the three-month period February-April. Most of the base goods that enter into mixed fertilizers sold during the season have already been manufactured and are in inventories before the season opens. Hence, the fertilizer producer is usually in a position not unlike that of a farmer who has already harvested his crop—he can sell his entire output at whatever it will bring, or he can store it for another year. Since the cost of storage, involving as it does product deterioration, tied-up working capital, and market risks, is fairly high, most producers attempt to unload most of their output even if they have to reduce prices substantially. The amount of price-cutting in a season depends largely on how accurately fertilizer producers have forecast the market. Each producer formally makes his forecast independently; but since all use the same basis for forecasting, all are likely to reach similar conclusions.

Producers generally accept the past year's sales of the various grades of fertilizers as a first approximation for sales in the coming season. They may then consult state control boards, state university agronomists, and the Department of Agriculture for recommended and approved changes in grades and analyses of fertilizers applicable to their sales territories.[33] If new grades are recommended, producers may substitute them for old ones. If the new grades call for radical changes in the traditional consumption patterns of farmers, however, producers are likely to proceed slowly in shifting to them. The estimated sales of various grades thus established are then adjusted for changes in total fertilizer consumption anticipated because of changes in farmers' cash income, and for changes in fertilizer production costs which are likely to affect prices. Since most fertilizer producers selling in the same territory base their estimates on essentially identical data, they are likely to adjust their outputs along similar lines. If they underestimate sales, prices generally rise; if they overestimate, prices are generally cut.

*Attempts at Price Leadership.* Having made estimates of the quantities that farmers will buy at given prices, each producer, especially the large producer, tries to play the role of price leader, hoping that his published price will be accepted by his rivals.[34] Price leadership in the industry,

---

[32] This discussion is based largely on information obtained in interviews with fertilizer producers, distributors, co-operatives, U. S. Dept. of Agriculture officials, and spokesmen for various farm organizations.

[33] Some producers make a more detailed study of their own market. For example, a New Jersey producer canvasses the local tomato canneries and catsup manufacturers to obtain their output estimates based on expected tomato crops. The output of fertilizer grades used by local tomato growers is adjusted accordingly. Similarly, a Delaware and a Maryland producer canvass all farmers who purchased fertilizer from them during the previous year to obtain information on expected crop changes.

[34] The initial price to the dealer usually results from a full-cost calculation, i.e., total costs including manufacturer's margins per unit of output, plus average delivery charges throughout the particular zone; suggested consumer prices include, in addition, the dealer's margin.

however, has not been systematic. At one time Virginia-Carolina Chemical Company was usually the first to announce prices in the South, and American Agricultural Chemical Company the first in the Middle Atlantic states. Under NRA, however, most southern producers stated when filing new price lists that they were doing so to meet competition from the F. S. Royster Guano Company; the rest stated that they followed the prices of "other producers." [35] In other regions Royster was among the price followers. In the postwar period co-operatives seem to have done the price leading in most territories, although several producers in the Delaware and Eastern Shore region have followed the prices of Swift & Company, particularly for price reductions.

Attempts at price leadership in the fertilizer industry apparently neither stabilize prices nor maintain them substantially above levels that would otherwise prevail. Published price lists issued by seven producers in the Delaware-Maryland area for the Spring of 1950 show little uniformity (Table 42). The earliest price list issued was that of a large national

TABLE 42

LIST PRICES [a] ON SPECIFIC GRADES OF FERTILIZER FOR
SEVEN PRODUCERS SELLING IN THE DELAWARE-MARYLAND
AREA, SPRING, 1950 [b]

| | Grade | | | |
|---|---|---|---|---|
| | 5-10-5 | 5-10-10 | 3-12-6 | 0-14-7 |
| Producer 1................ | $ 41.10 | $ 45.20 | $ 37.55 | $.......... |
| Producer 2............... | 40.05 | 46.35 | 40.05 | 35.10 |
| Producer 3............... | 41.18 | 45.23 | 38.93 | 36.23 |
| Producer 4............... | 40.09 | 44.01 | 37.84 | 35.14 |
| Producer 5............... | 40.05 | 44.10 | 37.80 | 35.10 |
| Producer 6............... | 40.50 | .......... | .......... | 34.00 |
| Producer 7............... | 45.22 | 47.02 | 41.62 | 40.00 |
| High.................. | $ 45.22 | $ 47.02 | $ 41.62 | $ 40.00 |
| Low.................. | $ 40.05 | $ 44.01 | $ 37.55 | $ 35.10 |

[a] Consumers' cash prices per ton delivered in 100-pound paper bags.
[b] Individual companies' price lists, Spring, 1950.

producer. Nearly two months later six other producers issued their price lists in rapid succession, all within a nineteen-day period. On only two grades, 5-10-5 and 0-14-7, were the prices of as many as two producers identical. The large national producers tended to be closer together on prices than the group as a whole, and the highest prices were quoted by a small regional dry-mixer and the lowest by a regional co-operative. List-price differentials for the Delaware-Maryland area are approximately the

[35] NRA Records G, *The Fertilizer Industry*, National Archives, p. 9.

same as those in other territories for which representative price lists are available.

List-price differentials afford fairly reliable evidence that such price leadership as is found in the fertilizer industry is not an instrument of collusive action. Moreover, competition has made actual prices throughout the fertilizer season more uniform and more flexible than list prices. Dealers and agents confronting farmers who have been offered the same fertilizers at lower prices must accept the lower prices or lose business.[36] Agents do not possess title to the fertilizer and are likely to request lower retail prices from their principals to avoid losing their commissions. If the principals do not comply, agents often absorb price differentials by accepting smaller margins. Dealers may, and usually do, meet their competitors' prices without consulting the manufacturer. However, most manufacturers recognize the necessity of meeting competition in order to move their product and have working agreements with their agents and dealers for the latter to pass such price reductions back to them. Where "joint" or "split" agents or dealerships are maintained, the working agreement is virtually inevitable; otherwise the dealer would sell only the brands of producers quoting the lower prices.[37]

Fertilizer prices have in fact been highly flexible. Although list prices are not revised often within a given season, actual prices paid by dealers and farmers generally change from month to month, and probably from week to week.[38] Fertilizer prices are also highly sensitive to general economic fluctuations. Between September, 1929, and April, 1933, the monthly index of fertilizer prices fell from 101.7 to 62.4; it registered cyclical declines between June, 1935, and April, 1936; between October, 1937, and May, 1938; and between April, 1949, and April, 1950.

*Profits in Fertilizer Manufacturing Are Low.* Excess capacity and numerous sellers in the fertilizer-manufacturing industry have reflected in profits substantially below those earned in manufacturing generally. For the period 1930-43 the average annual rate of return on total assets in the fertilizer industry was only 4.5 per cent; between 1930 and 1940 the average rate was only 0.9 per cent, and in only one year was the rate as high as four per cent (Table 43). When it is considered that account-

---

[36] This is not strictly true for all sellers in all territories. Some brands can sell at slightly higher prices in areas where they have been long established, but may sell at slightly lower prices in others; local producers can sometimes sell at higher prices because of the good will they built up during the depression by giving reliable farmers unlimited credit, and many farmers still select fertilizers by the "picture on the bag" instead of by the cost per unit of plant nutrient.

[37] The dealer's abuse of a bargaining position made possible through his first-hand knowledge of local conditions gave rise to an increased use of agents and producer-owned outlets in the Thirties. Before NRA, dealers frequently played one producer against the other in order to reduce the required remittance per ton, although they may not have reduced prices to farmers (OPA Records G, *The Fertilizer Industry*, National Archives, pp. 188 ff).

[38] Cf. Herbert Willett, *Fertilizer Prices and Price Indexes* (Washington: National Fertilizer Association, 1937; rev. ed., 1938 and 1941). Willett uses U. S. Bureau of Labor Statistics data. For postwar fertilizer prices paid by farmers, see *Agricultural Prices*, a monthly publication of the Bureau of Agricultural Economics, U. S. Dept. of Agriculture.

TABLE 43

RATES OF RETURN FOR CORPORATIONS IN THE
MANUFACTURED FERTILIZER INDUSTRY, BEFORE FEDERAL
INCOME TAXES, 1930-43.[a]

| Year | Rate of Return[b] | Year | Rate of Return[b] |
|------|-------------------|------|-------------------|
| 1930 | 0.7 | 1937 | 3.7 |
| 1931 | −4.4 | 1938 | 2.9 |
| 1932 | −4.2 | 1939 | 3.3 |
| 1933 | −1.2 | 1940 | 4.5 |
| 1934 | 2.2 | 1941 | 8.6 |
| 1935 | 2.2 | 1942 | 10.8 |
| 1936 | 4.2 | 1943 | 10.7 |

[a] Internal Revenue Service (formerly the Bureau of Internal Revenue).
[b] Net income as per cent of total assets.

ing profits make no allowance for imputed interest, it is quite evident that economic profits in the fertilizer industry for the decade of the 1930's were negative.

With the outbreak of World War II, demand for fertilizer increased and available supplies were rationed. Farmers purchased their fertilizer whenever it was made available to them and thereby spread demand much more evenly throughout the year. And between 1939 and 1947 the number of mixing plants in the United States declined from 764 to 704. With about twenty per cent of the excess capacity removed and operations adjusted to a more uniform monthly rate of output, profits rose. The annual average rate of return on total assets in the industry for the period 1940-43 was 8.6 per cent, considerably above the rate earned in the 1930's, but still only sixty-two per cent of the average annual rate of return earned by all manufacturing for the same four-year period.[39]

Probably the best evidence that strong competitive forces regulate fertilizer prices is the frequent attempts on the part of producers to circumvent them. As early as 1906 the Department of Justice charged the Virginia-Carolina Chemical Company and sixty other large fertilizer concerns with cartelizing the domestic fertilizer industry through a Canadian corporation.[40] In 1926, eight large fertilizer producers and certain individuals were charged in a criminal action with violating the anti-trust laws.[41] The thirty-seven defendants pleaded *nolo contendere* and were fined $95,000. In 1935 certain fertilizer producers, through the agency of the National Fertilizer Association, sought the Federal Trade Commission's approval of a code containing the open-pricing provisions which had enabled them to control price cutting under the NRA

[39] The rates of return before taxes on total assets for all manufacturing were as follows:

| 1940 | 8.8% | 1942 | 16.1% |
|------|------|------|-------|
| 1941 | 14.7% | 1943 | 17.3% |

(Internal Revenue Service [formerly the Bureau of Internal Revenue] *Source book* [unpublished], 1930-43.)

[40] *U. S. v. Virginia-Carolina Chemical Co.*, 163 Fed. 66 (C. C. M. Tenn. 1908).

[41] Arthur R. Burns, *Decline of Competition* (New York: McGraw-Hill, 1936), pp. 297-98.

Code of Fair Competition. The Commission did not approve the code, but suggested instead an alternative method of open pricing which the association considered too costly and too ineffective to adopt.

In 1941 the Department of Justice through a Grand Jury proceeding obtained an indictment charging sixty-nine corporations, the National Fertilizer Association, the Superphosphate Association, and thirty-six officials of the various companies and trade associations with having violated the anti-trust laws on 109 counts between the years 1927 and 1940.[42] Following the indictment, pleas of *nolo contendere* by the majority of the defendants resulted in fines amounting to $259,852.

Finally, in 1950 the Federal Trade Commission made public the results of another study of the fertilizer industry. The Commission in summarizing the industry's history stated that:

> The fertilizer cases . . . go no farther than to make it clear that concerted action to fix prices and restrain competition within the framework of distribution in use before 1940 was unlawful. Whether successful legal attack upon these specific methods and practices will serve in the future as an adequate warning against concerted action . . . cannot be stated with assurance. The most that can be said is that the outcome of these cases was a step in the direction of freeing competition in the fertilizer industry of some, but not necessarily from all, undue restraints.[43]

While the Commission does not explicitly state that in the absence of concerted action price behavior in the fertilizer industry is consistent with competitive pricing, it attributes most demonstrable departures from competitive pricing to concerted action. The foregoing appraisal leads to the same conclusion.

### D. THE FERTILIZER INDUSTRY AND DYNAMIC COMPETITION

Although competition in a particular market is often judged to be present or absent almost entirely on a basis of market structure and price behavior, competition embraces other phenomena as well. The equation of prices and costs—marginal costs in the short-run and average costs in the long-run—are static equilibrium concepts. The dynamic forces of competition, however, tend to destroy equilibrium rather than to create it. These are the forces usually associated with the creative entrepreneurship that constantly seeks to improve the techniques for producing a given product or to improve the product itself. In short, competitive equilibrium analysis is concerned with forces of adjustment to given data, whereas dynamic competition, as an allocative process, is concerned with progress, or with changes in the data themselves.

---

[42] *U. S. v. National Fertilizer Association,* U. S. District Court for the Middle District of North Carolina, Indictment No. 1167, returned February 10, 1941. In essence the associations were charged with having continued to operate for their members the NRA code after it had been declared illegal.
[43] FTC, *Report on The Fertilizer Industry,* p. 146.

Competition in fertilizer manufacturing conforms more to the static than the dynamic model. Except for those periods in the industry's history when producers were organized for collusive action, competition from the standpoint of structure and price behavior has been much in evidence. Sellers have been numerous; prices have rarely exceeded accounting costs by more than a slim margin; and profit rates have been low. In comparison with most manufacturing industries, however, and particularly in comparison with the chemical industry, of which it is a part, the fertilizer industry has been a static one. In fact, enterpreneurs apparently have not merely failed to innovate, they have even failed to transmit to buyers the benefits of creative enterprise in industries that supply their raw materials. For example, as late as 1910 the fertilizer industry relied heavily on such raw materials as cottonseed meal, castor pomace, animal tankage, fish scrap, low-grade potash salts, and twelve to sixteen per cent superphosphate. Almost any balanced combination of such materials yielded a mixed fertilizer containing a maximum of about fifteen per cent plant nutrients. The average plant nutrient content of mixed fertilizers in 1910 was 14.8 per cent (Table 44). Over the past forty years, however, the chemical industries have developed fertilizer materials having from four to ten times the plant nutrient content of those used in 1910. Chemical nitrogenous materials containing up to 82 per cent plant nutrients have replaced low-analysis organic sources of nitrogen. Kainite and manure salts containing twenty per cent potash, which were once the chief sources of potash for the fertilizer industry, have since 1920 been gradually replaced by sixty per cent muriate of potash. In 1910 superphosphate containing from twelve to sixteen per cent $P_2O_5$ was the chief source of phosphorus; over the past forty years the $P_2O_5$ content of superphosphate has increased to twenty per cent, and the production of concentrated superphosphate containing as much as fifty per cent $P_2O_5$ has greatly increased. While these substantial increases in plant-nutrient content were being registered in industries furnishing fertilizer materials, the average plant-nutrient content of mixed fertilizers increased from 14.8 per cent to only 21.6 per cent (Table 44).

With the development of such new materials plant-nutrient costs to fertilizer manufacturers declined substantially. Between 1925 and 1941 the wholesale price of a unit of N in natural organics declined from $4.95 to $4.10, and in sodium nitrate from $3.30 to $1.70, but by 1941 the expanding synthetic-ammonia industry had reduced the wholesale price of a unit of N in ammonia solutions to $1.15.[44] The wholesale price of muriate of potash declined from $34.65 to $28.53 per ton, or by

[44] U. S. Dept. of Agriculture, *Fertilizers and Lime in the United States*, Mis. Publication 586, 1946, p. 89.

TABLE 44

UNITED STATES CONSUMPTION OF COMMERCIAL
FERTILIZER MATERIALS, 1910-45 [a]

(1,000 Tons)

| Material | 1910 | 1920 | 1930 | 1940 | 1942 | 1945 |
|---|---|---|---|---|---|---|
| Chemical Nitrogen | | | | | | |
| Ammonia and solutions..... | | | 66 | 150 | 123 | 327 |
| Ammonium nitrate......... | | | | | | 271 |
| Ammonium sulphate........ | 135 | 373 | 611 | 652 | 830 | 964 |
| Calcium cyanamide........ | 3 | 18 | 94 | 80 | 90 | 118 |
| Sodium nitrate........... | 224 | 298 | 586 | 760 | 644 | 1,084 |
| Other nitrates............ | | 18 | 62 | 59 | 15 | 1 |
| Other chemical N........ | | | 18 | 79 | 20 | 110 |
| Organics | | | | | | |
| Castor pomace............ | 17 | 23 | 40 | 65 | 85 | 80 |
| Cottonseed meal........... | 444 | 447 | 205 | 115 | 68 | 60 |
| Fish scrap.............. | 90 | 110 | 74 | 34 | 12 | 11 |
| Guano and manures....... | 39 | 57 | 145 | 32 | 44 | 169 |
| Sludge, activated......... | | | 32 | 64 | 108 | 93 |
| Sludge, other............ | 2 | | 8 | 40 | 45 | 55 |
| Tankage, animal.......... | 226 | 209 | 68 | 60 | 15 | 10 |
| Tankage, garbage......... | 119 | 139 | 74 | 20 | 17 | 15 |
| Tankage, process.......... | 3 | 20 | 129 | 93 | 112 | 88 |
| Other organics........... | 64 | 53 | 42 | 43 | 41 | 25 |
| Phosphates | | | | | | |
| Ammonium phosphates..... | | 20 | 48 | 67 | 57 | 91 |
| Base goods, wet-mixed..... | 298 | 377 | 167 | 136 | 124 | 35 |
| Basic slag, open-hearth..... | 25 | 10 | 24 | 55 | 70 | 175 |
| Bone meal.............. | 139 | 170 | 94 | 55 | 33 | 20 |
| Superphosphate, double..... | 10 | 18 | 92 | 339 | 230 | 180 |
| Superphosphate, normal.... | 2,558 | 3,020 | 3,751 | 3,438 | 4,855 | 6,582 |
| Other phosphates.......... | 1 | 20 | 18 | 14 | 13 | 11 |
| Potash | | | | | | |
| Cotton-hull ashes.......... | 2 | 1 | 2 | 15 | 3 | 5 |
| Kainite, 20%......... | 447 | 414 | 124 | | | |
| Manure salts, 20%........ | 116 | 332 | 370 | 34 | | |
| Manure salts, 25%........ | | | | 10 | 154 | 136 |
| Manure salts, 30%........ | 15 | 15 | 30 | 8 | | 1 |
| Muriate of potash, 50%..... | 137 | 135 | 286 | 134 | 74 | 110 |
| Muriate of potash, 60%..... | | | 49 | 490 | 685 | 990 |
| Sulphates............... | 55 | 20 | 94 | 69 | 96 | 121 |
| Tobacco stems............ | 56 | 70 | 79 | 95 | 103 | 115 |
| Other potash............. | 86 | 120 | 18 | 20 | 18 | 18 |
| Miscellaneous | | | | | | |
| Gypsum................ | | | | 100 | 140 | 425 |
| Limestone and dolomite..... | 30 | 46 | 79 | 331 | 376 | 503 |
| Magnesia............... | | | | 4 | 4 | 9 |
| Other mg. materials........ | | | | 9 | 9 | 14 |
| Minor element............ | | | 2 | 21 | 31 | 75 |
| Nitrophoska, etc........... | | 5 | 13 | 2 | | |
| Peat, humus, and peanut hulls | 37 | 63 | 54 | 80 | 75 | 70 |
| Phosphate rock........... | | 2 | 39 | 156 | 240 | 477 |
| Other filler............. | 257 | 631 | 720 | 628 | 672 | 671 |
| Total filler material........ | 324 | 747 | 907 | 1,331 | 1,547 | 2,244 |
| TOTAL.............. | 5,635 | 7,254 | 8,407 | 8,656 | 10,331 | 14,315 |
| Per cent filler of total material.................. | 5.7 | 10.3 | 10.8 | 15.4 | 15.0 | 15.7 |
| Avg. plant nutrient content of mixed fertilizer....... | 14.80 | 13.90 | 17.90 | 19.74 | 20.0 | 21.6 |

[a] A. L. Mehring, *The American Fertilizer*, March 8, 1947.

eighteen per cent; but because of increases in its $K_2O$ content the price per unit of $K_2O$ declined from $0.62 to $0.47, or by twenty-four per cent.[45] Between 1925 and 1941 the price per unit of $P_2O_5$ in ordinary superphosphate declined by ten per cent, partly because superphosphate prices declined and partly because its $P_2O_5$ content increased. Greater reduction in $P_2O_5$ costs came with the expansion in concentrated super-phosphate production after 1945.

Entrepreneurs in the fertilizer industry have not overlooked the newer and more economical sources of plant nutrients for their fertilizer man-ufacturing operations. On the contrary, as the data (Table 44) demon-strate, they have substituted them for the older low-analysis ones on a large scale. In doing so they have reduced the price of fertilizer. Between 1925 and 1941 the average price paid by farmers for mixed fertilizers declined from $29.72 to $27.82 per ton, and from $1.86 to $1.43 per unit of plant nutrient.[46] But they have not transmitted the economic gains from technological progress by introducing and promoting the high-analysis fertilizers which they could produce and sell at lower costs per unit of plant nutrient. The plant-nutrient content of mixed fertilizers, largely because of the use of unnecessary diluents, has not increased nearly so rapidly as that of the materials from which the mixtures are made. Why they have not marketed the more economical fertilizers raises an old and complex issue, most often summed up in the simple query, "Why is there so much sand in the farmers' fertilizers?" This is the issue to which positive policy, as distinct from anti-trust policy, is addressed. The material markets—phosphate rock, sulphur, potash, and nitrogen— have been characterized by high concentration and substantial monopoly restraints. But through innovations producers of materials have sub-stantially reduced the real costs of production per unit of N, $P_2O_5$, and $K_2O$. The cost reductions have led in turn to significant price reductions per unit of plant nutrient to fertilizer manufacturers who have shifted to the new low-cost materials as they became available. The principal barriers to efficient resource allocation in these markets, where material producers are sellers and fertilizer manufacturers are buyers, are mo-nopolistic restraints. The principal remedies therefore lie in anti-trust policy. In contrast, manufactured-fertilizer markets have been character-ized by low concentration and fairly effective price competition. But in these markets, where fertilizer manufacturers and distributors are sellers and farmers are buyers, cost-reducing product and process innovations have proceeded slowly—so slowly that the fertilizers marketed have failed to keep pace with improvements in the materials from which they are

[45] Samuel P. Hayes, Jr. "Potash Prices and Competition," *Quarterly Journal of Economics*, LVI (November, 1942) p. 33.
[46] Willett, *op. cit.*

made. The problem of inefficient resource allocation in the fertilizer manufacturing industry, however, lies beyond the reach of anti-trust policy. The industry comprises over a thousand entrepreneurs, who can scarcely have conspired to retard innovation. Product improvement can be initiated successfully only when consumers buy intelligently. Farmers, it is often asserted, have been reluctant to substitute more efficient for less efficient fertilizers, even when available. The farmer's refusal to buy high-analysis fertilizers blocks the incentive to make them. The anti-trust laws cannot solve this problem. Public policy has accordingly been directed toward remedies of a different sort, not the least of which has been the partial socialization of the entrepreneural function in both the production and purchasing of fertilizers. Such remedies make up positive policy— a topic given considerable attention from this point on.

# Part V

## MARKET IMPERFECTIONS: THEIR MEASUREMENT AND THEIR POLICY IMPLICATIONS

# CHAPTER 9

# THE SOCIAL COSTS OF MONOPOLY AND THE ROLE OF ANTI-TRUST

THE prices farmers pay for plant nutrients depend in part on the effectiveness of competition. Monopolistic restraints in the nitrogen, phosphate rock, sulphur, and potash markets have raised the cost of manufactured fertilizers, and hence their prices, above the competitive level. But the farmer's fertilizer costs also depend on the rationality with which they buy the kinds and grades of fertilizers available in the market. In the 1952-53 fertilizer season farmers purchased 23.4 million tons of fertilizers —15.7 million tons as mixtures and 7.7 million tons as straight materials— containing 1.6 million tons of N, 2.3 million tons of available $P_2O_5$, and 1.7 million tons of $K_2O$. The tonnage sold as mixed fertilizers represented nearly 1,500 different grades, 177 of which accounted for 97.5 per cent of all mixtures.[1] Grades ranged from a 4-6-5 mixture containing only fifteen per cent plant nutrients to a 6-24-24 mixture containing fifty-four per cent plant nutrients. The prices farmers paid for a desired quantity of plant nutrients were materially affected by the types and grades of fertilizer they bought. Farmers buy fertilizers as productive agents and solely for their plant-nutrient content. They can therefore be said to buy irrationally when they buy fertilizers which do not yield the desired quantities of plant nutrients at the lowest possible cost. Since monopolistic restraints and irrational demand require different public policies, estimates of their social costs indicate the task confronting each policy—anti-trust in the case of monopolistic restraints and positive fertilizer policy in the case of irrational farmer demand.

## A. THE SOCIAL COSTS OF MONOPOLISTIC RESTRAINTS

Most of the monopoly element in fertilizer prices can be traced to the primary-material markets. The phosphate-rock, sulphur, nitrogen, and potash industries have all been characterized by a high order of oligopoly and by agreements in restraint of trade. These in turn have led to rates of return above those consistent with effective competition. From 1919 to 1951, individual sulphur producers earned rates averaging from nearly fourteen per cent up to twenty-five per cent; the industry as a whole averaged about twenty per cent (Table 19, p. 81). From 1936 to 1951,

[1] U. S. Dept. of Agriculture, Fertilizer and Agricultural Lime Section, Agricultural Research Service, *Commercial Fertilizers Consumption in the United States, 1952-53*, p. 2.

individual potash producers averaged from over nine per cent to thirty-four per cent (Table 23, p. 95). From 1937 to 1946 the phosphate-rock industry earned an average rate of 11.3 per cent, and in some years earned up to seventeen per cent (Table 31, p. 125). Profits of nitrogen producers are not available, but they have probably been above the competitive level. In comparison, producers of manufactured fertilizers, who buy these primary materials and sell them as mixtures or as straight materials to farmers, have earned low rates of return. Accordingly, the source of most of the social costs of monopoly in the fertilizer industry is the primary-material markets, where mining and chemical companies are sellers and fertilizer manufacturers and distributors are buyers.

While profits may not measure the social costs of monopoly with a high degree of accuracy, they are generally the only empirical data available from which such costs can be estimated.[2] Profits reported on company income statements usually are a composite of imputed interest on capital, monopoly returns, frictional gains, the rents of scarce capital resources, and the rewards of innovation. The portion that is imputed interest may possibly be estimated from long-term interest rates; for long periods of time frictional losses tend to offset frictional gains; and for most anti-trust issues it may be unnecessary to distinguish between the rents of scarce capital and monopoly profits. But no ready means exist for solving, or avoiding, the problem of measuring the rewards of innovation. The use of profits as a measure of the social costs of monopoly in the production of fertilizer materials raises these methodological problems. Sulphur, potash, and phosphate-rock producers exploit deposits which new entrants cannot duplicate. The profits they report probably include significant economic rents.[3] On the other hand, much of the technology nitrogen, potash, and phosphate-rock producers use was developed by the government. Hence, only a small portion of the profits they report can be regarded as rewards for private entrepreneural innovation. Appropriate adjustments for imputed interest and frictional gains and losses are about as difficult for the fertilizer-material industries as for other industries.

The particular profit data available on producers of fertilizer materials are superior in certain respects to profit data generally; in others they are inferior. Most large corporations are multi-products firms and usually do not report separately the profits they earn on each product. Profits earned on domestic sulphur, phosphate rock, and potash operations are available from the records of various anti-trust proceedings. But while they are

---

[2] See Joe S. Bain, "The Profit Rate as a Measure of Monopoly Power," *Quarterly Journal of Economics,* LV (February, 1941) 271-93; Fritz Machlup, *The Political Economy of Monopoly: Business, Labor and Government Policies* (Baltimore: The Johns Hopkins University Press, 1952) Chap. 12; and *Report of Attorney General's National Committee to Study the Anti-trust Laws* (March 31, 1955), pp. 323-24.

[3] This is probably true for potash companies, even though they operate almost entirely in the public domain and pay royalties to the government on the potash they recover.

available on a segregated basis, they are confined to the time period considered relevant for such proceedings. Profits on nitrogen are not reported separately by the multi-product chemical firms that produce it, and are not available from other sources. They can be estimated only by assuming that the profit per dollar of nitrogen sales on the average is approximately equal to that for sulphur, phosphate-rock, and potash sales. The profits earned by foreign potash and nitrogen companies on their exports to the United States cannot be ascertained.

For these reasons the monopoly profits earned by fertilizer-material producers cannot be calculated with slide-rule accuracy. For the purpose of indicating the respective roles of anti-trust and positive policy, however, it is doubtful that such accurate calculations would be much superior to reasonable estimates. For the period 1938-46 the profits sulphur, phosphate-rock, potash, and nitrogen producers earned per year on sales to domestic fertilizer manufacturers and distributors ranged from $13.7 million in the recession year of 1938 to $23.2 million in the highly profitable postwar year of 1946 (Table 45). Annual profits for the nine-

TABLE 45

PROFITS EARNED ON SULPHUR, POTASH, NITROGEN, AND PHOSPHATE-ROCK SALES TO THE FERTILIZER INDUSTRY, 1938-46 [a]

(Millions of Dollars)

| | Total Profits (Fertilizer and Non-Fertilizer Sales) | | | Total Profits on Sales to Domestic [b] Fertilizer Industry | Estimated Profits on Fertilizer Nitrogen Sales [c] | Estimated Profits on Sale of All Fertilizer Materials |
|---|---|---|---|---|---|---|
| | Sulphur | Potash | Phosphate Rock | | | |
| 1938 | $10.3 | $4.5 | $2.0 | $8.2 | $5.5 | $13.7 |
| 1939 | 12.2 | 5.1 | 1.5 | 8.9 | 5.9 | 14.8 |
| 1940 | 14.4 | 4.9 | 1.1 | 8.8 | 5.9 | 14.7 |
| 1941 | 16.6 | 4.2 | 1.1 | 8.6 | 5.7 | 14.3 |
| 1942 | 15.9 | 4.5 | .... | .... | .... | .... |
| 1943 | 17.8 | 4.5 | 1.4 | 9.4 | 6.3 | 15.7 |
| 1944 | 20.9 | 5.1 | 1.4 | 10.7 | 7.1 | 17.8 |
| 1945 | 23.5 | 4.6 | 1.8 | 11.1 | 7.4 | 18.5 |
| 1946 | 26.4 | 6.2 | 2.4 | 13.9 | 9.3 | 23.2 |

[a] *Moody's Manual of Industrial Investments*, New York, 1939-47 issues; FTC, *Report on the Sulphur Industry and International Cartels* (1947) pp. 31, 38, 41; FTC, *Report on International Phosphate Cartels* (1946) pp. 59-60; and files of the Federal Trade Commission.
[b] Adjusted for the portion of total output entering the fertilizer industry: 20 per cent in the case of sulphur, 96 per cent in the case of potash, and 80 per cent in the case of phosphate rock.
[c] Based on ratio of fertilizer-nitrogen sales to total fertilizer-material sales in the 1944-45 season. In 1944-45 total material sales amounted to about $240,000,000 and nitrogen sales to about $96,000,000. Since nitrogen sales accounted for 40 per cent of total sales, the fertilizer-nitrogen profits are estimated at 40 per cent of total profits made in the sale of all materials.

year period averaged about $16,000,000 and tended, in the prewar and war years alike, to cluster around $15,000,000. Over the same period sulphur producers earned an average rate of return of about eighteen per cent, potash producers about twenty per cent, and phosphate-rock producers about 8.3 per cent. The weighted average rate is nearly three times the five to six per cent usually considered to be the "normal" or competitive rate of return, and about four times the average long-term interest rate for the same period. Accordingly, for the period 1938-46, it can be reasonably concluded that monopoly profits amounted to from two-thirds to three-fourths of the total profits earned by producers of fertilizer materials, or to about $12,000,000 per year. This amounted to only 2.5 per cent of the $500,000,000 total expenditures on fertilizers in 1946, the last year for which monopoly profits can be estimated.

That $12,000,000 represents only a rough estimate of the annual monopoly returns to producers of fertilizer materials does not seriously handicap an analysis of the role of monopoly. As will be shown later, a sizable error in the statistical estimate would not materially alter the essential policy conclusions. A more crucial question is the extent to which the estimated monopoly returns reflect the social costs of monopoly in the manufacture and distribution of fertilizers and, in turn, indicate the task confronting anti-trust policy. Its answer is more a matter of judgment than of quantitative statistical refinement, and must be based on consideration of those factors which may cause a divergence between monopoly as measured in terms of abnormal profits and monopoly in contravention of the anti-trust laws.

In several respects the calculated average annual monopoly profits of $12,000,000 may understate the annual social costs of monopoly. First, they indicate only the costs of monopoly for those quantities of materials fertilizer manufacturers purchased at prices above the competitive level. Had prices been more competitive, fertilizer manufacturers and distributors presumably would have purchased them in larger quantities. Since the price elasticity of farmers' demand for fertilizers is estimated to be close to unity,[4] it follows that at lower prices manufacturers and distributors would have purchased the larger quantities of materials at a somewhat smaller total cost. Fertilizer material costs account for a large portion—but not all—of the price farmers pay for fertilizer. There are no substitutes for these materials. The derived demand for fertilizer materials therefore has a price elasticity of less than unity. Hence, at competitive prices fertilizer manufacturers and distributors would have acquired slightly larger quantities of materials, and at a slightly lower total cost than they incurred at higher prices. For this reason the calculated monopoly profits of $12,000,000 probably understate the social costs of monopoly in the fertilizer industry. Second, monopoly may exact a cost from society which does not reflect in monopoly profits. In calculating monopoly profits the sulphur, potash, phosphate-rock, and nitrogen industries were included because structurally they conformed to the model of oligopoly; they earned abnormally high rates of return; and

[4] *Supra*, pp. 144-45.

they have successfully pursued monopolistic practices. By using the same criteria, manufacturers and distributors of fertilizers, even those integrated with the phosphate-rock industry, were excluded. They have been numerous, have earned a rate of return substantially below that earned by industry generally, and their attempts at circumventing competition apparently have met with little success. Some of the monopolistic practices pursued by fertilizer material producers may have retarded cost-reducing innovations, affected the quantities produced of various materials, or have had other results which exacted a cost from society which did not reflect in monopoly earnings. Similarly, the attempts by fertilizer manufacturers and distributors to mitigate the forces of competition may have cost society something even though they were generally unsuccessful.

On the other hand, the calculated monopoly earnings may tend to overstate the annual social costs within the reach of anti-trust policy. First, while much of the technology used by producers of fertilizer materials were developed by the government, the producers themselves developed some of it. A portion, although probably small, of the abnormal earnings should be regarded as a reward for developing and introducing more efficient productive processes. Second, and more important, the objective of the anti-trust laws is not to reduce all abnormal earnings to the competitive level but rather to eliminate unreasonable restraints of trade and unreasonable monopoly. As was pointed out earlier, they have already been used effectively to this end; and as will be pointed out later, the monopoly that remains, irrespective of the amount of abnormal profits it earns, may well fall within the limit the anti-trust laws tolerate.

All these factors considered, it would appear that the social costs of monopoly in the fertilizer industry has exceeded the $12,000,000 abnormal profits earned annually by the producers of fertilizer materials. This follows from the virtual certainty that had materials been priced at the competitive level, fertilizer manufacturers would have been able to buy greater quantities of them at a smaller total cost than they incurred at the higher price, and from the probability that all the social costs of monopoly cannot be measured in terms of abnormal profits. These factors appear to outweigh the possibility that a portion of the profits in excess of a competitive return may reasonably be considered a reward for private innovation. It is evident, however, that the social costs of monopoly, by whatever amount they may exceed $12,000,000, overstates the task of anti-trust policy. Such costs would appear to fall somewhere between 2.5 per cent and five per cent of the nation's total expenditures on fertilizers; the amount that comes under the purview of the anti-trust laws would be less. But the apparent smallness of the amount does not mean that a review of the specific issues anti-trust confronts in the fertilizer industry is any less necessary; it may well suggest that the anti-trust laws have been, and continue to be, effective, and, therefore, all the more essential to a sound total fertilizer policy.

## B. THE ROLE OF ANTI-TRUST

The fertilizer industry raises two basic anti-trust issues, oligopoly and business practices in restraint of trade. Each has tended to strengthen the other. The phosphate-rock, sulphur, potash, and nitrogen industries, which sell the primary materials to fertilizer manufacturers and distributors, are oligopolies. In each of these industries agreements in restraint of trade apparently have effectively restrained competition. Fertilizer manufacturers and distributors, who buy from material producers and sell to farmers, are numerous. Their agreements in restraint of trade apparently have been relatively ineffective. The basic anti-trust issues are most clearly raised by the material-producing industries.

*Agreements in Restraint of Trade.* From 1923 to 1946 virtually all domestic phosphate-rock producers were bound together through the Phosphate Export Association and the Hard Rock Export Association. The associations entered into cartel agreements with foreign rock producers under which phosphate rock sold in international markets at fixed prices and quotas subject to a system of fines and penalties. Stabilized domestic rock prices and restrictions on domestic sales became by-products of the cartel agreements. Rock prices in the United States were stable between 1927, when the associations became strong, and 1946, when PEA was dissolved and the activities of Hardphos circumscribed. The associations encouraged other noncompetitive practices in the domestic market, the most important of which were exclusive licensing of the flotation-recovery process and restricting the use of Fernandina Terminal to Hardphos members.

Federal Trade Commission proceedings against PEA and Hardphos produced evidence that the associations priced phosphate rock consistent with a policy of multi-market price discrimination. In some foreign markets prices were higher than those on corresponding grades of rock in the United States; in others they were considerably lower. Whether multi-market price discrimination made for higher or lower domestic rock prices generally than would otherwise have prevailed cannot be determined. But it is clear that domestic prices, except for several weeks in 1935 when a domestic price war raged, reflected world-wide monopolistic pricing.

The Federal Trade Commission's recommendations and order to PEA and Hardphos pursuant to the proceedings identify the associations' general anti-competitive activities at issue. The Commission recommended that PEA rescind all cartel agreements and cancel all by-laws, rules, agreements, and understandings which restricted imports of phosphate rock into the United States, the rights of members to withdraw from PEA, the licensing of any patent used in mining or processing Florida pebble rock, or which restricted the sale of phosphate deposits. The Commission ordered PEA to cease and desist from entering into understandings which restricted the production, potential production, or marketing of pebble rock, and from agreeing on terms used by members in domestic-sales contracts. The Commission recommended that Hardphos and its members rescind all agreements which restricted the use of Fernandina Terminal facilities, which related to rock shipments by any other common carriers, or which provided that members' hard-rock domestic sales and non-members' hard-rock sales in Europe be deducted from Hardphos members' European quotas. PEA complied with the Federal Trade Commission's recommendations and order by dissolving itself; Hardphos, by submitting the required letter of compliance.

In 1922 the three leading United States sulphur producers formed the Sulphur Export Corporation (Sulexco), which immediately entered into an agreement with Sicilian sulphur interests to arrest declining world sulphur prices. Between 1922 and 1952, when it voluntarily dissolved itself, Sulexco participated in international cartel agreements which established prices and quotas and a system of fines and penalties on sulphur exports. It agreed with foreign producers to maintain the sulphur mining and manufacturing industry "as it at present exists," and toward this end tried to control patents on the recovery of sulphur from pyrites. Sulexco and non-member United States producers agreed not to compete with each other in the sulphur export trade, and Sulexco obligated itself to apply nonmember exports against its quota in foreign markets. When its members' customers found it profitable to buy sulphur in the United States and sell it abroad, Sulexco proposed to place its members under agreement not to sell sulphur to customers in excess of their domestic needs. It abandoned the proposal on the advice of the Federal Trade Commission. Sulexco succeeded in stabilizing natural and manufactured sulphur prices in the United States, and through agreements with foreign producers succeeded in increasing prices abroad.

In 1947 the Federal Trade Commission, following a proceeding against Sulexco under the Export Trade Act, recommended that Sulexco refrain from entering into agreements with domestic or foreign producers restricting the sale of sulphur, from acquiring or controlling patents used to manufacture and process sulphur, and from entering into any agreement or understanding to maintain the *status quo* in the sulphur industry. In its subsequent *Report on the Sulphur Industry and International Cartels* the Commission concluded that the two big sulphur companies, which controlled about ninety per cent of the output of domestic natural sulphur, possessed dominant market power over the sulphur industry which made their domestic and foreign sales activities inseparable. Their market power, co-ordinated through Sulexco, had been exerted to maintain artificially high export prices and stable domestic prices, and to retard the development of sulphur manufacture from pyrites. When Sulexco voluntarily dissolved itself in 1952, the formal organization for controlling the sulphur industry disappeared; the informal organization of conjectural interdependence associated with a four-firm oligopoly probably still exists.

The domestic potash industry dates its beginning with World War I. Before the war fertilizer manufacturers purchased nearly all their potash from the German potash cartel. Until the late 1930's they continued to purchase more than half their potash supplies from N.V. Potash Export My., a sales agency of the French-German potash cartel. The dominant supplier of potash until World War II therefore was not subject to the United States anti-trust laws.[5]

As each new domestic producer entered the market, it adopted the prices the cartel quoted at Atlantic and Gulf ports. Since the ocean-freight charge from European shipping points to United States ports in the 1930's was only about half the rail charge from Carlsbad or Searles Lake to the heavy fertilizer-consuming regions near the Atlantic and the Gulf, most of the potash market was in the cartel's freight-advantage area. But while this may explain why the four domestic producers adopted the cartel's prices, it made the practice no less inconsistent with competitive pricing. Under the multiple-basing-point system of pricing used, the greater the distance domestic producers shipped their potash, the lower the delivered price they charged. Prices at various delivery points bore no resemblance to competitive production costs plus transportation.

The pricing system did not arise altogether spontaneously. The cartel and the three domestic firms then operating collaborated in writing the NRA potash code. In 1935, coinciding with the Supreme Court's invalidation of NRA, the same three domestic producers and the cartel formed the American Potash Institute to promote potash through collective action. And as early as 1932 one domestic producer had entered into an exclusive sales contract with the cartel's Far East sales agency in exchange for an assurance of thirty per cent of the potash sales the agency made in Japan, Korea, and Formosa.

---

[5] In 1929 the Department of Justice brought action against the cartel's Potash Importing Company, a domestic corporation, under the Sherman Act (supra, pp. 86-87.). The action resulted only in a shift of Potash Importing Company's business to N. V. Potash Export My., a Netherlands corporation also owned by the cartel.

In 1939 a Grand Jury indicted the three domestic producers and N.V. Potash Export My. on charges of conspiracy to fix and maintain potash prices and eliminate competition, and to dominate and monopolize the production and distribution of potash. The Department of Justice later substituted a civil complaint for the criminal indictment, which was settled by a consent decree permanently enjoining the three United States firms from agreeing, combining, or conspiring among themselves or with any other potash producer to fix prices, from quoting prices only on the basis of c.i.f. recognized ports, and from refusing to sell potash to buyers not approved by all defendants. Thus, in 1940, action under the anti-trust laws effectively modified a basing-point system which had prevailed for two decades. The last vestiges of the system were discarded in 1949 when domestic producers began quoting only f.o.b. mine prices. But while anti-trust policy has eliminated the formal price-fixing arrangement, it is still confronted with the problem of a four-firm oligopoly.

Until World War I fertilizer manufacturers purchased most of their nitrogen, as they did their potash, from foreign cartels outside the jurisdiction of the United States anti-trust laws, principally sodium nitrate from the Chilean nitrate cartel. Expanded munitions production in World War I left most industrially developed countries, especially Germany, with excess by-product and synthetic nitrogen capacity. In the 1920's other nations intent on self-sufficiency developed their own nitrogen industries. Meanwhile, significant technological progress increased the capacity of old plants and lead to the construction of new ones. In the scramble for markets United States nitrogen prices by 1932 had declined to about one-fourth of their 1920 level. In the 1920's nitrogen prices reflected vigorous competition. The market place held the role of anti-trust to a minimum.

But outside the United States vigorous competition lead to vigorous cartel activity to check declining prices. In 1931, ninety-five per cent of the Chilean industry was reorganized under Cosach. In Germany the three major producing groups—by-product ammonia, synthetic ammonia, and cyanamide producers—organized under the German Nitrogen Syndicate. In Great Britain the industry was already highly concentrated. Led by German interests the major nitrogen producers outside the United States soon were organized as an international nitrogen cartel, allocating markets and setting prices by collective action.

The United States produced and consumed large quantities of nitrogen; arbitrage linked its market to those of other countries. The success of the international cartel therefore depended on the co-operation of United States producers. For nitrogen this was more difficult than it had been for potash. The two main branches of the United States chemical nitrogen industry were by-product and synthetic nitrogen. Neither comprised so few producers or was so highly concentrated as the potash industry, although du Pont and Allied Chemical & Dye accounted for nearly ninety per cent of the output of synthetic nitrogen.

The problems of organization apparently were solved. In 1939 the Department of Justice obtained five Federal Grand Jury indictments under the Sherman Act against the major nitrogen producers. The alleged anti-trust violations included: (1) agreements between the Barrett Company, a wholly owned subsidiary of Allied Chemical & Dye, and domestic by-product-nitrogen producers to fix prices on by-product-nitrogen; (2) agreements between Chilean nitrate producers and Allied Chemical & Dye and its subsidiaries to fix prices on nitrate of soda and indirectly on other nitrogen; (3) agreements between German producers and du Pont, Allied Chemical & Dye, and the Barrett Company to fix prices on synthetic nitrogen and indirectly on natural nitrates; and (4) agreements between Imperial Chemical Industries, Ltd., and United States producers to fix prices on synthetic-nitrogen products and indirectly on natural nitrates. All five indictments were *nolle pros.,* and the three civil complaints later substituted for them were settled by consent decrees. In sum, the voluminous injunctive provisions enjoined the defendants from entering into agreements to fix prices and other terms of sale, from refusing to sell f.o.b. at any port or point of production where defendants usually had nitrogen available, and from restricting exports and imports.

In the 1930's nitrogen prices were not set by the free interplay of competitive forces. Whether anti-trust alone would have made competition effective will never be known. The effects of the anti-trust actions were engulfed in the extraordinary wartime and postwar expansion of the nitrogen industry, which between 1940 and 1955 increased capacity sevenfold, the number of synthetic nitrogen producers increasing from seven to twenty-two, and reduced the share controlled by the three largest firms from ninety-two per cent to twenty-eight per cent. These developments have made the nitrogen industry competitive, and have significantly reduced the size of the task confronting anti-trust. Vigilance over collusive agreements and mergers would appear to be its future role—an easier task than that created by unworkably competitive oligopoly.

The domestic phosphate-rock, sulphur, potash, and nitrogen industries have tended to conform to the model of oligopoly; international cartel agreements have generally governed foreign trade in the fertilizer materials they produce. The combination of these two factors has brought most of the anti-trust actions against them. In the manufactured fertilizer industry anti-trust action has sprung from an enirely different source. Concentration has been relatively low, sellers numerous, and there have been no international cartel entanglements. Circumvention of competition in fertilizer manufacturing has required considerable organization and the vehicle of a central agency along the lines once prescribed by the National Industrial Recovery Act.

Four times in its history the fertilizer manufacturing industry, or a portion of it, has been so organized. In 1906 the Virginia-Carolina Chemical Company and sixty other superphosphate and mixed-fertilizer manufacturers allegedly attempted to cartelize the industry through their joint ownership and control of a Canadian corporation. In 1926 thirty-seven superphosphate and mixed-fertilizer manufacturers were found to have conspired to restrain trade in violation of the Sherman Act and fined $95,000. Under NRA the industry was among the first to submit its Code of Fair Competition; the National Fertilizer Association was the Code Authority. In 1941 a federal grand jury returned an indictment charging the National Fertilizer Association, the superphosphate and mixed-fertilizer manufacturers with having conspired to continue operating very much as they had under the Fertilizer Recovery Code, no longer legal after the Supreme Court invalidated NRA. Defendants, nearly all of which entered pleas of *nolo contendere,* were fined $259,852.

The anti-trust laws appear to have been used frequently and effectively to strike down agreements in various sections of the fertilizer industry in restraint of competition. In its survey of the entire industry in 1950 the Federal Trade Commission, summing up the anti-trust record, observed :

> Whether successful legal attack upon these [practices] will serve in the future as an adequate warning against concerted action . . . cannot be stated with assurance. The most that can be said is that the outcome of these cases was a step in the direction of freeing competition of some, but not necessarily from all, undue restraints.[*]

The Commission identified no undue restraints requiring action under the anti-trust laws and thereby gave greater emphasis to the success of past legal attacks on concerting action than it did in the context of its summary observation. But while such successful attacks may have provided a remedy for collusive action, the problem of noncompetitive behavior inherent in the structure of certain sectors of the industry remains unresolved.

*Oligopoly.* The term "oligopoly" as used in economic analysis denotes a particular kind of market power. The market power of a monopolist is complete and contained within a single decision-making unit; that of a cartel is derived from its members' abnegation of their entrepreneural independence, especially their independence to compete. The market power of oligopoly derives from an assumed pattern of behavior among rivals

[*] FTC, *Report on the Fertilizer Industry,* 1950, p. 146.

when they are few in number. Each firm, knowing beforehand that certain actions it may take will prompt its rivals to retaliate, will take only those actions that would leave it better off after its rivals have retaliated. When a monopoly price is beneficial to all, it presumably is the price that will eventually prevail. This is the *expected* result. The law, as the Attorney General's *Report* points out, cannot assume that actual market behavior will in fact correspond to the behavior theoretically expected.[7] In the law responsibility is individual; and although the law can learn from generalizations concerning human behavior, it cannot substitute them for established facts in a particular case.[8]

Inquiry into the role of the anti-trust laws must recognize this distinction between the law and economics on the significance of oligopoly. By economic standards at least two—possibly three—of the four fertilizer material industries would probably be judged as unworkably competitive oligopolies, not because the evidence clearly shows that the firms comprising them do not compete, but because the logic of oligopoly suggests that such industries generally are not competitive. Yet it may be impossible to marshall proof that the particular firms involved are guilty of specific illegal acts. By legal tests the industries may not offend the anti-trust laws. An assessment of the task of anti-trust is necessarily concerned more with what the law can reasonably be expected to accomplish than with economic standards of workable competition.

Concentration of control in the phosphate-rock, sulphur, and potash industries is high, especially in sulphur and potash where three or four sellers control the output. In comparison, concentration in the nitrogen industry is low. In 1956, largely because of the government's war-plant disposal program and the industry's rapid postwar expansion, twenty-two synthetic-nitrogen companies competed with numerous producers of by-product nitrogen for the fertilizer business. The largest four synthetic-nitrogen producers controlled only twenty-eight per cent of total capacity, and their share was rapidly declining as new firms entered the field. The structure of the nitrogen industry is workably competitive. The structure of the phosphate-rock, sulphur, and potash industries raises the issue of unworkably competitive oligopoly.

The phosphate-rock industry comprises about forty firms, ten of which are either inactive or scarcely more than prospecting operations. Seven large Florida producers account for about seventy-five per cent of total output. One of the remaining twenty-three active producers is the Tennessee Valley Authority; the others are small-scale operations, ten of which operate in the West. The seven large pebble companies are vertically

---

[7] *Op. cit.*, p. 340.
[8] *Ibid.*

integrated with fertilizer manufacturing. In 1957 they produced about forty per cent of the superphosphates and about thirty per cent of the mixed fertilizers manufactured in the United States. Because of their fertilizer operations they are also the largest buyers of potash and are among the large buyers of sulphur and nitrogen.

The seven integrated companies raise two issues for anti-trust policy: their large market share of phosphate rock and their vertical integration with fertilizer manufacturing. There is pursuasive evidence that concentration in the hands of seven integrated Florida producers, in combination with prewar export association activities, made for non-competitive pricing of phosphate rock. There is evidence, although somewhat less persuasive, that the same seven vertically integrated firms discouraged the introduction of new and more economical manufactured fertilizers. Since whatever power the "big seven" possess in fertilizer manufacture derives from their control of phosphate rock, deconcentration in rock mining resolves both issues.

In part, recent market developments have resolved the issues. Since World War II concentration has tended to decline, and price competition apparently has increased. The Federal Trade Commission's actions against the phosphate-rock export associations removed the principal means of organized collusion among Florida producers. The sharp rise in fertilizer consumption in the Midwest and West after the war stimulated exploitation of the western deposits and encouraged the entry of new firms. Between 1945 and 1954 western rock output increased from six per cent to thirteen per cent of the nation's total, and the number of active firms doubled. Between 1950 and 1957 the number of concentrated superphosphate producers increased from seven to fourteen. These developments have reduced the market shares of the seven large integrated Florida pebble producers and have made for greater price competition. According to closed bids rock producers submit to TVA on it rock requirements, competition for business on a price basis had increased perceptibly by 1949.

While these developments may not have made the phosphate-rock industry workably competitive, they probably have left little room for action under the anti-trust laws, especially since other and more feasible policies could very likely provide an equally effective remedy. Concentration in phosphate-rock production could be reduced by dissolution of the large Florida rock companies under the Sherman Act, or through policies designed to encourage entry and to increase competition between Florida and western producers. Dissolution of a geographically centralized strip-mining operation raises obvious technical difficulties. However, most of the large companies hold title to high-grade rock deposits of which they could be divested, or forced to lease, without substantially affecting their operations. Such a course of action would reduce concentration of control in ownership of high-grade deposits and remove the principal obstacle to entry in the Florida fields. But other policy measures besides divestiture can stimulate competition, and are probably more feasible. A large portion of the western phosphate reserves is owned by small firms or is in the public domain. In 1950 about twenty companies operated in the western fields; half of them were engaged in prospecting and developmental activities, and comprise an important potential source of competition. Their ability to compete with entrenched Florida and western firms depends on the deposits they discover, their access to efficient mining techniques, and relative transportation costs. Various agencies of the federal government influence these factors. The U.S. Geological Survey periodically investigates and carefully maps the location of phosphate deposits, and the Bureau of Mines makes extensive studies of their recovery costs. The Tennessee Valley Authority and other government agencies develop technical know-how on the production of concentrated phosphatic materials. Intensification and co-ordination of the research of these agencies and a preference to new over entrenched firms in leasing the public domain should increase the number of independent firms. To prevent increases in concentration through merger which would tend to offset the effects of these policy measures, it is obvious that in phosphate-rock mining Section 7 of the Clayton Act should be administered with special vigor.

The sulphur and potash industries present the issue of unworkably competitive oligopoly in its clearest form. Four firms control the output of natural sulphur; two firms—Texas Gulf and Freeport—account for ninety per cent of the total. Three firms control nearly all the output of potash; six small producers, including two that produce by-product potash from cement, account for the rest. Imports compete with domestic potash but in recent years have amounted to only ten per cent of United States potash consumption.

While concentration of control in sulphur and potash production is high, there is no obvious course of action under the anti-trust laws to reduce it. Natural-sulphur producers recover sulphur from domes (deposits) they discover themselves or which petroleum companies discover while drilling for oil. Most domes are found on petroleum company properties in Louisiana and Texas. Sulphur companies generally operate them under leaseholds obtained from petroleum companies. Sulphur firms can be no more numerous than commercially exploitable domes. In 1947 the four leading natural-sulphur producers operated five domes. Freeport operated Hoskins Mound in Brazoria County, Texas, and the Grande Ecaille deposits in Plaquemines Parish, Louisiana; Texas Gulf operated Boling Dome on one of the Gulf Oil Corporation's properties in Texas; Duval operated Orchard Dome at Fort Bend, Texas; and Jefferson Lake was in the process of closing down its depleted Clement Mound in Brazoria County and shifting operations to newly leased deposits at Fort Bend.[9] Apparently the only way to reduce concentration of control in natural sulphur is to limit the leaseholding and exploration activities of Freeport and Texas Gulf—the two largest producers. To do this under the Sherman Act would require a showing that they acquired leases on deposits with the intent to monopolize or which in fact monopolized, under the Federal Trade Commission Act a showing that such acquisitions constituted an unfair method of competition. Such possible actions raise complex issues of fact and law which this study cannot resolve.

Concentration of control in potash raises the same complex problems encountered in sulphur, but a remedy simpler than anti-trust prosecution is available. All the large potash producers operate in the public domain under leases subject to the Potash Leasing Act of 1927, as revised in 1945. The Act empowers the Secretary of the Interior to grant two-year prospecting permits and leases up to twenty years after a satisfactory showing of potash discovery. The typical lease requires the lessee to make prescribed investments in developments and improvements, to pay the government a rental fee on each acre of land and approximately a three per cent royalty on the gross value of all potash shipped, and to produce potash valued at least at $200,000 per year or to pay royalties on this amount if production is less.[10] The Secretary of the Interior may suspend action on prospecting permits to avoid overdevelopment of potash resources, and under the new 1945 regulations is empowered to purchase on one year's notice one-fourth of the potash produced from the leased land at not more than prevailing wholesale prices f.o.b. refinery.[11] The government can probably mitigate oligopoly in potash more effectively through the Potash Leasing Act, which gives it a measure of control over entry and distribution, than through the anti-trust laws.

### SUMMARY

Vigorous anti-trust law administration has doubtlessly held down the social costs of monopoly in various sectors of the fertilizer industry far below the level that otherwise would have prevailed. Agreements and conspiracies restricting competition in nitrogen, potash, and manufactured fertilizers have been prosecuted under the Sherman Act. Federal Trade

---

[9] FTC, *Report on the Sulphur Industry and International Cartels* (1947), pp. 3-4.
[10] Jules Backman, *The Economics of the Potash Industry* (American Potash Institute, Washington: 1946), pp. 40-41.
[11] *Federal Register*, January 9, 1945, p. 336.

Commission action put an end to the anti-competitive practices of PEA, Hardphos, and Sulexco in the domestic phosphate-rock and sulphur markets. Anti-trust action has not been confined to formal proceedings. The Federal Trade Commission and the Department of Justice periodically have conducted comprehensive investigations of the fertilizer industry. Commission reports were made public in 1916 and 1950; Justice's 1939 investigation, while never published, received much publicity and provided most of the facts for subsequent Sherman Act cases against nitrogen and potash producers. Such full-scale inquiries probably arrest certain monopolistic practices in their incipiency.

But anti-trust has not made all sectors of the fertilizer industry workably competitive. Oligopoly and monopoly profits, about $10,000,000 or $15,000,000 in 1946, still persist. In sulphur and potash three or four firms account for most of the output; and monopoly returns, primarily monopoly rents, remain especially high. There is no clear course of action under the anti-trust laws for remedying this situation. Oligopoly, in the absence of specific illegal acts to create and maintain it, is tolerated by the Sherman Act. The role of anti-trust in the fertilizer industry therefore appears to consist principally of preventing any further lessening of competition—the prosecution of mergers and other restrictive practices as the occur.

# CHAPTER 10

# IMPERFECT KNOWLEDGE

IN THE taxonomy of markets a distinction is drawn between monopoly and other impediments to efficient resource allocation. Competition is said to be "pure" when buyers and sellers of a homogeneous product are so numerous that no one of them can affect the price, to be "perfect" when no obstacles to efficient resource allocation are present.[1] Monopoly elements, on which the analysis heretofore has centered, are impurities. But market imperfections such as factor immobility and ignorance also involve social costs. In fact, some have concluded that the cost of ignorance probably exceeds that of any other market imperfection or impurity, and labeled it the "grand" imperfection.[2]

For obvious reasons empirical studies have accorded market imperfections less attention than market impurities. Monopoly profits, price-cost relationships, numbers of firms, and concentration of control are expressed as quantities; they are measurable. Market imperfections, such as ignorance, are not easily quantified, and, where consumer's tastes and preferences are involved, virtually defy empirical inquiry. Two washing machines may look and perform alike, but who is to say the housewife buys the costlier one out of ignorance? But while these difficulties seriously limit the number of situations where the social cost of ignorance can be analyzed, they do not preclude such analysis. For example, factor markets, in contrast with most consumer-goods markets, do not raise the problem of tastes. Entrepreneurs presumably purchase such factors solely on the basis of their relative productivities and prices. The productivities of factors and utilities of consumers goods can sometimes be reduced to comparable terms, e.g., the octane ratings of gasoline, the B.T.U. ratings of fuels, the cost-per-thousand readers for advertising displays in weekly magazines, and so forth.

Fertilizers are factors of production and can be compared on the basis of their plant-nutrient content. For example, a farmer desiring mixed fertilizers containing 1,000 pounds of N, 2,000 pounds of $P_2O_5$, and 1,000 pounds of $K_2O$ can obtain the desired quantities by purchasing five tons of 10-20-10, ten tons of 5-10-5, or twelve and one-half tons of

---

[1] E. H. Chamberlin, *The Theory of Monopolistic Competition* (6th ed.: Cambridge: Harvard University Press, 1956), p. 6; F. Machlup, "Monopoly and Competition: A Classification of Market Positions," *American Economic Review*, XXVII (1937), pp. 445, 448, 451; F. H. Knight, *Risk, Uncertainty and Profits* (Boston and New York: Houghton Mifflin, 1921) pp. 76-79.

[2] G. E. Hale and Rosemary D. Hale, "Market Imperfections: Enforcement of the Anti-trust Laws in a Friction-Afflicted Economy," *University of Pennsylvania Law Review* (December, 1953) p. 162; F. H. Knight, *op. cit., passim, esp.* pp. 86, 198, 213, and 225-26.

4-8-4.[3] Since fertilizers are purchased solely for the plant nutrients they contain, which of these he buys should depend on the price per unit of plant nutrient for each grade. If he buys on any other basis, he buys irrationally or out of ignorance. The social costs of such irrational buying can be measured in terms of the difference between the farmers' total outlays on mixed fertilizer and what they would have been had farmers bought the same plant nutrients in the cheapest grades available.

It is also possible to estimate a portion of the social costs of imperfections on the supply side of the fertilizer market. Fertilizers are sold by farmer-owned co-operatives and commercial mixers. Co-operatives presumably sell the most economical grades of fertilizers their members will buy at prices which yield a normal return on invested capital. The amount by which total fertilizer costs could be reduced if commercial mixers sold the kinds of fertilizers sold by co-operatives can be attributed in part to imperfections—or impurities—on the supply side of the market. Special considerations require that the resulting calculation be qualified somewhat, but the comparison provides a rough measure of the extent to which commercial mixers have failed to supply the kinds of fertilizers farmers demand, and which could be sold at prices which yield a normal return on investment.

These calculations do not cover all the costs of imperfect knowledge and other market imperfections. Farmers may not know precisely what kinds and quantities of plant nutrients their soils and crops require, the point at which the marginal application of fertilizer just pays for itself, the relative costs of straight materials and mixed fertilizers, and may not know what crops maximize the returns to their farms. Fertilizer manufacturers may lack knowledge on the most economical techniques of production and distribution. Qualitative information on such market imperfections can indicate whether their social costs generally tend to be great or small. But quantitative analysis of imperfect knowledge is limited by the nature of the data to the problems of how much farmers could reduce their plant-nutrient costs if they bought the most economical grades available in the market, and the extent to which fertilizer manufacturers fail to supply the kinds of fertilizers farmers demand.

## A . The Economics of High-Analysis Fertilizers

Fertilizers are generally priced according to grade and gross weight, e.g., grade 5-10-5 at $38.00 per ton. The grade, which under the laws of most states must be posted on the bag, indicates that the ton of fertilizer contains 100 pounds of N, 200 pounds of $P_2O_5$, and 100 pounds of

[3] Mixed fertilizers are graded according to the units (20 pounds) of N, $P_2O_5$, and $K_2O$ they contain.

$K_2O$—a total of 400 pounds, or twenty per cent by weight, of plant nutrients. The average ton of mixed fertilizer contains about 500 pounds of plant nutrients. Those containing more are referred to in the trade as high-analysis fertilizers; those containing less as low-analysis fertilizers. Because fertilizer materials contain plant nutrients, other compounds, and certain impurities, it is impossible to manufacture a mixed fertilizer containing one hundred per cent plant nutrients, although theoretically a ton of 28-16-20 fertilizer can be produced by mixing one-third of a ton each of eighty-four per cent anhydrous ammonia, forty-eight per cent superphosphate, and sixty per cent muriate of potash.

While high-analysis fertilizers sell at a higher price per ton, they are generally the cheapest source of plant nutrients. Mixing, bagging, handling, storage, and transportation costs per ton of fertilizer are about the same for all grades, making such costs per unit of plant nutrient less for high-analysis than for low-analysis fertilizers. Delivered costs per unit of plant nutrient also are generally less for the concentrated materials required to manufacture high-analysis fertilizers than for materials of low concentration. Detailed cost data for two midwestern mixing plants show the source of these production and distribution economies (Table 46). The cost of materials used to manufacture a ton of 0-20-20 fertilizer in Plant A is $25.75; to manufacture a ton of 0-12-12 fertilizer, $15.58. But while the material costs per ton for the high-analysis exceed those for the average-analysis fertilizer by $10.17, the material costs per unit of plant nutrient in the high-analysis fertilizer is $0.005 less. In Plant B the material costs per unit of plant nutrient for the high-analysis fertilizer is $0.009 less. The greater portion of the lower cost of plant nutrients in high-analysis fertilizers is attributable to lower labor, bagging, and transportation costs. Bags and labor cost $0.084 per unit less in high-analysis than in average-analysis fertilizers; and delivery costs range from $0.157 to $0.203 less per unit.[4] The total cost of producing and delivering forty units of plant nutrients is $9.72 less for the grade 0-20-20 than for the grade 0-12-12 fertilizer. The cost of forty units of plant nutrients in the grade 4-24-12 range from $10.48 to $12.16 less than for forty units in the grade 2-12-6. These are significant differences.

The cost data show that the grades 0-20-20 and 4-24-12 fertilizers are a cheaper source of plant nutrients for farmers than comparable average-analysis grades. But they also show that producers tend to minimize the production costs of each grade, and that in doing so they may use considerable quantities of inert filler. For example, in Plant B

[4] In 1957, the difference would be considerably greater because of the freight rate increases which have occurred over the intervening years. In 1947 the cost per unit of $P_2O_5$ was nearly as great in concentrated superphosphate as it was in ordinary superphosphate in the Midwest, but by 1951 the difference had become significant.

## TABLE 46

### HIGH- AND AVERAGE-ANALYSIS FERTILIZER PRODUCTION AND DISTRIBUTION COSTS FOR TWO MIDWESTERN PLANTS, APRIL 10, 1947 [a]

| | PLANT A | | | | | | | |
|---|---|---|---|---|---|---|---|---|
| | 0-20-20 | | 0-12-12 | | 4-24-12 | | 2-12-6 | |
| Materials | lbs. | Cost | lbs. | Cost | lbs. | Cost | lbs. | Cost |
| Ordinary Superphosphate (48%).. | 711 | $4.80 | 1,263 | $8.52 | 671 | $4.53 | 1,263 | $8.52 |
| Concentrated superphosphate (79%)............... | 552 | 9.47 | | | 734 | 12.59 | | ....... |
| Muriate of potash (60%)........ | 667 | 11.37 | 400 | 6.82 | 400 | 6.82 | 200 | 3.41 |
| Anhydrous ammonia (82¼%)... | ....... | ....... | ....... | ....... | 60 | 2.01 | ....... | ....... |
| B 2 A (40.8%)................ | ....... | ....... | ....... | ....... | 75 | 1.87 | 50 | 1.24 |
| B liquor (24.7%)............. | | | | | | | 79 | 0.79 |
| Sulphuric acid (60%)........... | ....... | ....... | ....... | ....... | 60 | 0.23 | 40 | 0.16 |
| Lime........................ | 70 | 0.11 | 70 | 0.11 | ....... | ....... | 68 | 0.10 |
| Filler....................... | | | 267 | 0.13 | | | 300 | 0.15 |
| Total........ | 2,000 | $25.75 | 2,000 | $15.58 | 2,000 | $28.05 | 2,000 | $14.37 |
| Material costs per unit of plant nutrient.................. | ....... | 0.644 | ....... | 0.649 | ....... | 0.702 | ....... | 0.718 |
| Advantage of high over average-fertilizers per unit of plant nutrient: | | | | | | | | |
| Material costs............. | ....... | $0.005 | | | ....... | $0.017 | | |
| Bags and labor............ | | 0.084 | | | | 0.084 | | |
| Delivery costs[b]............ | | 0.157 | | | | 0.203 | | |
| Total advantage per unit........ | ....... | $0.246 | | | ....... | $0.304 | | |
| Total net advantage per 40 units of plant nutrients............. | | $9.84 | | | | $12.15 | | |

| | PLANT B | | | | | | | |
|---|---|---|---|---|---|---|---|---|
| Ordinary superphosphate (18%).. | 750 | $4.79 | 1,334 | $8.52 | 636 | $4.06 | 1,333 | $8.52 |
| Concentrated superphosphate (47%)................ | 558 | 9.26 | | | 769 | 12.77 | | ....... |
| Muriate of potash (60%)........ | 667 | 10.96 | 400 | 6.57 | 400 | 6.57 | 200 | 3.29 |
| Anhydrous ammonia (82¼%)... | ....... | ....... | ....... | ....... | 60 | 2.07 | ....... | ....... |
| B 2 A (40.8%)................ | ....... | ....... | ....... | ....... | 75 | 1.88 | 50 | 1.25 |
| B liquor (24.7)............. | | | | | | | | |
| Sulphuric acid (60%)........... | ....... | ....... | ....... | ....... | 60 | .028 | 40 | 0.19 |
| Lime........................ | 25 | 0.02 | 25 | 0.02 | ....... | ....... | 68 | 0.06 |
| Filler....................... | | | 241 | 0.14 | | | 230 | 0.13 |
| Total........................ | 2,000 | $25.03 | 2,000 | $15.25 | 2,000 | $27.63 | 2,000 | $13.44 |
| Unit Material Costs............. | ....... | 0.626 | ....... | 0.635 | ....... | 0.690 | ....... | .0672 |
| Advantage of high- over average-analysis fertilizers per unit of plant nutrient: | | | | | | | | |
| Material Costs............. | ....... | 0.009 | | | ....... | —0.018 | | |
| Bags and labor............ | | 0.077 | | | | 0.077 | | |
| Delivery costs[b]............ | | 0.157 | | | | 0.203 | | |
| Total Advantage per unit........ | ....... | 0.243 | | | ....... | .262 | | |
| Total advantage per 40 units of plant nutrients............. | | $9.72 | | | | $10.48 | | |

[a] Records of Swift & Company.
[b] Based on 1947 freight rates and average shipping distance for the two plants.

the manufacturer used 558 pounds of concentrated superphosphate (47.5 per cent $P_2O_5$) and 750 pounds of ordinary superphosphate (eighteen per cent $P_2O_5$) to get twenty units of $P_2O_5$ in a ton of grade 0-20-20 fertilizer, and 1,334 pounds of ordinary superphosphate to get twelve units of $P_2O_5$ in a ton of grade 0-12-12 fertilizer. A unit of $P_2O_5$ in the concentrated superphosphate cost the manufacturer $0.70; in the ordinary superphosphate, $0.71. Seemingly, the manufacturer has foregone an opportunity to reduce production costs by not substituting concentrated for ordinary superphosphate. But a closer examination shows that it takes about 111 pounds of ordinary superphosphate to get a unit (20 pounds) of $P_2O_5$ into the mixture, and only about forty-two pounds of concentrated superphosphate. Hence, to keep the total weight and $P_2O_5$ content unchanged, for each substitution of forty-two pounds of concentrated superphosphate for 111 pounds of ordinary superphosphate, about sixty pounds of inert filler must be added. Because each hundred pounds of filler costs $0.06, sixty pounds of filler and forty-two pounds of concentrated superphosphate would cost $0.74, or $0.03 more than 111 pounds of ordinary superphosphate. Even by using no concentrated superphosphate the manufacturer could not make a ton of grade 0-12-12 fertilizer without adding 241 pounds of inert filler. The production of low-analysis mixed fertilizers requires the addition of considerable quantities of filler and the avoidance of the more economical concentrated fertilizer materials, both of which unnecessarily increase production and delivery costs. These factors explain why high-analysis fertilizers are the farmers' cheapest source of plant nutrients.

An abundance of mixing and transportation cost data[5] for various regions show that as the analysis of mixed fertilizers is increased, mixing and transportation costs per unit of plant nutrient generally tend to decline. The point is further demonstrated by cost data for a fertilizer mixing plant in Maine (Table 47.) The mixer could have produced forty units of plant nutrients containing N, $P_2O_5$, and $K_2O$ in the ratio of 1-2-2 in several alternative forms. For example, he could have produced 1 3/5

TABLE 47

RELATIVE COSTS AND PRICES OF FORTY UNITS OF
PLANT NUTRIENTS DELIVERED TO THE FARMERS IN
MAINE IN FOUR GRADES OF FERTILIZER, 1950 [a]

| Grade | Quantity | Per cent of Total Cost | | Delivered to Farm (5-10-10 = 100) | Delivered Price to Farmers |
| | | Blending, Packaging, and Distribution | Delivered Materials | | |
|---|---|---|---|---|---|
| 5-10-10 | 1 3/5 tons | 57 | 43 | 100 | $77.76 |
| 6-12-12 | 1 1/3 tons | 50 | 50 | 92 | ————[b] |
| 7-14-14 | 1 1/7 tons | 48 | 52 | 89 | ————[b] |
| 8-16-16 | 1 ton | 42 | 58 | 84 | 66.00 |

[a] K. D. Jacob, ed., *Fertilizer Technology and Resources in the United States*, Vol. III of *Agronomy: A Series of Monographs* (Academic Press, New York: 1953), pp. 395-412.
[b] Price quotations not available for 1950.

[5] For examples, see FTC, *Report on The Fertilizer Industry* (1950), pp. 129-37; Martin A. Abrahamsen, *Manufacturing Costs as Reported for Co-operative Fertilizer Plants in the North Central States*, U. S. Dept of Agric. Special Report No. 218 (1951); and OPA Records on the Fertilizer Industry, National Archives.

tons of 5-10-10, 1 1/3 tons of 6-12-12, 1 1/7 tons of 7-14-14, or 1 ton of 8-16-16. However, because transportation and mixing costs per ton of fertilizer are the same regardless of analysis or grade, the higher the analysis the lower the costs per unit of plant nutrient. Under 1950 transportation rates and factor prices the cost of producing and delivering 1 ton of 8-16-16 was sixteen per cent less than that for 1 3/5 tons of 5-10-10; 9.5 per cent less than that for 1 1/3 tons of 6-12-12; and 6.0 per cent less than that for 1 1/7 tons of 7-14-14. On the grades for which quoted delivered-to-the-farm prices in 1950 are available, prices just about reflected the differences in delivered costs. The cost of producing and delivering the forty units of plant nutrients in the form of 1 ton of 8-16-16 fertilizer was eighty-four per cent of the cost of 1 3/5 tons of 5-10-10; the delivered price of 1 ton of 8-16-16 was eighty-five per cent of the delivered price of 1 3/5 tons of 5-10-10.

## B. The Social Costs of Imperfect Knowledge

*Mixed Fertilizers.* Fertilizer manufacturers offer farmers a wide variety of mixed fertilizer grades ranging from twelve per cent to nearly sixty per cent in plant-nutrient content. The price per unit of plant nutrient varies considerably among grades. When farmers buy those grades which do not give them the plant nutrients they want at the lowest total cost it can be assumed that they do so irrationally or out of ignorance. The amount farmers could save by substituting more economical grades for those they actually buy should reflect a portion of the cost of irrational demand or imperfect buyer knowledge. In computing such costs, however, comparisons must be made between fertilizers having N, $P_2O_5$, and $K_2O$ in the same ratio. For example, a ton of mixed fertilizer, grade 8-12-8, contains twice the plant nutrients of a ton of grade 4-6-4. If the delivered price to the farmer of one ton of 8-12-8 is less than twice the delivered price of one ton of 4-6-4, it is a more economical fertilizer to buy. Price comparisons of fertilizers containing plant nutrients in different ratios are hardly meaningful, since they raise the problem of comparing prices of different commodities.

During the fertilizer year ending June 30, 1949, American farmers bought 12.6 million tons of mixed fertilizers of 894 specific grades.[6] Forty-one grades ranging from sixteen per cent to forty per cent in plant-nutrient content accounted for 90.3 per cent of the total tonnage purchased. Nineteen of these forty-one grades containing from eighteen to twenty-one per cent plant nutrients accounted for sixty-four per cent (Table 48). The weighted average plant-nutrient content per ton of fertilizer was

[6] The year 1949 was selected for analysis because it was the first postwar year in which fertilizers were not generally in short supply.

### TABLE 48
### AVERAGE PLANT-NUTRIENT CONTENT OF THE FORTY-ONE PRINCIPAL GRADES OF FERTILIZERS SOLD IN THE UNITED STATES, 1949 [a]

| Plant-Nutrient Content | No. of Grades | Thousands of Tons Purchased |
|---|---|---|
| 16% | 2 | 184.5 |
| 18% | 5 | 1,985.4 |
| 20% | 9 | 4,337.9 |
| 21% | 5 | 1,701.8 |
| 22% | 1 | 116.7 |
| 24% | 5 | 713.9 |
| 25% | 2 | 504.5 |
| 26% | 3 | 233.8 |
| 27% | 2 | 1,043.5 |
| 28% | 1 | 41.3 |
| 30% | 3 | 359.7 |
| 40% | 3 | 141.9 |
| | 41 | 11,364.9 |

Average Plant-Nutrient Content.................22.47%

[a] U. S. Dept. of Agriculture, Bureau of Plant Industry, Soils, and Agricultural Engineering, *Consumption of Commercial Fertilizers in the United States*, 1948-49.

3.87 per cent N, 10.87 per cent $P_2O_5$, and 7.73 per cent $K_2O$, or an average total plant-nutrient content of 22.47 per cent.

While only a few of the grades for which average prices and quantities are available can be paired with corresponding grades of high-analysis fertilizers having identical plant-nutrient ratios, the number of such pairs is sufficient to indicate the annual cost of imperfect buyer knowledge. The price per unit of plant nutrient for thirteen commercial grades of fertilizer are shown in Table 49. The thirteen grades represent six widely used plant-nutrient ratios that accounted for 17.5 per cent of the total tonnage of mixed fertilizers purchased in 1949. Seven of the thirteen grades contain from twenty per cent to twenty-five per cent plant nutrients; the weighted average plant-nturient content per ton for the seven grades is 22.2 per cent, or approximately the same as the weighted average plant-nutrient content (22.47) of all mixed fertilizers purchased in 1949. The remaining six grades contain from twenty-eight per cent to forty per cent plant nutrients; the average plant-nutrient content for the six high-analysis grades is approximately 35.3 per cent. Each of the high-analysis grades can be compared with at least one low-analysis grade with a corresponding N, $P_2O_5$, and $K_2O$ ratio.

For all six ratios the average cost per unit of plant nutrient delivered to the farm was considerably less in the high-analysis than in the corresponding low-analysis grades. Had all the farmers who bought the 1,987,800 tons of low-analysis grades bought instead the same quantity of

TABLE 49

COST PER UNIT OF PLANT NUTRIENT IN SELECTED GRADES OF
HIGH- AND LOW-ANALYSIS MIXED FERTILIZERS HAVING
IDENTICAL PLANT-NUTRIENT RATIOS, 1949-50 [a]

| N, $P_2O_5$, $K_2O$ Ratio | Low Analysis | | | High Analysis | | | Possible Savings to Farmers if High-Analysis Had Been Substituted for Low-Analysis [c] |
|---|---|---|---|---|---|---|---|
| | Grade | Quantity [b] | Price per Unit | Grade | Quantity | Price per Unit | |
| 1-1-1 | 7-7-7 | 53.8 | $2.345 | 10-10-10 | ....[d] | $2.107 | $269.5 |
| 0-1-1 | 0-12-12 | 251.0 | 1.750 | 0-20-20 | 67.9 | 1.388 | 2,183.2 |
| 1-4-2 | 3-12-6 | 859.7 | 11.844 | 4-16-8 | ....[d] | 1.684 | 2,912.3 |
| 0-2-1 | 0-14-7 | 148.1 | 1.655 | 0-20-10 | 94.8 | 1.500 | 481.4 |
| 1-2-2 | { 4-8-8 | 217.6 | 2.000 | 8-16-16 | 37.1 | 1.650 | 4,884.6 |
| | } 5-10-10 | 457.6 | 1.944 | | | | |
| 2-2-1 | 8-8-4 | ......[d] | 2.763 | 12-12-6 | ....[d] | 2.592 | ...... |
| TOTAL | .......... | 1,987.8 | .......... | .......... | 199.8 | ........ | $10,731.0 |

[a] Prices are average delivered prices paid by farmers in April, 1950, as reported in *Agricultural Prices* (Bureau of Agricultural Economics, U. S. Dept. of Agriculture); or are average delivered cash prices to farmers as computed from published price lists for the Spring, 1950, season. The quantities consumed of each grade are from *Consumption of Commercial Fertilizers in the United States, 1948-49* (Bureau of Plant Industry, Soils, and Agricultural Engineering, U. S. Dept. of Agriculture).
[b] Thousands of tons.
[c] Thousands of dollars.
[d] Very small.

plant nutrients in the form of high-analysis grades, they would have saved $10.73 million on the purchase price of fertilizers. And, since the total tonnage of high-analysis fertilizers required to obtain the given quantity of plant nutrients would have been only 63.7 per cent of the total tonnage of low-analysis fertilizers actually purchased,[7] reductions in on-the-farm costs of handling and applying fertilizers to the soil would have resulted in additional savings.

If it is assumed that the average difference in cost per unit of plant nutrient between high- and low-analysis fertilizers was approximately the same for the remaining 82.5 per cent of the mixed fertilizers purchased in 1949 as it was for the 17.5 per cent accounted for in Table 49, American farmers could have obtained the same quantity of plant nutrients at a saving of $61.32 million by using high-analysis fertilizers. Total expenditures on mixed fertilizers in 1950 were approximately $586.8 million; by

[7] For a given quantity of plant nutrients the total weight of the fertilizer varies inversely with the plant-nutrient content; e.g., if the total weight is 1,987,800 tons when the plant-nutrient content is 22.5 per cent, then it is $\frac{22.5 \times 1,987,800}{35.3}$ tons, or 1,265,036 tons, when the plant-nutrient content is 35.3 per cent.

using only high-analysis fertilizers farmers could have reduced their mixed-fertilizer bill by 10.5 per cent.

Seemingly the cost of irrational demand and imperfect buyer knowledge is about 10.5 per cent of the total cost of mixed fertilizers. But this conclusion assumes that fertilizer manufacturers would supply the additional quantities of the more economical high-analysis fertilizers if farmers wished to buy them. While the fact that manufacturers sell high-analysis fertilizers in competition with their other less economical grades would appear to support this assumption, it is nonetheless possible that the fertilizers farmers buy are limited to the quantities manufacturers produce. In short, the reason farmers do not shift from low- to high-analysis fertilizers may be that manufacturers do not produce enough of them.

*The Test of Farmer-Controlled Distribution.* In 1953 about 105 farmer-owned co-operative fertilizer plants manufactured and distributed twelve per cent of the nation's fertilizer supplies.[8] Their share of sales varies considerably among regions, amounting to as much as twenty-five per cent in the Middle Atlantic states and to as little as two per cent in the Rocky Mountain and Pacific Coast states. Since farmer-owned co-operatives are operated to promote the best interests of their members, the types of fertilizers they distribute should be the types that farmers wish to buy. Comparing the types of fertilizers distributed by commercial producers with those distributed by co-operatives in the same market area should indicate whether commercial fertilizer producers have failed to adjust their production to meet the demands of farmers.

But such a comparison has some obvious shortcomings. The Tennessee Valley Authority and the Department of Agriculture have tried to promote innovation and intelligent buying among farmers. Specifically, the Tennessee Valley Authority has encouraged the use of high-analysis fertilizers by making them available on favorable terms to farmers who pledge themselves to use the best-known principles of agronomy. TVA has distributed much of its fertilizer to farmers through farmer-owned co-operatives.[9] The co-operatives for which the necessary data are available have contracts with TVA to distribute its high-analysis fertilizer materials. By carrying out the terms of the contracts, such co-operatives distribute fertilizers of higher than average analysis. And although the hypothesis cannot readily be tested, co-operative memberships probably include the more enterprising farmers. If this is true, co-operatives can probably distribute better grades of fertilizer than those the commercial firms can sell to the entire farm population. For these reasons it should

[8] Claud L. Scroggs, "Co-operative Fertilizer Production and Distribution—New Facts and Figures," a paper presented to the American Institute of Co-operation, Columbia, Mo., 1953.
[9] After 1950 the Authority made its high-analysis materials available to a few commercial fertilizer producers who complied with certain contractual provisions (see Chap. 11).

be expected that farmer-controlled co-operatives would distribute relatively larger quantities of the more economical high-analysis fertilizers than would commercial firms.

On the other hand, the types of fertilizers distributed by co-operatives are limited to those they can produce from their supplies of raw materials. Co-operatives have frequently complained that commercial producers of high-analysis materials do not make available to them the quantities they would be willing to purchase at prevailing prices. If all high-analysis phosphate, nitrogen, and potash materials were sold in highly competitive markets, co-operatives would possibly distribute fertilizers of higher analysis than they do.

Still another shortcoming of the comparison of co-operatives and commercial firms is that the managers of both imitate each other's production policies and so reduce the differences between them that would otherwise exist. Co-operative managers tend to keep in touch with commercial firms' practices, and commercial firms have been forced to follow co-operatives' practices and policies when they tended to bid away their market.

The foregoing qualifications aside, it can be shown that farm-owned co-operatives in some regions produce and distribute fertilizers of higher analysis than those produced and distributed by the industry as a whole. In the North Central states the weighted average plant-nutrient content of phosphate-potash mixtures sold by co-operatives in 1949 was 37.52 per cent, while that for mixtures sold by all producers was 29.69 per cent (Table 50); co-operative nitrogen-phosphate-potash mixtures averaged 27.29 per cent plant-nutrient content, while all producers' mixtures averaged 24.68 per cent; and co-operative nitrogen-phosphate mixtures averaged 24.90 per cent plant-nutrient content, while all producers' mixtures averaged 21.50 per cent. For mixed fertilizers of all kinds, those sold by co-operatives in 1949 averaged 28.97 per cent plant-nutrient content; those sold by all producers averaged 25.19 per cent; and in 1952, mixtures sold by co-operatives averaged 31.27 per cent, while non-co-operative mixtures averaged 28.99 per cent.

Co-operatives in the North Central states clearly distribute more high-analysis fertilizers than do their non-co-operative competitors, but the plant-nutrient content is not substantially higher. In 1949 the average ton of mixed fertilizer distributed by co-operatives contained 3.8 more units of plant nutrients than that distributed by all producers; in 1952 it contained 2.3 units more than that of the non-co-operatives. Most of the difference in both years is accounted for by the higher $P_2O_5$ content of the co-operative mixtures, and is therefore explained in part by TVA's concentrated superphosphate program. Farmer co-operatives in the

TABLE 50

WEIGHTED AVERAGE ANALYSIS OF FERTILIZER MIXTURES
DISTRIBUTED IN NORTH CENTRAL STATES COMPARED WITH
THAT OF MIXTURES DISTRIBUTED BY REGIONAL
CO-OPERATIVES, 1949 AND 1952 [a]

| Type of Fertilizer | Regional Co-operatives | | | | All Producers | | | |
|---|---|---|---|---|---|---|---|---|
| | %N | %P₂O₅ | %K₂O | Total | %N | %P₂O₅ | %K₂O | Total |
| | | | | 1949 | | | | |
| Phosphate-potash mixtures......... | ..... | 21.52 | 16.00 | 37.52 | ..... | 14.94 | 14.75 | 29.69 |
| Nitrogen-phosphate-potash mixtures.. | 3.32 | 13.50 | 10.47 | 27.29 | 3.01 | 12.15 | 9.52 | 24.68 |
| Nitrogen-phosphate mixtures......... | 5.86 | 19.04 | ...... | 24.90 | 4.60 | 16.90 | ...... | 21.50 |
| All mixtures....... | 2.84 | 15.13 | 11.00 | 28.97 | 2.69 | 12.63 | 9.87 | 25.19 |
| | | | | 1952 | | | | |
| All mixtures....... | 3.58 | 15.14 | 12.55 | 31.27 | 3.71[b] | 13.39[b] | 11.89[b] | 28.99[b] |

[a] Adapted from data supplied by Co-operative Research and Service Division, Farm Credit Administration, U. S. Dept. of Agriculture.
[b] Non-co-operative producers only.

North Central states, in comparison with commercial firms and other co-operatives, are generally considered unusually progressive and enterprising. For example, in 1948 Minnesota consumed 131,903 tons of commercially mixed fertilizers containing an average of 27.8 units of plant nutrients per ton; the average cost per unit to farmers was $1.8959. In the same year a large Minnesota co-operative sold 24,592 tons of mixed fertilizers containing an average of 39.2 units of plant nutrients per ton; the average cost per unit to farmers was $1.5494, or $0.3465 less per unit than the commercial industry's average. By buying the co-operative's high-analysis fertilizers farmers saved a total of $334,196.84, or an average of $13.18 per ton.[10] Such instances suggest that an aggressive organization can reduce materially the fertilizer costs of enlightened buyers. But the over-all relatively small difference in plant-nutrient con-

[10] Co-operatives distribute fertilizers at prevailing or slightly less than market prices, and appear to do so profitably. However, certain difficulties arise in comparing prices and profits of co-operatives with those of non-co-operative firms. Co-operatives have usually published prices on various grades about equal to the industry's average. In recent years, non-co-operative firms have begun to regard co-operatives as price leaders in most areas where they account for a significant percentage of total sales. It is not known whether farmers consider the co-operatives' published prices or the published prices less some expected patronage refund per ton to be the price at which they buy. When settlements are made at the end of the fertilizer season, they can be regarded either as price adjustments or as a distribution of profits. This is particularly true of time sales, where patronage refunds are frequently applied against the individual farmers' accounts.

All the savings that accrue to patrons of co-operatives as a result of the types of fertilizers they distribute cannot be treated as co-operative profits. Co-operatives have purchased some of their concentrated superphosphate at TVA costs, an option not open to commercial firms generally; they also have certain tax exemptions that commercial firms do not have. All these things considered, it is probably true either that co-operatives sell high-analysis fertilizers at prevailing market prices and earn slightly more than the average rate of return for the industry, or that they sell at slightly lower prices and earn about the average rate of return for the industry.

tent between co-operative and commercial fertilizers in the North Central states suggests that commercial firms do not restrict their sales of high-analysis fertilizers to significantly smaller quantities than farmers are willing to buy.

In the South co-operatives and non-co-operatives distribute almost identical grades of mixed fertilizers. In 1949 the average plant-nutrient content of mixed fertilizers sold by all producers was about 19.6 per cent; that of three regional co-operatives, about 20.2 per cent (Table 51). In

TABLE 51

WEIGHTED AVERAGE PLANT-NUTRIENT CONTENT OF ALL MIXED FERTILIZERS DISTRIBUTED IN VARIOUS AREAS OF THE SOUTH COMPARED WITH THAT OF MIXED FERTILIZERS DISTRIBUTED BY SOUTHERN REGIONAL CO-OPERATIVES, 1949 [a]

| Market Area Served by: | Regional Co-operatives | | | | All Producers | | | |
|---|---|---|---|---|---|---|---|---|
| | % N | % $P_2O_5$ | % $K_2O$ | Total | % N | % $P_2O_5$ | % $K_2O$ | Total |
| Co-operative No. 1 | 4.64 | 9.36 | 6.11 | 20.11 | 5.17 | 8.83 | 5.33 | 19.33 |
| Co-operative No. 2 | 5.48 | 9.16 | 5.48 | 20.12 | 5.12 | 8.89 | 5.39 | 19.40 |
| Co-operative No. 3 | 5.25 | 9.79 | 5.25 | 20.29 | 5.38 | 9.43 | 5.38 | 20.19 |

[a] Adapted from data supplied by the Fertilizer Distribution Section of The Tennessee Valley Authority.

the area served by Co-operative No. 1, the average plant-nutrient content of fertilizers sold by the co-operative was 20.11 per cent, and that for all producers was 19.33 per cent; in the area served by Co-operative No. 2, that for fertilizers sold by the co-operative was 20.12 per cent, and that for all producers was 19.40 per cent; and in the area served by Co-operative No. 3, the average for the co-operative was 20.19 per cent, and that for all producers was 20.19 per cent. For all three areas the average for co-operatives was only 0.6 units of plant nutrients higher than that for all producers, of which 0.4 units were $P_2O_5$. TVA's concentrated superphosphate program carried on through co-operatives probably accounted for most of the difference.

The similarity in plant-nutrient content of mixed fertilizers distributed by co-operative and commercial firms suggests that imperfect buyer knowledge and irrational demand are the principal obstacles to the marketing of more economical fertilizers. Co-operatives clearly have no incentive to restrict the output of high-analysis fertilizers below the quantities their members will buy. They sell only slightly higher grades than commercial firms in the North Central states and about the same grades as the rest of the industry in the South. A reasonable inference is that both co-operative and non-co-operative producers handle the grades of fertilizers farmers generally want.

Other evidence supports this conclusion. Fertilizer manufacturers and distributors are numerous. While they have sometimes conspired to fix prices, it is doubtful that so many sellers could have conspired to hold down the plant-nutrient content of their fertilizers. In fact, they generally try to find out in advance of the fertilizer season what grades farmers will want. Nearly all of them consult the lists of recommended grades put out by state agricultural colleges and the U.S. Department of Agriculture. Many have their dealers and agents canvass the farmers in their territories. Some conduct extensive market surveys.

Swift & Company conducted such a survey in 1946 in connection with its investigation of the long-run demand for concentrated superphosphate.[11] Swift's fertilizer-plant managers and sales agencies were required to estimate for their respective markets the ratio high-analysis fertilizers,[12] if made available and properly promoted, would bear to total fertilizer sales in 1946, 1950, and 1955. Swift requested similar estimates from most of the state agricultural colleges, and had its Plant Food Division make its own independent estimate. All three estimates revealed that farmers in the Midwest would probably buy more high-analysis fertilizers if they were properly promoted. But for only one state, Wisconsin, did the estimates show that high-analysis fertilizer sales might possibly exceed forty per cent of total fertilizer sales (Table 52). For all other regions, high-analysis fertilizer sales were estimated at less than thirty per cent, and for most southern states at twenty per cent or less.

The survey cannot be easily interpreted, because terms such as "properly promoted" are not easily defined. But the survey represented an attempt to find out the fertilizer demand for high-analysis fertilizers; the low estimates reflected a prevailing opinion that most farmers would not buy them. Reports from individual managers and agricultural colleges, especially those from the border and southern states, revealed some of the reasons why. They reported a general disinterest in high-analysis fertilizers among dealers and farmers; some stated that farmers would probably apply the same tonnage per acre regardless of the grade used and, accordingly, would find high-analysis fertilizers more costly; others stated that some southern farmers did not own machinery for applying high-analysis fertilizers; and still others stated that landlords in the South resisted the use of high-analysis fertilizers because they did not believe that tenant farmers knew how to use them properly. Tests conducted by the U.S. Department of Agriculture as early as 1929 had shown that most fertilizer applicators then in use could efficiently apply fertilizers

---

[11] See Chap. 8.
[12] Swift & Co. refers to high-analysis as "multiple-grade" fertilizers and defines them as those containing 40 per cent or more plant nutrients. Except for certain straight potassic materials, it is almost impossible to manufacture a fertilizer containing as much as 40 per cent plant nutrients without using concentrated superphosphate.

TABLE 52

RATIO OF PROJECTED HIGH-ANALYSIS FERTILIZER SALES TO
TOTAL FERTILIZER SALES; BY STATE AND REGION, 1950 [a]

| State | Per Cent High Analysis in 1950 |
|---|---|
| Midwest: | |
| Indiana | 40 |
| Illinois | 40 |
| Michigan | 40 |
| Iowa | 40 |
| Wisconsin | 50 |
| Ohio | 30 |
| Kansas | 30 |
| East: | |
| New York | 30 |
| Pennsylvania | 30 |
| West Virginia | 20 |
| Massachusetts | large[b] |
| New Jersey | slight[b] |
| South: | |
| Missouri | 20 |
| Kentucky | 20 |
| Tennessee | 20 |
| Arkansas | 30 |
| Oklahoma | 20 |
| Maryland | slight[b] |
| Virginia | 10 |
| North Carolina[d] | 20[c] / slight[b] |
| South Carolina | slight[b] |
| Georgia[d] | 5[c] / slight[b] |
| Louisiana[d] | 25[c] / 5 |
| West: | |
| California[d] | slight[b] |
| Washington and Oregon | 25 |

[a] Records of Swift & Company.
[b] Specific percentages not given.
[c] Highest of several estimates.
[d] Entire state not represented.

containing nearly ninety per cent plant nutrients.[13] The reasons given can therefore be reduced to imperfect buyer knowledge.

Finally, fertilizer manufacturers appear to have no incentive to restrict the supply of high-analysis fertilizers. At 1949 factor costs a unit of plant nutrient could be produced cheaper in high-analysis fertilizers; at 1949 prices plant nutrients were cheaper for the farmer in high-analysis fertilizers; and while profit margins on various grades of fertilizer for 1949 are not available, those for earlier years show that manufacturers

[13] The tests made by the Department's Bureau of Plant Industry, Soils and Agricultural Engineering (then the Bureau of Chemistry and Soils) showed that 1929 model fertilizer applicators could be adjusted to spread fertilizers five times as concentrated as the average ton of mixed fertilizer sold in 1929. In 1929 the average ton of fertilizer contained about eighteen per cent plant nutrients. (A. L. Mehring and G. A. Cumings, *Factors Affecting the Mechanical Application of Fertilizers to the Soil*, U. S. Dept. of Agric. Technical Bulletin No. 182 [Washington: 1930], *esp.* pp. 160-62).

have a profit incentive to produce more high-analysis and less low-analysis fertilizers. According to studies made for the Office of Price Administration by the Federal Trade Commission (Table 53), in 1941 the average

TABLE 53

PROFIT MARGINS ON SPECIFIC GRADES OF FERTILIZERS, 1941 AND 1942 [a]

| | 1941 | | | 1942 | | |
|---|---|---|---|---|---|---|
| Grade | No. Plants | Average Profit Per Ton | Per Unit | No. Plants | Average Profit Per Ton | Per Unit |
| 3-8-5 regular (16%) | 12 | $0.53 | $0.03 | 13 | $3.45 | $0.22 |
| 3-8-5 tobacco (16%) | 14 | 1.27 | 0.08 | 16 | 3.04 | 0.19 |
| 4-8-4 (16%) | 20 | 1.07 | 0.07 | 21 | 3.48 | 0.22 |
| 3-8-6 (17%) | 4 | 1.78 | 0.10 | 6 | 3.28 | 0.19 |
| 5-7-5 (17%) | 8 | 0.40 | 0.02 | 9 | 3.34 | 0.19 |
| Average for 16%—17% grades | | $1.01 | $0.06 | | $3.32 | $0.21 |
| 4-12-4 (20%) | 21 | 1.66 | 0.08 | 23 | 4.15 | 0.21 |
| 2-12-6 (20%) | 25 | 2.45 | 0.12 | 25 | 4.03 | 0.20 |
| 0-12-12 (24%) | 23 | 2.21 | 0.09 | 23 | 4.39 | 0.18 |
| Average for 20%—24% grades | | $2.11 | $0.10 | ........... | $4.14 | $0.20 |

[a] FTC, *Costs, Prices and Profits in the Fertilizer Industry—1942* (an unpublished study conducted for the OPA).

profit per ton of fertilizer containing from twenty per cent to twenty-four per cent plant nutrients was $2.11, whereas that on fertilizers containing sixteen per cent and seventeen per cent was only $1.10; in 1942 the corresponding profit margins were $4.14 and $3.32. In 1941 the average profit per unit of plant nutrient for the twenty per cent to twenty-four per cent grades was $0.10, and for the sixteen per cent and seventeen per cent grades was $0.06; in 1942 the corresponding margins were $0.20 and $0.21. For the two years combined, the average profit per unit of plant nutrient for the higher grades was $0.15, for the lower grades, $0.135. Had farmers bought the same quantity of plant nutrients, but bought them all in the form of the higher grades, fertilizer manufacturers would have made larger profits. They presumably would have bought more because the price per unit of plant nutrient would have been less, and profits would have been still larger. A reasonable inference is that manufacturers did not produce more of the higher grades because farmers, who buy with imperfect knowledge, did not prefer them.

## C. MIXED FERTILIZERS *vs.* STRAIGHT MATERIALS

Of the total tonnage of fertilizers sold in the United States, nearly seventy per cent reaches the farmer as mixed fertilizers and the remaining thirty per cent as straight materials. If at prevailing prices farmers would purchase greater quantities of separate materials were they available, fertilizer manufacturers do not supply the most economical types of fertilizers. For example, if in view of the fertility of their soils and the crops they propose to raise, farmers would purchase straight concentrated superphosphate, but are forced to buy the desired quantities of $P_2O_5$ by purchasing mixed fertilizers containing superfluous quantities of potash and nitrogen, a certain amount of economic waste results. While it is obviously impossible to compare the actual plant nutrients each farmer buys with those he should buy, a comparison of co-operative and commercial sales should show whether commercial firms restrict the sales of straight materials. Nor is it possible to compare the costs of home-mixed and pre-mixed fertilizers. To make such a comparison would require cost data on home-mixing operations. These are not available. It is possible only to compare the delivered-to-the-farm costs of the plant nutrients farmers buy in mixed fertilizers with what farmers would have paid for the same plant nutrients in straight materials. The difference between the two indicates how much farmers pay to have their plant nutrients arrive at the farm mixed in the desired ratios, but whether it is greater or less than the cost of home mixing cannot be determined.

In 1949 American farmers consumed 12,839,506 tons of mixed fertilizers containing 496,889 tons of N, 1,395,654 tons of $P_2O_5$, and 992,494 tons of $K_2O$. The average analysis of all mixed fertilizers was 3.87—10.87—7.73, or about the average analysis obtained by mixing two tons of 4-12-8 with one ton of 3-9-6. The weighted average delivered-to-the-farm price for one ton of such a mixture was $45.70. Hence, it can be estimated that the total bill for mixed fertilizers in 1949 was approximately $586,765,424.20 (12,839,506 X $45.70). Had American farmers not purchased the 12.8 million tons of mixed fertilizers, but had they purchased instead 1.5 million tons of 33.5 per cent ammonium nitrate, 3.1 million tons of forty-five per cent concentrated superphosphate, and 1.7 million tons of sixty per cent muriate of potash, they would have obtained the same quantities of N, $P_2O_5$, and $K_2O$ for $418,863,550 (Table 54). If it could be assumed that farmers would have purchased these particular separate materials instead of mixtures, the price American farmers paid to have their fertilizers mixed was $167,901,874, or an average of $13.07 per ton. But in view of the imperfect knowledge on the demand side of the fertilizer market, many farmers would have purchased less economical materials. The actual difference in costs between mixtures and straight materials, and therefore the computed cost of mixing, would have been somewhat less.

Whether a reduction in costs of $13 a ton would pay farmers to mix their own fertilizers obviously depends on the cost of mixing equipment and the alternative employment open to farm labor. Public agencies con-

TABLE 54

DELIVERED-TO-THE-FARM COSTS OF PLANT NUTRIENTS
DISTRIBUTED IN THE UNITED STATES IN 1949, MIXED
AND UNMIXED FORM[a]

| | Delivered-to-the-Farm Costs |
|---|---|
| 1. Mixed fertilizers—12,839,506 tons ............................... | $586,765,424.20 |
| | |
| 2. Equivalent plant nutrients as separate materials: | |
| Ammonium nitrate (33.5%): 1,483,250 tons @ $78.30 ............ | $116,138,475.00 |
| Concentrated superphosphate (45%): 3,101,450 tons @ $67.10 ............ | 208,107,295.06 |
| Muriate of potash (60%): 1,654,157 tons @ $57.20 ............ | 94,617,780.00 |
| | |
| 3. Total cost of separate materials ................................ | $418,863,550.06 |
| | |
| 4. Total cost of mixing (1-3) ..................................... | $167,901,874.14 |
| | |
| 5. Average mixing costs per ton ................................... | $ 13.07 |

[a] Adapted from data appearing in various publications of the Bureau of Plant Industry, Soils and Agricultural Engineering, U. S. Dept. of Agriculture. Prices used in the computations were those reported in *Agricultural Prices* for April 15, 1949 (Bureau of Agricultural Economics, U. S. Dept. of Agriculture).

cerned with fertilizer policy look upon home mixing as a means of reducing fertilizer costs. The Department of Agriculture found that home mixing would reduce the cost of fertilizers to farmers when factors such as "the need for a particular type of fertilizer not commercially available, local price and supply situations, and the need for utilizing farm labor during slack periods" [14] were important. So that farmers who considered home mixing would not lack the technical know-how, the Department published detailed instructions on how to mix various fertilizer materials. The Tennessee Valley Authority requires co-operative and commercial distributors of its high-analysis materials to make a portion of them available to farmers as straight materials. While such actions do not suggest that farmers would purchase more separate materials if made available to them, they reflect a judgment on the part of public agencies concerned with the nation's fertilizer problem that some substitution of straight materials for mixtures would reduce the farmer's fertilizer costs.

*The Test of Farmer-Controlled Distribution.* The portion of total fertilizer sales accounted for by straight materials for commercial and farmer-owned co-operatives varies considerably by geographical region (Table 55). In 1952 co-operatives accounted for twenty-three per cent of all fertilizer sales in New England, but for only seven per cent of the

[14] U. S. Dept. of Agriculture, *Mixing Fertilizers on the Farm*, Farmers' Bulletin No. 2007, Washington, 1949.

## TABLE 55

### PER CENT OF FERTILIZERS DISTRIBUTED AS MIXTURES AND AS STRAIGHT MATERIALS, COMMERCIAL FIRMS AND CO-OPERATIVES; BY REGION, 1952[a]

| Regions | Mixtures | | | Materials | | | All Fertilizers | | |
|---|---|---|---|---|---|---|---|---|---|
| | Commercial Firms | Co-operatives | Total | Commercial Firms | Co-operatives | Total | Commercial Firms | Co-operatives | Total |
| New England........ | 81 | 19 | 100 | 93 | 7 | 100 | 83 | 17 | 100 |
| Middle Atlantic...... | 79 | 21 | 100 | 70 | 30 | 100 | 77 | 23 | 100 |
| South Atlantic....... | 95 | 5 | 100 | 96 | 4 | 100 | 96 | 4 | 100 |
| East North Central... | 84 | 16 | 100 | 82 | 18 | 100 | 84 | 16 | 100 |
| West North Central.. | 76 | 24 | 100 | 82 | 18 | 100 | 78 | 22 | 100 |
| East South Central... | 93 | 7 | 100 | 79 | 21 | 100 | 87 | 13 | 100 |
| West South Central.. | 91 | 9 | 100 | 92 | 8 | 100 | 91 | 9 | 100 |
| Mountain........... | 100 | ...... | 100 | 98 | 2 | 100 | 98 | 2 | 100 |
| Pacific............. | 99 | 1 | 100 | 98 | 2 | 100 | 98 | 2 | 100 |
| Total—Continental United States...... | 89 | 11 | 100 | 88 | 12 | 100 | 88 | 12 | 100 |

[a] Dr. Claud L. Scroggs, "Co-operative Fertilizer Production and Distribution—New Facts and Figures," a paper presented to the American Institute of Co-operation, Columbia, Mo., August, 1953, p. 5 of "Materials for Discussion."

sales of straight materials. In the East South Central states they accounted for thirteen per cent of all fertilizer sales, but for twenty-one per cent of the sales of straight materials. In New England commercial firms sell proportionately more straight materials than do co-operatives; in the East South Central states, they sell proportionately less. But in all regions combined, co-operatives and non-co-operatives make the same proportion of their total sales in the form of straight materials. Co-operatives account for twelve per cent of all fertilizer sales and for twelve per cent of the sales of straight materials; commercial firms, for eighty-eight per cent of all fertilizers, and for eighty-eight per cent of the straight materials.

As was previously pointed out,[15] comparisons between co-operative and commercial fertilizer sales are subject to several qualifications. But co-operatives that distribute mixed fertilizers must first buy the straight materials used in their manufacture. They presumably operate to serve best the interests of their members and therefore have no incentive to manufacture mixtures out of materials their members prefer to buy unmixed. Since co-operatives and commercial firms sell the same proportion of their fertilizers as mixtures, a reasonable inference is that commercial firms generally sell straight materials in the quantities farmers demand.

[15] But see *supra*, this Chap., for the limitations of this comparison.

## D. The Role of Concentrated Superphosphate in the Manufacture of High-Analysis Fertilizer

Because the average mixed fertilizer contains almost as much $P_2O_5$ as it does N and $K_2O$ combined, it is nearly impossible to produce fertilizers containing more than twenty-five per cent plant nutrients without using concentrated superphosphate. Each unit (20 pounds) of $P_2O_5$ in the mixture requires 100 pounds of twenty per cent superphosphate. Mixing 467 pounds of thirty per cent ammonium nitrate, 1,300 pounds of twenty per cent superphosphate, and 233 pounds of sixty per cent muriate of potash theoretically would produce exactly one ton of grade 7-13-7 fertilizer. But because the mixture would need a small amount of an inert conditioning agent, the materials containing plant nutrients must weigh less than 2,000 pounds. The mixture must therefore contain less than twenty-seven per cent plant nutrients. If forty-eight per cent concentrated superphosphate were used, a mixture containing the 27 units of plant nutrients would weigh only 1,242 pounds, making it possible to produce about 43 units to the ton.

The growth of the concentrated superphosphate industry is therefore in part dependent on the demand for high-analysis fertilizers. As was shown earlier, although a unit of $P_2O_5$ may cost a little less in concentrated than in ordinary superphosphate, fertilizer manufacturers may not find it economical to use concentrated superphosphate to produce low-analysis mixtures. To the extent that imperfect buyer knowledge and irrational demand have restricted the sales of high-analysis fertilizers, they have retarded the growth in concentrated superphosphate production. Competition between western and Florida phosphate-rock producers depends in part on the growth of the concentrated superphosphate industry;[16] TVA's fertilizer distribution program is designed to stimulate wider use of concentrated superphosphate;[17] and greater acceptance of the high-analysis fertilizers requiring concentrated superphosphate to manufacture will reduce the cost of plant nutrients to farmers. For these reasons imperfect buyer knowledge and irrational demand have involved social costs which though not measurable are probably substantial.

The tonnage of concentrated superphosphate actually produced has been significantly less than that which could have been produced and distributed profitably had demand reflected more perfect knowledge and more rational choice. According to OPA records and to studies made by the Agricultural Adjustment Administration, under 1941 prices a unit of $P_2O_5$ was cheaper in concentrated superphosphate in all states west of the Mississippi River and in Illinois, Indiana, Michigan, Ohio, and

[16] See Chap. 7, pp. 135 ff.
[17] See Chap. 11, pp. 218 ff.

Kentucky; in Mississippi and Vermont the delivered price per unit of $P_2O_5$ was the same in concentrated as in ordinary superphosphate; and in all the remaining states ordinary superphosphate was the cheapest source of $P_2O_5$. Had concentrated superphosphate been purchased wherever it was the cheapest source of $P_2O_5$, total sales would have amounted to 662,208 tons (Table 56); they amounted instead to 325,111 tons. And

TABLE 56

TONNAGES OF ORDINARY AND CONCENTRATED SUPERPHOPHATE
ACTUALLY SOLD COMPARED WITH TONNAGES WHICH WOULD
HAVE PROVIDED THE CHEAPEST SOURCE OF $P_2O_5$, 1941 AND 1951 [a]

|  | 1941 | 1951 |
|---|---|---|
| Tons actually sold: | | |
| Ordinary superphosphate (18% basis)........ | 4,493,900 | 9,357,945 |
| Concentrated superphosphate (45% basis).... | 325,111 | 686,855 |
| Tons which would have provided the cheapest Source of $P_2O_5$: | | |
| Ordinary superphosphate (18% basis)........ | 3,825,727 | 1,100,525[b] |
| Concentrated superphosphate (45% basis).... | 662,208 | 3,704,480 |

[a] Adapted from various issues of *Fertilizer Consumption in the United States*, an annual publication of the Bureau of Plant Industry, Soils, and Agricultural Engineering, U. S. Dept. of Agriculture; *Agricultural Prices*, a monthly publication of the Bureau of Agricultural Economics, U. S. Dept. of Agriculture; *The Fertilizer Industry* (OPA Records, National Archives); and files of the Tennessee Valley Authority. Prices of ordinary and concentrated superphosphate are comparable within each state but are not necessarily comparable among states because of the different sources used.
[b] Alabama and South Carolina only.

ordinary superphosphate sales would have amounted to 3,825,727 tons, whereas they actually amounted to 4,493,900 tons.

By 1951 the area in which concentrated superphosphate was the cheapest source of $P_2O_5$ included practically the entire United States. The only state in which ordinary superphosphate was definitely the cheapest source of $P_2O_5$ was Alabama. The cheapest source for South Carolina could not be determined because of insufficient price data.[18] Had concentrated superphosphate been purchased wherever it was the cheapest source of $P_2O_5$, total sales would have amounted to 3,704,480 tons; they amounted instead to only 686,855 tons. And ordinary superphosphate sales would have amounted to only 1,100,525 tons instead of 9,357,945 tons (Table 56, above).

The foregoing calculations probably overstate the differences between the sales of ordinary and concentrated superphosphate actually made and those that should have been made on the basis of price per unit of plant nutrient. And the differences cannot be attributed entirely to imperfect

[18] Nor were comparable prices on ordinary and concentrated superphosphate available for New England and most of the Middle Atlantic states. However, since concentrated superphosphate was the most economical source of $P_2O_5$ in these areas as early as 1945, it is virtually certain to have been the most economical source in 1951.

buyer knowledge and irrational demand. While the factors of production used to manufacture ordinary and concentrated superphosphate are similar, they are not identical. A significant shift in demand from ordinary to concentrated would probably have increased the supply price of concentrated relative to ordinary, thereby making the differences somewhat smaller. Entry to the superphosphate industry requires several million dollars capital, familiarity with the industry's technology, and considerable study of alternative plant locations and processes.[19] Concentrated superphosphate producers, most of which also produce ordinary superphosphate, may not quickly adjust their output in response to shifts in demand. But imperfect buyer knowledge and irrational demand are the most important reasons why concentrated superphosphate has not displaced ordinary on a much larger scale. In every year following the immediate postwar shortage, except 1950, producers' concentrated superphosphate inventories increased.[20] And in most years the Tennessee Valley Authority encountered consumer resistance to its concentrated superphosphate, though it was made available to them on attractive terms.[21] Manufacturers clearly had little incentive to produce more than they did, though farmers had a strong incentive to buy it in much larger quantities.

## E. Summary

In markets where fertilizer manufacturers sell to farmers, demand reflects imperfect buyer knowledge and irrational choice. The social cost of these market imperfections is high; in truth, in recent years it appears to have been higher than that of monopoly and restraints of trade. It does not follow from this that the anti-trust laws should be administered with greater or less vigor. Practices of fertilizer manufacturers which contravene the law are no less illegal because farmers buy unwisely. But it does follow that much of the efficiency in production associated with effective competition is unattainable through anti-trust policy. In its recent study the Federal Trade Commission came to this conclusion, although it missed an essential part of the problem, when it stated:

> To a probably greater extent, however, the distribution barriers [to efficient fertilizers] are due to the existence of an archaic, expensive system of distribution which seems to be firmly embedded in the industry's way of doing business. To the extent, then, that this system has become an institution which is not dependent upon monopolistic practices, it, of course, cannot be reached by the antitrust laws.[22]

But imperfect buyer knowledge and irrational demand have helped

[19] Cf. case study of Swift & Co. (*supra*, pp. 154-56).
[20] U. S. Bureau of Mines, *Minerals Yearbook*, 1954, p. 903.
[21] See Chap. 11, p. 226 and Table 62.
[22] FTC, *Report on the Fertilizer Industry*, 1950, p. 157.

foster the inefficient production and distribution system. Selling to uninformed buyers, entrepreneurs have had no strong incentive to create a more efficient one. An individual producer may well consider the cost of promoting rational and informed buying prohibitive when he stands to gain no more than any of his rivals by doing so; he can patent neither his high-analysis fertilizers nor his "enlightened" customers.

Accordingly, the task of reducing the cost of uninformed buying has fallen to public agencies such as the Department of Agriculture, the Tennessee Valley Authority, and various state institutions. In performing their task they have sometimes taken over, and have often participated in, decisions customarily left to private business firms—they have assumed a quasi-entrepreneurial role. The sum of their activities cannot appropriately be described as public utility regulation, as the prescription of standards such as is done by the Bureau of Standards and the Pure Food and Drug Administration, or as an extension of anti-trust policy, although it includes features of them all. For the sake of brevity, the sum of these activities is called positive policy.

# CHAPTER 11

# POSITIVE POLICY: THE ROLE OF GOVERNMENT

## A. The Background of Government Activity

THE government's interest in fertilizers has been largely ancillary to its concern with agriculture. Paradoxically, while the economic philosophy of laissez faire sprang from societies dominated by agriculture and other small-scale enterprise, the complete divorcement of agriculture from government came to an end in the United States over a century ago. As early as 1839 Congress appropriated funds for collecting farm statistics and for distributing seeds and plants to farmers.[1] In 1862 Congress passed the Homestead Act, the Land-Grant College Act, and the Department of Agriculture Act. The Homestead Act provided for distributing the public domain so as to promote family unit farming; the Land-Grant College Act for the teaching of those branches of learning relating to agriculture and mechanical arts; and the USDA Act for establishing a Federal Department of Agriculture to diffuse among farmers information on agricultural subjects and to procure, propagate, and distribute to farmers new and valuable seeds and plants.[2]

It was soon recognized that mere provision for the dissemination of agricultural information was not enough. Individual farmers in the normal process of farming could not take the initiative in developing technical know-how, and the general treatises on agricultural subjects used as textbooks in land-grant colleges as late as the 1880's were much more applicable to European than to American agriculture. Accordingly, in 1887 Congress passed the Hatch Act, which provided federal funds to establish state agricultural experiment stations for the purpose, among other things, of developing useful agricultural know-how.[3]

The program still contained a fundamental weakness. It lacked the means of communicating its technological advances to farmers. Few farmers consulted state experiment stations, and still fewer attended state agricultural colleges. To overcome this weakness, Congress passed in 1914 the Smith-Lever Agricultural Extension Act, which provided federal aid for disseminating and encouraging the application of practical information on agriculture and home economics. The Act established a

---

[1] U. S., Senate, Committee on Agriculture and Forestry, *Long-Range Agricultural Policy and Program Report* (pursuant to Senate Resolution 147, February 9, 1948), 1948 p. 55.
[2] See U. S., *Statutes at Large*, XII, pp. 387, 392, and 504.
[3] See U. S., *Statutes at Large*, XXIV, p. 440. Funds were not appropriated to carry into effect provisions of the Hatch Act until February 1, 1888 (see U. S., *Statutes at Large*, XXV, p. 32).

system of county agents through which such information could reach individual farmers and farm groups.

Before World War I the basic objective of the federal government's agricultural program was efficiency. It had been built on two assumptions: The family-size farm was the desirable producing unit, but small-scale agriculture could not create and diffuse among farmers a satisfactory body of technical know-how. Accordingly, public land policy was directed toward promoting small-scale farms; and the federal government, acting primarily through state land-grant colleges, assumed an entrepreneural function—the responsibility for developing and introducing more efficient agricultural technology. Beyond this, resource allocation in agriculture was left to the market place.

After World War I agricultural policy became concerned with agricultural-resource conservation and farmers' welfare as well as efficiency. But the three objectives were not explicitly recognized in the numerous laws. As Professor Schultz has observed,

> [Objectives of policy] . . . more often than not . . . are inconsistent one with another, for all too seldom are they integral parts of a comprehensive system of means and ends. One of the major sources of this difficulty arises from the fact that the beliefs and values underlying the objectives of policy are not made explicit, they are mostly hidden, like the bulk of an iceberg afloat at sea. So it is with agricultural policy.[4]

The Bankhead-Jones Research Extension Act of 1935 provides funds for research on the basic economic problems of agriculture.[5] The Hope-Flanagan Act of 1946 provides additional funds for this purpose.[6] The Bankhead-Jones Farm Tenant Act of 1937 provides for the rehabilitation of destitute but potentially profitable farms and for the retirement of submarginal farms. The Tennessee Valley Authority's test-demonstration farm program is designed to encourage the reallocation of resources on farms to more profitable uses, also an objective of the Soil Conservation Service's program. The Bureau of Agricultural Economics and staff members of land-grant colleges apply the techniques of variable input-output analysis to agricultural data. The purpose of such programs is a more efficient allocation of agricultural resources. The parity price-support program is concerned with farmers' welfare. But it tends to encourage inefficient agricultural resource allocation.[7] Sometimes policy measures designed to promote conservation serve incidentally to reallocate resources more efficiently. The promotion of cover-crop and pasture programs,

---

[4] Theodore W. Schultz, *Production and Welfare of Agriculture* (New York: Macmillian Co., 1949), p. 1.

[5] See U. S., *Statutes at Large*, XLIX, p. 436.

[6] See U. S., *Statutes at Large*, LX, p. 1,083.

[7] For a lucid discussion of how the federal farm price support program has interfered with efficient resource allocation in agriculture, see William H. Nicholls, "America's Biggest Farm Surplus—Too Many Farmers," *Readings in Economics*, ed. Paul A. Samuelson, *et al.* (New York: McGraw-Hill, 1952), pp. 171-80.

better terracing and contour farming—all important features of conservation programs—educate the farmer to use his resources more efficiently. But often such programs encourage farmers to shift resources to unprofitable types of agriculture; when they do so, they conflict with the policy objectives of improved farmers' welfare and more efficient use of agricultural resources.

The federal government's fertilizer policy has reflected the inconsistencies and conflicts of over-all agricultural policy. Its primary objective as expressed in fertilizer policy statements is more efficient fertilizers.[8] Agencies concerned with this objective have sought methods for reducing the social costs of imperfect knowledge. They have concerned themselves especially with promoting more rational buying and more efficient use of fertilizers, and with improving the technology of fertilizer production. But agencies primarily concerned with conservation have sometimes failed explicitly to recognize the policy objective of greater efficiency. They have often used fertilizer programs to promote conservation practices. Such programs have sometimes encouraged farmers to use uneconomical fertilizers. Agencies promoting conservation have therefore worked at cross-purposes with those promoting efficiency.

## B. Positive Policy Programs

State and federal agencies influenced fertilizer practices long before explicit statements of a national fertilizer policy defined the objectives they should pursue. Connecticut's state agricultural experiment station studied the cost of plant nutrients in various types of fertilizers as early as 1875.[9] Congress made its first appropriation for fertilizer research to the Bureau of Soils in 1911. Section 124 of the National Defense Act of 1916 authorized the President to investigate all known nitrogen-fixing processes and to build government nitrogen-fixing plants.[10] Section 5 of the TVA Act authorized the Authority to produce and distribute fertilizer materials.[11] In 1935 Congress authorized the Agricultural Adjustment Administration (now the Production and Marketing Administration) to make commodity payments to farmers in fertilizers instead of cash. A year later the AAA began distributing fertilizer to farmers for conservation purposes. Other federal agencies that have played a role in the nation's fertilizer program include the Bureau of Agricultural Economics, the Farm Credit Administration, the Department of Commerce, and the

[8] The first express statement of a national fertilizer policy appeared in the *Report of the Inter-bureau Co-ordinating Committee on Fertilizer* (U. S. Dept. of Agriculture, Washington, D. C., 1941, mimeographed). A recent restatement appears in *A National Program for More Efficient Use of Fertilizer and Lime* (U. S. Dept. of Agriculture, Office of the Secretary, Washington, 1952).
[9] *Infra*, Table 64.
[10] See U. S., *Statutes at Large*, XXXIV, p. 215.
[11] See U. S., *Statutes at Large*, XLVIII, p. 58.

Department of Interior. Their fertilizer activities, however, are ancillary to both the nation's fertilizer policy and their own principal activities. The fundamentals of positive policy are to be found in the activities of agencies having a large concern with fertilizers. These agencies are the U.S. Department of Agriculture's Bureau of Plant Industry, Soils, and Agricultural Engineering and Production and Marketing Administration, the Tennessee Valley Authority, and the state fertilizer-control boards, land-grant colleges, and extension services.

*The Bureau of Plant Industry, Soils, and Agricultural Engineering.* The Bureau of Soils, predecessor agency to the Bureau of Plant Industry, Soils, and Agricultural Engineering, was the first federal agency to launch a fertilizer program. Its efforts have been directed largely toward improving fertilizer technology.[12] The Bureau of Soils initiated research on chemical methods of fixing nitrogen from the atmosphere in 1914, two years before the Defense Act of 1916 authorized the President of the United States to investigate nitrogen-fixing processes for defense purposes. The Bureau made important contributions toward placing the synthetic ammonia and urea industries on a commercial basis in the United States. During World War II it participated with other government agencies and industry, especially TVA, in the development of ammonium-nitrate fertilizers.

The Bureau's early studies of electric- and blast-furnace techniques for producing phosphoric acid contributed to the successful large-scale operation of both processes; its subsequent research on superphosphate helped perfect processes for producing better types of phosphate fertilizers. In co-operation with the fertilizer industry the Bureau studied the reactions of free ammonia with superphosphates. With the aid of state agricultural experiment stations the Bureau determined the plant-nutrient value of the resulting nitrogen-phosphate. Such studies have led to wider use of anhydrous ammonia and solutions of ammonium nitrate and urea.

After 1933 the center of technological research on phosphates shifted from the Bureau to the Tennessee Valley Authority. But the Bureau continued its phosphate research program, and its recent discoveries promise significantly to alter traditional phosphate fertilizer practices in some areas of agriculture. By the use of radioactive materials the Bureau developed tracer techniques for determining the relative importance of residual and applied fertilizers to plant growth. Until 1951 the Bureau's experiments were limited to radioactive phosphorus; they were recently extended to potassium, rubidium, sodium, zinc, and calcium.

But while the Bureau's research on nitrogen, phosphorus, and potash

[12] See K. D. Jacob, "Fertilizer Technology Research in the United States Department of Agriculture," *Transactions of the Fertilizer Society* (London, April, 1950), for a more detailed account of the Bureau of Soil's technological research.

has undoubtedly contributed to more economical fertilizers, its research on mixed fertilizers has more clearly fulfilled its policy mandates. Other federal agencies and private producers shared in developing technology that led to lower cost fertilizer materials, but the Bureau remained up to 1948 [13] the sole federal agency concerned with lowering the costs of mixed fertilizers—the form in which seventy per cent of the fertilizer reaches the farmer. Its research on mixed fertilizers developed useful information on chemical reactions in mixed fertilizers, granulation, segregation, caking, moisture absorption, drillability, and other physical and chemical properties of fertilizer mixtures. For over twenty years the Bureau has given special attention to an old public issue—the use of fillers and conditioning agents in mixed fertilizers in relation to the preparation and application of high-analysis mixtures. As technological developments have increased the plant-nutrient content of fertilizer materials, the Bureau has recommended correspondingly higher percentages of plant nutrients in mixed fertilizers. In particular, it has urged that chemical fertilizers not be diluted with surplus inert filler, and that the plant-nutrient content of mixed fertilizers be raised to thirty per cent or more.[14]

The effectiveness of its mixed-fertilizer program is difficult to assess. The Bureau has made rather modest claims, stating that in the increase in the average plant-nutrient content of mixed fertilizers from 13.9 per cent in 1920 to 24.19 per cent in 1951 its research on fillers and conditioning agents was an "important factor." [15] The effectiveness of its program in reducing the social costs of imperfect buyer knowledge depends largely on state agencies. The Bureau maintains direct and effective channels of communication with fertilizer producers. Its research on fertilizer production problems has brought the Bureau in direct contact with the industry's representatives with whom it has frequently collaborated. It has conducted many of its survey studies jointly with the National Fertilizer Association and its members. As scientists, Bureau and industry researchers are interested in similar problems, speak the same language and belong to the same professional societies. But the channels of communication between the Bureau and farmers are indirect. The state experiment stations and land-grant colleges are the immediate recipients of the information it disseminates. They in turn rely upon the State

---

[13] In 1948 TVA began to direct some of its research efforts toward this problem also.
[14] For typical statements see the following articles by A. L. Mehring: *Filler in Relation to Plant Food Units* (Mimeographed summary of an address given at Virginia Polytechnic Institute, July 16, 1936); "What the Southern Farmer Pays for the Filler in His Fertilizer" (*Commercial Fertilizer Yearbook*, 1936); "Higher Analysis Fertilizers Are More Economical" (*The Bulletin of the North Carolina Department of Agriculture*, 11, No. 1, 1936, pp. 237-8); "Materials Used as Fertilizers" (*The American Fertilizer*, March 8, 1947); and by J. O. Hardesty and R. Kumagai, "Some Properties of Fertilizer Conditioning Agents" (*The American Fertilizer*, December 10, 1949).
[15] K. D. Jacob, "Fertilizer Technology Research in the United States Department of Agriculture," *Transactions of the Fertilizer Society* (London, April, 1950), p. 8.

Extension Services' county agents to transmit such information to the farmer. The effectiveness of the Bureau's research in overcoming imperfect buyer knowledge and irrational fertilizer buying habits depends on how effectively county agents use such information to educate farmers.

*The Agricultural Conservation Program.* The Agricultural Conservation Program (ACP) of the Production and Marketing Administration (PMA) dates from the Soil Conservation and Domestic Allotment Act of 1936. The Act tied assistance to farmers with conservation after the Supreme Court had declared unconstitutional the earlier AAA payments to support farm prices and control production. It authorized annual appropriations up to $500,000,000 to pay farmers to carry out soil conservations practices—to be construed as including acreage control and parity price supports.

Until 1942-43, ACP was clearly more concerned with maintaining farm income than with conservation, as evidenced by the fact that most payments for the period 1936-42 were to compensate farmers for conforming with acreage allotments.[16] After the removal of marketing quotas and acreage allotments in World War II, nearly all payments were to cover a part of the costs of specific conservation practices, usually those recommended by either land-grant colleges or the Soil Conservation Service. Nearly half the conservation payments were to cover the costs of fertilizers (Table 57).

A program having conservation and commodity control as its principal

TABLE 57

COST OF CONSERVATION PRACTICES CARRIED OUT UNDER THE
AGRICULTURAL CONSERVATION PROGRAM, 1951 [a]

| | 1951 | |
| --- | --- | --- |
| | Millions of Dollars | % of Total |
| Conservation Practice: | | |
| Fertilizers................................... | $108.0 | 42.36 |
| Protective and Pasture Crops.................... | 42.6 | 16.59 |
| Mechanical Erosion Control..................... | 30.9 | 12.02 |
| Drainage....................................... | 9.1 | 3.54 |
| Irrigation...................................... | 9.7 | 3.77 |
| Pasture and Range............................. | 47.4 | 18.47 |
| Forestry....................................... | 1.2 | 0.48 |
| All other...................................... | 7.1 | 2.77 |
| Total.................................. | $256.7[b] | 100.00 |

[a] U. S. Dept. of Agriculture, PMA, *1951 Statistical Summary, Agricultural Conservation Program,* 1952, pp. 1-5, 91.
[b] Cumulative, 1936-51, $3,925.2 million.

[16] Charles M. Hardin, "The Politics of Conservation: an Illustration," *The Journal of Politics,* XIII (1951), 467.

objectives is not likely to give much attention to the problem of efficient fertilizer usage; it might possibly overlook the problem altogether. ACP's fertilizer program has sometimes given the problem less attention than it deserved, and sometimes completely ignored it. ACP's phosphate fertilizer distribution program has ignored it. In 1936 the AAA (now the PMA) launched a program of supplying farmers with lime and phosphate fertilizers to restore soil fertility. Initially the program combined the purposes of introducing high-analysis fertilizers in areas where they were not available, conservation, and aid to farmers. Between 1939 and 1942, ACP distributed 240,200 tons of TVA's surplus concentrated superphosphate (forty-eight per cent $P_2O_5$) and about 1.5 million tons of ordinary superphosphate (twenty per cent $P_2O_5$) for such purposes, large portions of which ACP purchased outright and distributed directly to farmers through government warehouses. But the introduction of high-analysis phosphate apparently was soon subordinated to other objectives. Commercial producers and distributors of twenty per cent superphosphate argued that the government's program hurt their business. To get the co-operation of commercial producers, ACP offered to buy at contract prices all twenty per cent superphosphate production that could not be sold commercially or used in mixed fertilizers. To still the complaints of distributors, ACP initiated the "purchase order" plan, whereby farmers acquired superphosphate from distributors who later billed the government. In its efforts to satisfy everybody, ACP compromised its objective of efficient fertilizer usage.

But the best evidence that ACP neglects the problem of efficient fertilizer usage is its system of honoring purchase orders at "fair" prices. Farmers using fertilizers for approved soil programs can obtain fertilizers from commercial distributors by presenting a purchase order approved by their county ACP committee. ACP pays the distributor all or part of the cost computed at fair prices; the distributors bill the farmer for any balance ACP payments do not cover. Fair prices are established in each local market by county committees and published in state ACP *Handbooks*.

In thirty states fair prices are set to cover the highest cost source of $P_2O_5$, and in seventeen they are graduated in accordance with prevailing and estimated ordinary and concentrated superphosphate prices.[17] In all forty-seven states farmers can purchase either ordinary or concentrated superphosphate and be assured that ACP will pay a large part or all of the costs. Their incentive to purchase $P_2O_5$ in its most economical form is therefore much smaller that it would be if ACP allowances were based on

---

[17] In the one remaining state, West Virginia, ACP phosphate fertilizer payments vary from county to county, but payment schedules are not published (see *West Virginia ACP Handbook*, 1952).

the cheapest source of $P_2O_5$; that is, they pay only a small fraction of the difference between the cost of $P_2O_5$ in its most economical and in its least economical form.

In most of the seventeen states using graduated allowances the ACP program probably discourages farmers from using the cheapest source of $P_2O_5$. In these states the allowance per unit of $P_2O_5$ is generally less for concentrated superphosphate than for ordinary superphosphate (Table 58). In no state is the allowance for a unit of $P_2O_5$ higher in concentrated

TABLE 58

FAIR PRICE ALLOWANCES PER POUND OF AVAILABLE $P_2O_5$ IN 20 PER CENT AND IN 48 PER CENT SUPERPHOSPHATE, 1952 [a]

| State | 20% Superphosphate | 48% Superphosphate |
|-------|--------------------|--------------------|
| Alabama | $0.0361 | $0.0346 |
| Arkansas | 0.040 | 0.031 |
| Georgia | 0.0355 | 0.03125 |
| Illinois | 0.035 | 0.035 |
| Indiana | 0.045 | 0.045 |
| Kentucky | 0.048 | 0.038 |
| Michigan (Northern Peninsula) | 0.060 | 0.060 |
| North Carolina | 0.035—0.038 | 0.035 |
| Ohio | 0.0475 | 0.0406 |
| Oregon (50% of cost of material not to exceed $0.05 per lb. of $P_2O_5$) | | |
| Pennsylvania | 0.040 | 0.040 |
| South Carolina | 0.025 | 0.024 |
| Tennessee | 0.0470 | 0.0369 |
| Texas | 0.048 | 0.042 |
| Virginia | 0.0350 | 0.0325 |
| Washington | 0.05 | 0.04 |
| Wisconsin | 0.05 | 0.04 |

[a] State Agricultural Conservation Program, 1952 *Handbook*.

than in ordinary. Since prevailing and estimated market prices are used as a basis for calculating PMA allowances, concentrated superphosphate is the cheapest source of $P_2O_5$ in these states. In the absence of credit allowances, farmers who buy rationally would buy the concentrated material. But under prevailing ACP payment allowances they can afford to ignore the price differentials. And because farmers have no incentive to buy concentrated superphosphate, distributors have no incentive to handle it. The ACP program therefore tends to discourage the use of economical fertilizers.

The social costs of such PMA practices exceed the unnecessary costs of the immediate quantities of phosphate fertilizers involved. The far-flung PMA organization touches the lives of virtually the entire farm population. It is a rural government within a government, and conspicuously well-situated to encourage farmers to adopt sound fertilizer purchasing practices. It serves as one of the main channels through which farmers' wants are made known in Washington, and could be equally as effective a channel for disseminating information that would lead to greater efficiency in agriculture. In failing to shape its fertilizer program to implement those of other agencies concerned with promoting enlightened fertilizer purchasing practices, ACP has further perplexed American farmers, who in dealing with the complex problems of buying and using fertilizers already act on highly imperfect knowledge.

*The Tennessee Valley Authority.* The scope of TVA's fertilizer program is spelled out in Section 5 of the Act creating a Tennessee Valley Authority,[18] which authorizes TVA's Board of Directors:

(a) To contract with commercial producers for the production of such fertilizers or fertilizer materials as may be needed in the Government's program of development and introduction in excess of that produced by Government plants.

(b) To arrange with farmers and farm organizations for large-scale practical use of the new forms of fertilizers under conditions permitting an accurate measure of the economic return they produce.

The board, to implement this responsibility and to link TVA's fertilizer program with existing agricultural institutions and conservation objectives, has permissive power:

(c) To co-operate with national, state, district, or county experimental stations or demonstration farms, with farmers, landowners and associations of farmers or landowners, for the use of new forms of fertilizers or fertilizer practices during the initial or experimental period of their introduction, and for promoting the prevention of soil erosion by the use of fertilizers and otherwise.

Further,

(d) The board in order to improve and cheapen the production of fertilizer is authorized to manufacture and sell fixed nitrogen, fertilizer, and fertilizer ingredients at Muscle Shoals by the employment of existing facilities, by modernizing existing plants, or by any other process or processes that in its judgment shall appear wise and profitable to the fixation of atmospheric nitrogen or the cheapening of the production of fertilizer.

(e) The board may make donations or sales of the product of the plant or plants operated by it to be fairly and equitably distributed through the agency of county demonstration agents, agricultural colleges, or otherwise as the board may direct, for experimentation, education, and introduction of the use of such products in co-operation with practical farmers so as to obtain information as to the value, effect, and best methods of their use.

The board is further authorized:

(f) To establish, maintain, and operate laboratories and experimental plants, and to undertake experiments for the purpose of enabling the Corporation to furnish nitrogen products for military purposes, and nitrogen and other fertilizer products for agricultural purposes in the most economical manner and at the highest standard of efficiency.

[18] 48 *Stat.* 58 (May 18, 1933).

While the Act granted TVA's board wide discretionary powers in the conduct of the Authority's fertilizer program, it emphasized TVA's role as a producer and distributor of fertilizers, and in no way limited the Authority's fertilizer program by subordinating it to regional development objectives. That the board has viewed the Authority's fertilizer program as essentially national in scope is attested by the fact that TVA has distributed over seventy per cent of its fertilizers outside the Valley states.[19]

One of the first fertilizer policy decisions the board reached was to work in co-operation with the land-grant colleges. A concomitant decision had to be reached on whether the Authority's program would be built upon nitrates, as the Act seemed to imply but did not make mandatory, or upon some other fertilizer product. The land-grant colleges and the American Farm Bureau Federation supported a phosphate program, but other considerations were important factors in the board's decision to produce phosphates, and to use the electric-furnace method: (1) Scientists who were to administer the production program believed that phosphate technology had not been as thoroughly developed as had the technology of nitrate production. (2) Between the first World War and 1933 the old nitrate plants at Muscle Shoals had become hopelessly obsolete, although a portion of one of them could be used in the electric-furnace process for superphosphate production. (3) The nearby Tennessee phosphate-rock deposits were a source of raw materials. (4) Low-cost electric power from TVA generators would be available for the electric-furnace process. (5) And elemental phosphorus, a munition of war, is an intermediate product in the electric-furnace process. A phosphate fertilizer program based on the electric-furnace process preserved some of the defense purposes of the original Muscle Shoals plants.

In 1933 TVA launched a phosphate fertilizer production and research program built on the electric-furnace process. From the beginning the Authority adopted a policy of limiting its activities to fertilizers not in general use. It began with concentrated superphosphate, which though produced commercially was not in general use. Between 1934 and 1952, TVA accounted for about twenty per cent of the concentrated super-phosphate produced in the United States (Table 59). In 1935 it began research on calcium metaphosphate (sixty per cent to sixty-two per cent $P_2O_5$), and had built a pilot plant by the outbreak of World War II when research was discontinued. By 1949, TVA had a commercial-scale furnace in operation, and by 1952 had produced 157,900 tons. In 1945, TVA began producing fused tricalcium phosphate (about twenty-eight per cent $P_2O_5$), building on a process developed earlier by the Bureau of Plant

[19] *Annual Report of the Tennessee Valley Authority*, 1951, p. A 32.

TABLE 59

## TVA PHOSPHATES AND AMMONIUM NITRATE PRODUCTION, 1934-52 [a]
(Net 1,000 tons for fiscal years ending June 30)

| | Concentrated Superphosphate | Calcium Metaphosphate | Fused Tricalcium Phosphate | Dicalcium Phosphate | Ammonium Nitrate |
|---|---|---|---|---|---|
| 1934 | 4.0 | ........ | ........ | ........ | ........ |
| 1935 | 18.2 | ........ | ........ | ........ | ........ |
| 1936 | 28.7 | ........ | ........ | ........ | ........ |
| 1937 | 35.0 | ........ | ........ | ........ | ........ |
| 1938 | 47.3 | 4.5 | ........ | ........ | ........ |
| 1939 | 67.7 | 4.6 | ........ | ........ | ........ |
| 1940 | 79.1 | 4.0 | ........ | ........ | ........ |
| 1941 | 96.4 | 11.5 | ........ | ........ | ........ |
| 1942 | 55.4 | 12.1 | ........ | ........ | ........ |
| 1943 | 60.2 | 7.1 | ........ | ........ | 12.8 |
| 1944 | 48.0 | 3.0 | ........ | 9.0 | 130.7 |
| 1945 | 22.4 | 4.3 | 1.0 | 6.4 | 111.4 |
| 1946 | 68.0 | 8.1 | 15.4 | 24.8 | 153.0 |
| 1947 | 128.1 | 8.2 | 23.1 | 21.7 | 154.3 |
| 1948 | 152.5 | 6.4 | 27.3 | 24.0 | 154.9 |
| 1949 | 158.7 | 3.5 | 15.2 | 36.6 | 151.2 |
| 1950 | 125.4 | 16.4 | 17.5 | 49.6 | 136.6 |
| 1951 | 142.9 | 31.3 | 17.5 | ........ | 136.1 |
| 1952 | 132.2 | 32.9 | 14.8 | ........ | 197.2 |
| Total | 1,470.2 | 157.9 | 131.8 | 172.1 | 1,338.2 |

[a] *Annual Report of the Tennessee Valley Authority,* various issues.

Industry, Soils, and Agricultural Engineering. By 1952, TVA had produced 132,000 tons and had begun distributing it to farmers on an experimental basis. It has also carried on extensive research on various nitrogen-phosphate and nitrogen-phosphate-potash fertilizers, and has developed to the pilot-plant stage several nitric-acid processes for producing superphosphates.

Every phosphate manufacturer in the United States has probably benefited directly or indirectly from TVA's research, but those that have benefited directly comprise an impressive list. At least sixteen companies have obtained designs or detailed operating information, or both, on TVA installations and processes; five have employed TVA personnel to assist them with initial plant operations; five other phosphate manufacturers and several engineering and construction companies have sent representatives and operators to Wilson Dam for training in TVA plants; and two fertilizer producers have built plants using one of TVA's nitric-phosphate processes.[20]

Most of TVA's activities have been directed to its policy objective of new and cheaper fertilizers, but some have grown out of the needs for national defense. During World War II, TVA became the principal source of elemental phosphorus for military purposes. In 1943, at the request of

[20] TVA Records, Wilson Dam, Alabama.

the War Food Administration, TVA began producing dicalcium phosphate, a mineral supplement for stock feed then in short supply. Between 1943 and 1950, TVA produced and sold 171,800 tons of the material. It discontinued the operation in 1950 on the grounds that it contributed little to research knowledge or soil-building objectives, and turned over all accumulated information on manufacturing processes and marketing channels to potential commercial producers. And during the war TVA manufactured ammonium nitrate for defense purposes. At the end of the war TVA adapted its facilities to produce ammonium-nitrate fertilizer. By 1952 it had produced nearly one-and-a-half million tons (Table 59).

As a matter of policy TVA has distributed only its own fertilizers, although the TVA Act authorized it to distribute those of commercial firms as well. It has therefore had to use channels of distribution especially suited to experimental fertilizers. TVA has tried to co-ordinate its fertilizer distribution with its soil conservation, flood control, and regional development program; the channels used also had to serve these purposes. And TVA as a matter of policy has relied heavily upon local institutions to organize and administer its distribution program. In truth, it is alleged that TVA has been as much concerned with promoting the local institutions themselves as it has with its more immediate fertilizer objectives.[21] Distributive channels serving these purposes do not reach directly a large proportion of the farmers who use commercial fertilizers, and hence are not necessarily the most effective means for overcoming farmers' imperfect knowledge and irrational fertilizer buying practices.

TVA has distributed its fertilizer through four principal channels (Table 60). It has distributed nearly ninety-nine per cent of it through demonstration farms, other government agencies, and other sales, primarily co-operatives. The rest has been used in co-operation with state agricultural experiment stations and the USDA for purposes of testing and evaluating TVA fertilizers, a program carried out through contracts with eleven states.

*TVA's Test-Demonstration Program.* A little over ten per cent of TVA's fertilizers have gone into practical farm test-demonstrations, but the small percentage understates considerably the importance TVA attaches to this channel of distribution. The test-demonstration farm is an educational device county agents have found effective. In educational work with farmers they have relied heavily on the "example" approach. Test-demonstration farms are examples. They serve also as the counterpart

---

[21] See Philip Selznick, *TVA and the Grass Roots* (Berkeley and Los Angeles: University of California, 1949), pp. 37, 205-13; for a more moderate interpretation see Norman I. Wengert, *Valley of Tomorrow, The TVA and Agriculture* (University of Tennessee Record Extension Series, XXVIII, No. 1 [Knoxville, 1952], p. 18).

TABLE 60

TRIBUTION OF TVA FERTILIZERS, CUMULATIVE TO JUNE 30, 1951 [a]

| | Concentrated Superphosphate | | Calcium Metaphosphate | | Fused Tricalcium Phosphate | |
|---|---|---|---|---|---|---|
| | Tons | % | Tons | % | Tons | % |
| Preliminary investigation..... | 4,629.97 | 0.35 | 1,839.92 | 1.49 | 994.71 | 0.83 |
| Practical farm test-demonstration................... | 274,123.36 | 21.05 | 87,258.17 | 70.57 | 117,919.84 | 97.92 |
| Other TVA purposes........ | 3,705.63 | 0.28 | 57.85 | 0.05 | 1,188.58 | 0.99 |
| Sales to other govt. agencies.. | 339,130.86 | 26.04 | 3,877.01 | 3.13 | 3.68 | 0.00 |
| Other sales............... | 680,852.95 | 52.28 | 30,612.73 | 24.76 | 320.00 | .27 |
| Total.................. | 1,302,442.77 | 100.00 | 123,645.68 | 100.00 | 120,426.81 | 100.01 |

| | Ammonium Nitrate | | Other Fertilizer Materials | | Grand Total | |
|---|---|---|---|---|---|---|
| | Tons | % | Tons | % | Tons | % |
| Preliminary investigation..... | 1,099.45 | 0.10 | 1,667.95 | 0.09 | 10,232.00 | 0.22 |
| Practical farm test-demonstration................... | 27,849.12 | 2.44 | 17,847.84 | 0.92 | 524,998.33 | 11.37 |
| Other TVA purposes........ | 395.40 | 0.03 | 37,871.43 | 1.96 | 43,218.89 | 0.94 |
| Sales to other govt. agencies... | 78,608.00 | 6.89 | 784,302.46 | 40.62 | 1,205,922.01 | 26.11 |
| Other sales............... | 1,033,491.65 | 90.54 | 1,089,113.23 | 56.41 | 2,834,390.56 | 61.37 |
| Total.................. | 1,141,443.62 | 100.00 | 1,930,802.91 | 100.00 | 4,618,761.79 | 100.01 |

[a] *Annual Report of the Tennessee Valley Authority*, 1951.

of pilot plants in industry. Results of greenhouse and plot experimentation are not indicative of a commercial farm's production possibilities; they show only the outputs associated with a given input—a certain type of fertilizer. Inputs on the "whole" farm include not only fertilizers, but, among other things, farm management, livestock, labor, machinery, and water. The test-demonstration farm is an instrument for ascertaining economical combinations of farm inputs as well as economical fertilizer practices.

There is a strong presumption that farmers accept the results obtained on test-demonstration farms—production establishments that closely resemble their own—with more confidence than those obtained in greenhouse and plot experimentation. But farmers are not the only beneficiaries of test-demonstration farm results. Fertilizer producers are able to test new products on the "practical" farm, and on a whole range of crops, soil types, and climatic conditions. Because TVA produces new and untested fertilizers, and tries to distribute them in ways which promote more economical fertilizer practices, conservation, and better resource allocation on farms, its program requires a channel of distribution that serves as a testing and educational device. The test-demonstration farm serves these purposes.

Between 1935 and 1952, TVA used about 68,000 test-demonstration farms. Seventy-five per cent of the total were in the Tennessee Valley watershed area, ten per cent in the seven Valley states outside the watershed area, and fifteen per cent in non-Valley states. Altogether, the farms represent a total of nearly ten million acres of farm land. Until July, 1951, test-demonstration farms were divided into two classes: unit test-demonstrators, which were interspersed with other farms in rural communities, and area test-demonstrators, which were organized to carry out a community agricultural program. From 1935 until 1948 test-demonstrators received TVA fertilizers by paying only the handling and freight charges. In return, unit test-demonstrators committed themselves to increase food and livestock feed production, to adjust land-use practices to prescribed principles of soil conservation, to keep records, and to make their farms accessible to extension service personnel and other farmers. Area test-demonstrators received TVA fertilizers by participating in a watershed or community development program. A community organization, usually formed on the initiative of the county agent, drew up the plans under which each co-operating farmer participated. TVA discontinued area test-demonstrations in July, 1951.

Between 1948 and 1952, reflecting several years of deliberate reappraisal of its policies, TVA made important changes in its test-demonstration program.[22] In 1949, TVA, the co-operating Valley state colleges, and test-demonstration farmers worked out a graduated payment plan whereby the longer farmers participated in the program the higher the percentage of the total costs of fertilizer they would pay.[23] The plan met one of the most damaging criticisms of the test-demonstration program as an educational medium; namely, that farm adjustments made possible by relatively free fertilizers would not necessarily be profitable for non-participating farmers, or for participating farmers after they left the program. However, TVA officials found the graduated payment plan difficult to administer, and discontinued it in July, 1951. Since that date all test-demonstration farmers, regardless of length of participation, have paid substantially uniform prices as established by TVA's board, plus freight and handling charges. The board has generally set prices at approximately one-third of the fertilizer's market value.

TVA's policy reappraisal also produced a new definition of purpose for test-demonstrations. The objectives of test-demonstration farms in the national fertilizer program were "to determine farmer acceptance of experimental fertilizer materials and to promote the selective use of these materials in improved farming systems." [24] For these purposes plans called for approximately fifty test-demonstration farms in each participating state outside the Valley area. Farms selected to carry out the program were to participate for a maximum of five years. The test-

---

[22] This change was requested by the 80th Congress (see Wengert, *op. cit.*, p. 39).
[23] Set forth in TVA's Test-Demonstration *Project Authorization,* Serial No. 511, drafted May 18, 1951.
[24] *Ibid.*

demonstration program for the Valley area called for a larger number of participating farms and for a longer period of participation for a selected number of farms.[25] According to the Project Authorization:

The greater number of test-demonstrations in the Valley is to obtain representation of the great variety of soil-agricultural combinations within this region and to further TVA's special interest in the use of its products for agricultural development and the improvement of water-shed-stream flow relationships in the Valley. . . . In further response to TVA's special interests in the Valley, provision is made for the selection of long-term farms from those that have participated for five years or more to remain in the program for indefinite periods. The purpose of this group of farms, which shall not exceed one-fourth of the total number of Valley test-demonstration farms, is to determine and demonstrate the effects of improved fertilization in good farming systems over long periods and through varying economic conditions. . . . [They] will serve as community guides and educational devices to encourage co-ordination of effort among the several agencies working in the Valley.

In redefining its test-demonstration program TVA distinguished more clearly than it ever had before between its objectives inside and outside the Valley, and in doing so eliminated some of the confusion between TVA's fertilizer program and its broader agricultural program.

From its inception TVA's test-demonstration program, in keeping with TVA's policy of administering through local institutions, has been virtually under the complete control of the state land-grant-college extension services. Test-demonstration farms have usually been selected by community groups. The county agent, as an influential member of local farm groups, exerts considerable influence on the selection.[26] Test-demonstration farms so selected have obtained TVA fertilizers by promising to adjust their land-use practices to conform to those recommended by the land-grant colleges, or jointly by them and TVA. County agents translate the recommendations to the participating farmers. To help administer the program TVA has provided funds for assistant county agents. Assistant county agents are selected by and responsible to the extension services.

TVA's test-demonstration program has probably stimulated the development of more efficient fertilizers. It hastened the growth of large-scale concentrated superphosphate commercial operations, and made some farmers more aware of the value of fertilizers generally, of the advantages of high-analysis fertilizers, and of the possible advantages of separate materials over mixed fertilizers. While many farmers still use large quantities of low-analysis phosphate fertilizers when it is uneconomical for them to do so, the relatively small number of test-demonstrations could scarcely have been expected to stamp out deep-rooted and pervasive

---

[25] *Project Authorization,* Serial No. 511, called for 1,350 test-demonstrations outside the Valley and 2,100 in the Valley by 1954—an average of 50 per non-Valley state and 20 per Valley county. As of December, 1952, the program included 845 non-Valley and 2,708 Valley farms; 376 of the latter were long-term farms.
[26] Selznick, *op. cit.,* pp. 129 ff.

irrational buying and imperfect buyer knowledge in less than a single generation. But TVA's test-demonstration program has suffered from obvious defects. Neither TVA nor the land-grant colleges have clearly distinguished between soil conservation and efficient farm management. In fact, the entire test-demonstration farm program was administered for many years as though good farm-management practices consisted chiefly of good soil conservation, and its effectiveness was measured largely in terms of conservation criteria. This defect has been compounded by the Authority's and the extension service's reliance on physical rather than economic techniques of measurement. In a comprehensive study of Valley state test-demonstrations in 1940, made jointly by the land-grant colleges, the Department of Agriculture, and TVA,[27] results were measured almost entirely in terms of acreages in pastures and small grains, the number of trees planted, changes in livestock population per farm, and so forth. More recent studies have used similar yardsticks of progress.[28] But such yardsticks provide no basis for determining the effect of test-demonstration on farm management, of which economical fertilizer practices are a part, and suggest that fertilizer practice objectives are subordinated to, if not largely obscured by, those of soil conservation.

*TVA Distribution Through Farm Co-operatives and Commercial Firms.* Because TVA carries on a fertilizer research, development, and production program with commercial-size plants, it has also carried on a commercial-scale distribution program. Yet, as a matter of policy, TVA has tried to avoid duplicating and competing with commercial manufacturers and distributors; it has tried to maximize the educational value of fertilizers rather than the profits of its fertilizer operations. TVA has distributed about sixty per cent of its fertilizer materials through farmer-owned co-operatives and commercial distributors (Table 60) under contracts that limited the use of such materials to experimental and educational activities.

TVA's use of co-operatives and commercial firms as distributive channels is a logical final step in its program of developing more economical fertilizers and encouraging farmers to use them. The real test of success for a particular fertilizer produced by TVA is whether, after a reasonable period for testing and demonstration, it can be sold in the market at a price that covers all costs. This requires that TVA produce and sell fertilizer under conditions reasonably similar to those private firms encounter. By 1945, TVA had in operation commercial-scale concentrated-superphosphate, calcium-metaphosphate, and ammonium-ni-

---

[27] TVA, *Results of Cooperative Tests of Tennessee Valley Authority Plant-Food Materials by the Valley States Land-Grant Colleges*, Part 2, December, 1941 (Mimeographed). Subsequent reports on test-demonstrations made by individual states have been equally as remiss on this score.

[28] See TVA, *Food at the Grass Roots, The Nation's Stake in Soil Minerals*, Knoxville, 1947, pp. 64-65.

trate plants, and was planning large-scale production of other experimental fertilizer materials, notably fused tricalcium phosphate. State experiment stations had tested the materials for their agronomic value, and TVA's test-demonstration program had tested them on farms. Contracts with farm co-operatives and industrial firms were to provide for their large-scale distribution under simulated market conditions. Under the terms of the contracts, distributors obligated themselves to furnish TVA with detailed distribution costs and to sell TVA fertilizers only to farmers who agreed to put them into an "improved-use" program.[29] TVA's sales program, therefore, imposes fewer restrictions on the use of TVA fertilizers than does its test-demonstration program, and more successfully divorces economical fertilizer practices from soil and water conservation objectives. Yet the restrictions tend to keep TVA fertilizers out of conventional commercial channels where the sole requisite to possession is payment of the prevailing price.

In 1952 TVA sold fertilizer outside the Valley area through three regional co-operatives and seven commercial firms. The three regional co-operatives had fifty-seven affiliates that sold in thirty-six states, and the commercial firms sold in fourteen states. In the Valley area TVA sold directly through six federated co-operatives and six county co-operatives, and indirectly through another federated co-operative. Nearly all the fertilizer materials TVA produced on a commercial scale in 1952 reached the farmer through these channels (Table 61), whereas earlier large

TABLE 61

PER CENT OF TVA FERTILIZERS DISTRIBUTED THROUGH
VARIOUS CHANNELS, SELECTED YEARS[a]

|  | Year Introduced % | 1947 % | 1952 % |
|---|---|---|---|
| Concentrated Superphosphate: | | | |
| Testing and demonstration............ | 100.00 | 17.58 | 0.4 |
| Other............................... | ......... | 0.71 | ......... |
| Sales............................... | ......... | 81.71 | 99.6 |
| Calcium Metaphosphate: | | | |
| Testing and demonstration............ | 100.00 | 99.82 | 17.9 |
| Other............................... | ......... | 0.18 | ......... |
| Sales............................... | ......... | ......... | 82.1 |
| Fused Tricalcium Phosphate: | | | |
| Testing and demonstration............ | 100.00 | 99.84 | 62.8 |
| Other............................... | ......... | 0.16 | ......... |
| Sales............................... | ......... | ......... | 37.2 |
| Ammonium Nitrate: | | | |
| Testing and demonstration............ | ......... | 0.07 | 0.1 |
| Other............................... | ......... | 17.19 | ......... |
| Sales............................... | ......... | 81.91 | 99.9 |

[a] *Annual Report of the Tennessee Valley Authority*, 1935-52 issues.

[29] An improved use of fertilizers could relate to a specific crop as well as to whole farm planning, and was based on fertilization practices recommended by the land-grant colleges and the U. S. Dept. of Agriculture (from *Selective Uses of TVA Fertilizers*, a three-page Mimeographed statement, dated April 2, 1952 [TVA files, Fertilizer Distribution Division, Knoxville, Tennessee]).

quantities were used in preliminary testing and demonstrations. From 1934 until 1938 virtually all of TVA's concentrated superphosphate went into testing, demonstrations, and the AAA program. Even as late as 1947, two years after TVA initiated its direct-distribution program, 17.6 per cent of its concentrated superphosphate and nearly all of its calcium metaphosphate and fused tricalcium phosphate went into testing and demonstrations. By 1952, TVA's fertilizers, except for fused tri-calcium phosphate, were distributed almost entirely through its direct sales program. The Authority's ammonium nitrate was transformed from an experimental to a fully accepted fertilizer in only a few years, but the ready acceptance of ammonium nitrate by farmers was due in part to the post-war nitrogen shortage.

TVA has generally followed a policy of selling its fertilizer materials to distributors at delivered prices in the lower market range of delivered prices on comparable commercial fertilizers. Prices in effect on various days in August, 1952 (Table 62), show that TVA's average delivered

TABLE 62

COMPARISON OF TVA AND COMMERCIAL MARKET
PRICES, AUGUST, 1952 [a]

(Price Per Unit of Plant Nutrient)

| | TVA Prices | | Commercial Market Prices | |
|---|---|---|---|---|
| | F.O.B. Sheffield | Average Delivered [b] | F.O.B. Producers Plant | Average Delivered [b] |
| Ammonium nitrate (33.5%) | $1.71 | ....... | $1.91—$2.00 | ........ |
| Concentrated superphosphate (48%) | 0.92 | $1.14 | 0.87 | $1.205 |
| Calcium metaphosphate (62%) | 0.8755 | 1.097 | ............. | ........ |

[a] Price data compiled by Fertilizer Distribution Branch, Tennessee Valley Authority, Knoxville, Tennessee.
[b] Average delivered price to fifty-five cities in twenty-five states. TVA delivered prices are quoted f.o.b. Sheffield prices plus transportation charges. Commercial concentrated superphosphate prices are based on f.o.b. Tampa prices.

price on concentrated superphosphate was approximately five per cent less per unit of $P_2O_5$ than on commercial superphosphate in the same area; its price on calcium metaphosphate was about 10 per cent less per unit than commercial concentrated superphosphate. TVA justifies this price differential on the grounds that buyers must be induced to accept the "improved-use" restriction and the risk and uncertainty associated with TVA's newer fertilizers materials.

But while prevailing market prices generally determine TVA's base prices (prices f.o.b. Sheffield), the extent to which they do so depends largely upon how wide an area TVA wishes its sales program to cover. Because its sales program is designed to channel fertilizer materials into improved uses and to stimulate more economical fertilizer practices on the farm, TVA's pricing policy differs considerably from that of a commercial firm attempting to maximize its profits. In the postwar years TVA could have increased profits by raising base prices and selling its entire output in the Midwest and other nearby areas comprising its natural market area. Instead, it set base prices that permitted nationwide sales. Commercial firms unencumbered with a fertilizer educational program could have obtained higher total revenue from the sale of the same fertilizers.

*TVA also incurs certain costs it would not incur if it operated strictly as a commercial firm. Its fertilizer research program is more extensive than its own contemplated production program alone would justify. Its production facilities are geared as much to developmental and experimental work as they are to minimizing production costs. It maintains sufficiently flexible plant and equipment to serve both defense and peacetime needs, and maintains facilities at Muscle Shoals, notably those used to produce concentrated superphosphate, that could operate at lower costs elsewhere. And it performs certain public services that commercial firms are not generally expected to perform. On the other hand TVA obtains electric power at lower rates than those paid by private industry, does not pay certain taxes, and is not liable for certain damages.

But while TVA's revenues are lower and its costs possibly higher than those for a private firm of comparable size, its fertilizer operations are self-sustaining. The net income from TVA's fertilizer program for fiscal 1951 was over $0.2 million, and for fiscal 1952, almost $1.5 million (Table 63). These net incomes represent a rate of return on next fixed assets of 1.1 per cent in 1951 and 6.9 per cent in 1952.[30] If TVA's income statement could be made comparable to that of a commercial firm the rates of return on assets would probably be higher. The elimination of research, testing, and demonstration costs alone would increase the rate of return for 1951 to 6.6 per cent, and for 1952 to 16.9 per cent.

These data suggest that high-analysis fertilizers of the types produced by TVA can be produced profitably. TVA's direct sales activities, in providing a reasonably sound basis for this conclusion, bestow a measure of success on TVA's entire fertilizer program. But the data also reveal weaknesses in the Authority's program as an effective guide for private industry. While its total fertilizer operations may have been profitable, the profitability of various materials has varied widely. TVA's ammonium-nitrate operations have been highly profitable; its phosphate operations—where

---

[30] According to the *Annual Report of the Tennessee Valley Authority,* 1951 and 1952, total net assets used in fertilizer production were valued at $19.9 million in 1951 and at $21.6 million in 1952.

TABLE 63

NET INCOME ON VARIOUS TVA FERTILIZER OPERATIONS
FOR FISCAL YEARS 1951 AND 1952 [a]
(In Thousands of Dollars)

| | Total | | Phosphorus and Concentrated Superphosphate | | Calcium Metaphosphate | | Fused Tricalcium Phosphate | | Ammonium Nitrate | |
|---|---|---|---|---|---|---|---|---|---|---|
| | 1951 | 1952 | 1951 | 1952 | 1951 | 1952 | 1951[f] | 1952 | 1951 | 1952 |
| Sales.............. | $16,106 | $18,694 | $ 7,554 | $ 6,376 | $ 1,379 | $ 1,596 | ...... | $ 138 | $ 7,173 | $10,587 |
| Test-demonstration shipments[b]......... | 1,226 | 616 | 167 | 24 | 381 | 354 | $ 667 | 225 | 11 | 13 |
| Total revenue......... | $17,332 | $19,314 | $ 7,721 | $ 6,400 | $ 1,760 | $ 1,950 | $ 667 | $ 363 | $ 7,184 | $10,600 |
| Production and distribution cost......... | 16,184 | 14,842 | 6,951 | 6,353 | 1,718 | 2,280 | 641 | 678 | 5,874 | 5,532 |
| Gross income from products[c]............. | $ 2,148 | $ 4,471 | $ 770 | $ 47 | $ 42 | ($330) | $ 26 | ($315) | $ 1,310 | $ 5,068 |
| General expenses[d]..... | 820 | 817 | ...... | ...... | ...... | ...... | ...... | ...... | ...... | ...... |
| Net income before research, etc......... | $ 1,328 | $ 3,654 | ...... | ...... | ...... | ...... | ...... | ...... | ...... | ...... |
| Research, tests, and demonstrations costs... | 1,101 | 2,170 | ...... | ...... | ...... | ...... | ...... | ...... | ...... | ...... |
| Net income from fertilizers and munitions[e] | $ 227 | $ 1,484 | ...... | ...... | ...... | ...... | ...... | ...... | ...... | ...... |

[a] *Annual Report of the Tennessee Valley Authority,* 1951 and 1952 issues.
[b] Estimated at prices comparable to TVA sales prices but in the aggregate less than total cost.
[c] ( ) Indicates loss.
[d] TVA does not allocate general, research, and testing and demonstration costs over its various fertilizer materials.
[e] $163,000 loss in 1950.
[f] Includes small quantities of dicalcium phosphate.

TVA has put most of its research and development efforts—operated at a $1.4 million loss in 1952, and about broke even in 1951.

The losses can possibly be explained in terms of extraordinary conversion costs, pilot-plant and development costs, and other costs unique to TVA's operations. But the long-run effectiveness of TVA's fertilizer program depends on the Authority's ability to foster fertilizer-consumption patterns consistent with production costs. Its principal guide in pricing its new products as they are shifted from testing and demonstrations to direct sales need be, not TVA's own costs, but the best estimates of what competitive costs for commercial firms would be. TVA has priced its ammonium nitrate considerably above and its phosphate materials generally below their respective costs. While its pricing policy has made TVA's fertilizer operations self-sustaining, its prices on each material may not have reflected competitive costs. For this reason the fertilizer consumption they foster may not be entirely consistent with what TVA seeks to promote: namely, greater consumption of those fertilizers which can be produced and delivered to farmers at the lowest cost per unit of plant nutrient.

*State Agencies.* State agencies play a vital role in the nation's fertilizer policy. The Bureau of Plant Industry, Soils, and Agricultural Engineering relies on the state agricultural college to make known to farmers the results of its fertilizer research; TVA leaves the administration of its test-demonstration program almost entirely to the extension services; PMA (ACP) leaves fertilizer recommendations to the state agricultural colleges; and state departments of agriculture and state colleges rely on the extension services to disseminate among farmers the fertilizer practices they recommend. Most state and federal fertilizer programs ultimately reach farmers through the extension service county agents; the effect they have on farmers' fertilizer practices depends largely on how well county agents perform. Furthermore, the power to regulate and police fertilizer markets—unlike that for food and drug markets—has been left to the states. There is no federal statute comparable to the Pure Food and Drug Act to regulate the sale of fertilizers. State control boards regulate the registration of brands and grades of fertilizers—a prerequisite to their sale—and prohibit the sale of certain kinds of fertilizers. State inspectors police fertilizer markets for discrepancies between the actual and stated chemical composition of fertilizers, and have the power to invoke a prescribed system of fines and penalties. State control boards and county agents have considerable influence on the kinds and quantities of fertilizers farmers buy.

The county agency system is generally regarded as uniquely an American institution. Visiting representatives of foreign countries, especially agrarian countries, may return home with mingled reactions to much that is American, but those who observe rural America closely appear to give unanimous approval to the institution of the county agent. Not only do they approve of it; they understand it and they imitate it. It is founded on the laudable principle that practical knowledge should be made available to all who wish access to it. Few would contend that it has failed to pay for itself; many would contend that it has not been expanded to the point where the marginal costs of the system are equal to the marginal benefits derived from it. And if this is in fact the case, most criticisms of it, including those discussed below, should in truth be viewed as inevitable consequences of an understaffed system.

Some have looked upon the county agency system and found room for improving it.[31] According to Gladys Baker the system's principal weakness stems from loose and poorly defined lines of state and federal supervision. Under the Smith-Lever Law, county agents became joint agents of their state agricultural college and the United States Department of Agriculture. The latter, in keeping with its traditional policy of grass-

[31] See esp. Gladys Baker, *The County Agent* (Chicago: Univ. of Chicago, 1939). For comprehensive general descriptions of the system see Lincoln D. Kelsey and Cannon C. Hearne, *Cooperative Extension Work* (rev. ed.; Ithaca: Cornell Univ., 1955); and Edmund de S. Brunner and Elwood Hsin Pao Yang, *Rural America and the Extension Service* (New York: Teachers College, Columbia University, 1949).

roots administration, forfeited the supervisory powers given it by the Act to the state colleges. The state colleges, perhaps mindful of the voices of local representatives in state legislatures, in turn bowed to local senti- ment. Thus, the county agent, "who satisfies the local people, whether it be through courting the favor of a few dominant and influential farmers and political leaders or by really effective extension work which reaches a large percentage of the farmers, is allowed to remain in the county and pursue his work along certain broad lines." [32]

Out of this lack of effective direction has arisen the criticism that county agents orient their activities toward the more influential and well-to-do members of the farm community—the upper third. It is often made by spokesmen for the poorer farm groups,[33] and one that circum- stantial evidence appears to support. TVA's test-demonstration farms have averaged larger in size than farms generally. In some states, especially southern states, the average size of test-demonstration farms has been three times the state average.[34] A similar though smaller dif- ference in average size exists between farms receiving ACP aid and all farms; farms receiving ACP aid are on the average twenty-five per cent larger. County agents play an important role in selecting test-demon- stration farms and in making farmers acquainted with the ACP program.

The principal weakness of the county agency system lies as much in the changing nature of the county agent's job as in his tendency to serve only influential farmers. The early county agent had to teach only a few well-established methods of farming. New technology and New Deal farm legislation have thrust upon the county agent programs he has not been trained to administer, and have required that he become much more a central-office administrator and much less an itinerant teacher.[35] The complexities of his duties and the quasi-political nature of his job have probably left the county agent little time to promote more economical fertilizer-purchasing practices among farmers, especially the back-area farmers who seldom visit his office.[36]

While the evidence that county agents do not, or cannot, serve all farmers equally may be inconclusive, it is clear from the high cost of

---

[32] Baker, *op. cit.*, p. 134.

[33] See minority report of the President's Committee on Farm Tenancy, cited in *ibid.*, p. 100; see also pp. 99-101, and 212.

[34] However, the method of classifying farms used by the Census Bureau understates the average size of the full-time farm. The difference between the size of test-demonstration farms and all farms is therefore overstated. Data on the size of test-demonstration farms were provided by the Tennessee Valley Authority; data on all farms were obtained from the Census Bureau.

[35] Baker, *op. cit.*, pp. 207-8.

[36] The writer's field study of county agents' activities in the summer of 1952 supports this con- clusion. In their preoccupation with restoring permanent pastures damaged by the 1952 drought, county agents paid little attention to relative costs in making their fertilizer recommendations. The Mimeo- graphed instructions sent out to farmers by one county agent (by reputation one of the most informed and most progressive agents in his state) contained the following statement "nitrogen applied now will give you a longer grazing period on your permanent pastures this Fall. Use 300 lbs. nitrate of soda (or its equivalent) or more per acre" (dated August 7, 1952 [name of county and county agent withheld by request]). At the time the recommendation was made a unit of nitrogen in ammonium nitrate cost only 58 per cent of what it cost in nitrate of soda.

imperfect knowledge[37] that more farmers need their services. These may be farmers whom county agents see but do not properly advise, or seldom if ever see. But whatever the reasons, public policy should be directed to correcting the weaknesses and inadequacies of the county agent system. The success or failure of virtually every state and federal fertilizer program depends largely on how the county agent administers it.

*State Fertilizer Control Boards.* The initial purpose of state control laws was to protect farmers from the excesses of imperfect knowledge and exploitation of them by fertilizer manufacturers. States enacted laws requiring producers to register their brands and to label them according to their plant-nutrient content. Farmers apparently needed such protection. Around 1876 the state of Connecticut employed chemists to determine the actual plant-nutrient value of fertilizers purchased by Connecticut farmers. Chemical analysis showed that they often bought mixed fertilizers at prices about thirty times the estimated value of their plant-nutrient content (Samples 3 and 4, Table 64). In other words apparently the same

TABLE 64

ACTUAL COSTS AND ESTIMATED VALUES OF FERTILIZERS
SOLD IN CONNECTICUT AROUND 1876 [a]

| Sample Number | Actual Cost Per Ton | Estimated Value Per Ton |
|---|---|---|
| 1 | $30.00 | $31.40 |
| 2 | 30.00 | 33.54 |
| 3[b] | 32.00 | 1.03 |
| 4[c] | 32.00 | 0.99 |
| 5 | 45.00 | 32.96 |
| 6 | 38.00 | 46.30 |
| 7 | 35.00 | 33.04 |
| 8 | 25.00 | 44.73 |
| 9 | 30.00 | 46.44 |
| 10 | 35.00 | 38.85 |

[a] *Annual Report of the Connecticut Agricultural Experimental Station* for 1877, New Haven, 1878, pp. 1-30.
[b] 16.7% moisture and 65.27% sand, soluble silica, and oxides of iron and alumina.
[c] 15.41% moisture and 68.12% sand, soluble silica, and oxides of iron and alumina.

conditions prevailed.

State laws requiring the labeling of fertilizers according to their plant-nutrient content may have made more informed buying possible, but many farmers continued to buy fertilizers according to their color, smell, texture, and other physical characteristics. To protect farmers from their own irrational purchasing habits and to reduce the excessive quantities of worthless filler in fertilizers, states gradually established minimum plant-nutrient requirements.

[37] *Supra,* Chap. 10.

But while state control laws have protected farmers from the excesses of imperfect knowledge, they have not served the farming community as well as they might have. They have generally failed to keep pace with developments in the fertilizer industry and the agronomic sciences. Less than 2.5 per cent of the mixed fertilizers sold in 1951 contained as little as eighteen per cent plant nutrients. In 1951 only twenty-six states required a minimum plant-nutrient content of at least twelve per cent (Table 65); of these only Minnesota required a minimum of as much as

TABLE 65

PARTIAL SUMMARY OF STATE FERTILIZER CONTROL LAWS, 1951 [a]

| Minimum % Plant-Nutrient Requirements | Number of States |
|---|---|
| 27% | 1 |
| 18%—20% | 11 |
| 15%—17% | 9 |
| 12%—14% | 5 |
| 0%—11% | 22 |
| Total | 48 |

| Annual Brand Registration Fee | |
|---|---|
| $50 | 3[b] |
| 35 | 1 |
| 30 | 1 |
| 20-25 | 15 |
| 10 | 4[c] |
| 0.50—6.0 | 17 |
| 0.0 | 7 |
| Total | 48 |

| Annual Per-Ton Inspection Fee | |
|---|---|
| $0.50 | 2 |
| 0.35 | 1 |
| 0.30 | 3 |
| 0.20—0.25 | 14 |
| 0.10—0.15 | 13 |
| 0.05—0.08 | 5 |
| 0.01 | 3 |
| 0.00 | 7 |
| Total | 48 |

| Filler Content Provisions | |
|---|---|
| Requires listing of pounds of filler per ton of fertilizer | 4 |
| Requires listing name of filler material | 5 |

[a] Minimum plant-nutrient requirements from U. S. Dept. of Agriculture; all other data from J. D. Conner, "State Fertilizer Controls," *Agricultural Chemicals,* Nov. and Dec. 1951, and Jan. 1952.
[b] Includes one state that charges from $15 to $50, depending upon tonnage sold.
[c] Includes one state that charges $25 the first year the brand is registered and $10 each year thereafter.

twenty-seven per cent; and only nine of the twenty-six required a minimum of as much as twenty per cent. The remaining twenty-two states had minimum requirements of less than eleven per cent. Such requirements no doubt afforded the untrained farmer a moderate amount of protection twenty or thirty years ago, but three decades of chemical progress have made them obsolete. The obsolete laws probably retard the use of the more economical high-analysis fertilizers offered for sale. The fact that a fertilizer is registered is likely to lead farmers to conclude that it has the endorsement of the state agronomists and control authorities, especially those farmers who began using it twenty years ago when it was recommended as an economical fertilizer. Hence, simply to permit the registration of low-analysis fertilizers is likely to encourage their sale.

In some instances state control boards have actually impeded the sale of economical high-analysis fertilizers. Shortly after the end of World War II the Mathieson Chemical Company began producing high-analysis fertilizers containing as much as forty per cent plant nutrients. Mathieson encountered considerable difficulty getting state boards to approve them. Swift & Company and the Davison Chemical Company encountered similar difficulties. Fertilizer mixers once tried to remove a 3-9-6 fertilizer from the approved list in North Carolina because of its relatively low analysis. When the board failed to do so because the grade was popular with farmers, mixers continued to supply it. Connecticut's state experiment station does not recommend the use of a 5-8-7 fertilizer because it is not economical. But because farmers want it, and because its analysis meets with the required state minimum, the 5-8-7 grade accounts for thirteen per cent of the total tonnage of mixed fertilizers used in the state. Virginia's state experiment station has not recommended the use of 3-12-6 fertilizer for years. Although in 1950 the Virginia state control board finally approved the registration of a 4-16-8 fertilizer having 33 1/3 per cent more plant nutrients, the 3-12-6 remains on the approved list and accounts for nearly twenty-five per cent of the total tonnage of mixed fertilizers sold in the state. Fertilizer officials of both states agree that farmers would oppose the removal of such low-analysis fertilizers from the approved lists, but they also agree that farmers would be better off if they were removed.[38]

The state control boards' failure to keep regulatory standards abreast of technological progress can be largely explained by farmers' buying habits. But the method of financing the fertilizer-control programs used by most states provides control boards with an economic incentive for approving low-analysis fertilizers. All forty-eight states finance their fertilizer-control programs from registration and inspection fees collected from fertilizer producers and distributors. In some states annual registration fees run as high as $50 per brand, and inspection fees as high as $0.50 per ton (Table 65). Forty states levy inspection fees by the bag or

---

[38] All information was obtained in interviews in 1951 with agricultural experiment station and state agricultural college officials of Connecticut, North Carolina, and Virginia, and with officials of Mathieson Chemical Company, Davison Chemical Company, and Swift & Company.

ton, regardless of their plant-nutrient content. The annual revenues they collect vary directly with the volume of fertilizer sold. Because fewer tons of high-analysis fertilizers are required for a given quantity of plant nutrients, control boards stand to lose revenues when they substitute high-analysis for low-analysis fertilizers on the approved list.

While state control boards have a financial incentive to keep minimum plant-nutrient requirements low, it does not follow that they have actually done so. However, the fact that some states rely on their fertilizer registration and inspection fees as an important source of revenue makes the objectives of their control program questionable. In fiscal year 1950, Mississippi collected $219,711 from fertilizer stamp sales and tonnage taxes, although operating expenditures for the state's entire Department of Agriculture amounted to only $153,579.[39] In the same year North Carolina collected $338,631 in fertilizer fees, but spent only $216,579 on inspecting, sampling, and testing all agricultural commodities; and Georgia collected $360,252 from fertilizer fees, but spent only $68,440 on its fertilizer inspection program. In fiscal year 1951, Alabama's fertilizer fee collections amounted to $335,872, while expenditures on its fertilizer control program amounted to only $104,000. When states rely so heavily on the revenues obtained from a single inspection program to finance other activities, financial considerations might easily influence the program's administration.

State fertilizer control programs also raise problems of co-ordination. Soil characteristics and crops, the two principal determinants of the kinds and quantities of fertilizer farmers use, are unaffected by state boundaries, and fertilizer production and distribution are primarily interstate in character. Manufacturers must produce a multiplicity of fertilizer grades to comply with the approved lists of all the states in which they do business. The differences in many grades may be of little agronomic significance but the multiplicity of grades probably increases fertilizer production costs. Some states have recognized the likelihood of such diseconomies and have begun working toward co-ordinated control. State officials of Virginia, North Carolina, and South Carolina have begun to hold joint meetings prior to the annual preliminary grade hearings. In 1951, New England agronomists made joint recommendations on fertilizer grades for the New England states. In 1952, a joint meeting of agronomists from thirteen states [40] and fertilizer industry representatives, sponsored by the Middle West Soil Improvement Committee, recommended increased sales of straight nitrogenous, phosphate, and potash materials, a minimum plant-

[39] All data are from Robert B. Highsaw, "Memorandum on State Departments of Agriculture, Tennessee Valley States," p. 28. Professor Highsaw kindly gave permission for the use of his manuscript and to quote therefrom.
[40] Ohio, Indiana, Illinois, Michigan, Wisconsin, Minnesota, Iowa, Missouri, Kentucky, Kansas, Nebraska, South Dakota and North Dakota.

nutrient content of thirty per cent for mixed fertilizers, and a reduction in the number of grades of mixed fertilizers.[41] In 1950, the Association of American Fertilizer Control Officials proposed a model state fertilizer bill, and has urged that states adopt it.[42] While it is too early to appraise the effects of these attempt at co-ordinated control, they evidence a fairly wide-spread recognition of the shortcomings of completely independent state regulation.

## C. A Positive Policy for Reducing Imperfect Knowledge

For over a half-century, state and federal governments have recognized the problem of farmers' imperfect knowledge and have undertaken programs to solve it. The states have imposed minimum plant-nutrient requirements on sellers of fertilizer to prevent farmers from buying excessive quantities of worthless filler. The Department of Agriculture and the land-grant colleges have tried to educate farmers to adopt more efficient practices. The Tennessee Valley Authority has tried to encourage widespread use of efficient high-analysis fertilizers. The Department of Agriculture has distributed high-analysis fertilizers to farmers, and all three of its statements on national fertilizer policy identify the increased use of more economical high-analysis fertilizers as an important objective. The problem of imperfect buyer knowledge in the fertilizer market does not persist because it has been ignored. A positive policy has been created to solve it. But while it no doubt has mitigated some of the earlier excesses of buyer ignorance characteristic of fertilizer demand, positive policy has not satisfactorily solved the problem. It has not done so because fertilizer programs have lacked co-ordination; their objectives have not been clearly defined; and channels for communicating knowledge to farmers have been ineffective.

In the administration of their respective programs public agencies have often worked at cross-purposes with each other. TVA has sought to introduce and promote the widespread use of high-analysis phosphate-fertilizer materials where they are the cheapest source of $P_2O_5$, but PMA has used a system of fair-price credit allowances which discourages their use. In 1951 high-analysis phosphate materials used in TVA's test-demonstration and direct-sales programs were the cheapest source of $P_2O_5$ for most farmers. But in forty-seven states PMA fair-price allowances on phosphate materials used in the Agricultural Conservation Program covered the costs of the most expensive sources of $P_2O_5$, generally ordinary superphosphate. Farmers therefore had little incentive to buy the high-analysis

---

[41] "Agronomists' Recommendations for Year Beginning July 1, 1933," from report of joint meeting of agronomists with fertilizer industry, sponsored by Middle West Soil Improvement Association.
[42] "Proposed Model State Fertilizer Bill," *Official Publication of the Association of American Fertilizer Control Officials*, No. 4 (October, 1950), pp. 71-81.

materials; and while such agencies as the Bureau of Plant Industry, Soils, and Agricultural Engineering, and TVA have designed programs encouraging farmers to buy economical fertilizers, the land-grant colleges' extension services, on which the Bureau and TVA rely almost entirely for their contact with farmers, have often ignored plant-nutrient costs in their fertilizer recommendations. Co-ordination of activities is a high-sounding principle of public administration, more easily enunciated than attained. This is especially true of the nation's fertilizer policy, the administration of which is not the primary responsibility of a single agency but an ancillary activity of many. But programs designed to stimulate rational fertilizer demand cannot be expected to succeed so long as they work at cross-purposes.

A problem closely related to inadequate co-ordination is that of unclear definitions of policy objectives. Although frequently not made explicit, more efficient fertilizer buying practices is presumed to be an objective of all agencies concerned with fertilizer policy. But because it is an objective only by implication, it is often subordinated to others or overlooked altogether. Yet, the attainment of most primary objectives of fertilizer programs is largely dependent on intelligent fertilizer buying. The U.S. Department of Agriculture and the land-grant colleges place great emphasis on adequate fertilization. TVA's fertilizer program emphasizes low-cost fertilizers and the promotion of improved fertilization as an integral part of improved farm management. But "adequate" and "improved" fertilization must be defined in the context of farm-firm decisions. It is inconceivable that farmers will use fertilizers economically —to the point where the last dose is just expected to pay for itself—so long as their demand reflects imperfect knowledge. But if more perfect buyer knowledge is a prerequisite to the attainment of other objectives, the agencies involved should explicitly recognize it as a primary objective and give it high priority. The appropriate remedy consists chiefly of recognizing the importance of stimulating intelligent buying and of using all available opportunities to achieve it. Specifically, TVA should price its fertilizer materials on a per-unit-of-plant-nutrient basis rather than by the ton, and should contractually obligate co-operatives and commercial firms that distribute its fertilizers to do so. Land-grant colleges should consider the relative costs of various fertilizer materials and mixed fertilizers in their recommendations to farmers. And ACP should adopt a system of payment allowances which encourages farmers to buy low-cost fertilizers.

While such revisions in fertilizer policy should bring about more intelligent fertilizer purchasing, a revamping of state fertilizer control programs would hasten the process. When states initially imposed minimum plant-nutrient requirements on fertilizers, they presumably did so to outlaw uneconomical fertilizers and thereby to prevent farmers from buying unwisely. Control laws no longer provide this protection. The average plant-nutrient content of mixed fertilizers has increased far more rapidly than state minimum requirements. As of 1952 the average ton of mixed fertilizer contained about twenty-two per cent plant nutrients, whereas the minimum requirement in thirty-six states was seventeen per cent or less, and in only one state did the minimum requirement exceed twenty per cent. But state control laws do not merely fail to prevent the sale of uneconomical fertilizers. Farmers who rely on the laws for protection generally assume that fertilizer grades approved by the state are economical fertilizers. State-board approval is viewed by many as state-board recommendation. The lag in state minimum requirements behind developments in fertilizer manufacturing therefore encourages the use of outdated high-cost fertilizers.

Finally, no fertilizer program, however co-ordinated and up-to-date, can effectively reduce the wastes of ignorance if inadequately communicated to farmers. Land-grant college, USDA, and TVA programs reach farmers through the state extension services. The wide discrepancy between the state of knowledge at fertilizer research and experiment centers and fertilizer practices on the farm suggests that the extension services can perform this role more efficiently than they do. In part this is a problem in education. A multiplicity of agricultural programs has been thrust upon county agents which they were inadequately trained to administer. In part it is a problem of inadequate staff.[43] The administration of such programs has made the county agent more and more a central office administrator and less and less an itinerant teacher. Accordingly, he has lost touch with those who need his services most, farmers who do not as a matter of good farm practice seek their county agent's advice at his office place.

Better co-ordination of existing fertilizer programs, improved extension services, and more up-to-date state control laws would no doubt reduce the social costs of unintelligent buying. A more effective positive policy would also make competition more effective. Mixed-fertilizer manufacturers are numerous and generally have to compete for customers. If farmers bought fertilizers intelligently, manufacturers would be forced to compete on a price per unit of plant-nutrient basis, the basis on which intelligent farmers buy. But because many farmers buy fertilizers unintelligently, manufacturers compete in terms of the criteria uninformed

[43] In 1954 the United States had one county agent for every 1,000 farmers, while the Netherlands had one county agent for every 240 farmers, Denmark one for every 360 farmers, Germany one for every 420 farmers, and Great Britain one for every 800 farmers. Among Western nations using the county agency system only France and Italy had a higher ratio of farmers to agents than the United States (*Le Monde*, October 24, 1954, Financial and Economic Supplement).

buyers use as bases for their choice. They often choose according to the price per ton of total material, the color of the fertilizer, custom, or similar irrational criteria. When farmers, by using such criteria, select high-cost over low-cost fertilizers, manufacturers have little incentive to compete on a price basis. The principal obstacle to effective competition in the fertilizer industry, therefore, derives not from its structure nor from collusive agreements (though these more familiar barriers to competition have at times been much in evidence), but from the highly imperfect knowledge underlying the demand for fertilizers. Hence, positive policy rather than anti-trust provides the remedy for the competitive barrier most urgently in need of attention. Until imperfect knowledge is reduced, competition in fertilizer markets where farmers are buyers cannot be effective; or as the problem has been historically and popularly stated, there will continue to be excessive quantities of "sand" in the farmers' fertilizer.

# INDEX

241